A note to readers:

Research completed since this edition of *Five Fur Traders of the Northwest* was published in 1965 has established that the original unsigned diary attributed to Thomas Connor (see pages 245–278) was in fact written by North West Company partner John Sayer.

Evidence that Thomas Connor could neither read nor write led to comparisons of the original diary with known samples of John Sayer's handwriting by the Royal Canadian Mounted Police Detection Laboratory in Ottawa, which confirmed Sayer's authorship.

For more details, see Douglas A. Birk and Bruce M. White, "Who Wrote the 'Diary of Thomas Connor'? A Fur Trade Mystery," and "John Sayer 'Guilty as Charged,'" both in *Minnesota History,* 46:170–188 (Spring 1979) and 47:162 (Winter 1980), respectively.

—*Minnesota Historical Society Press*

Five Fur Traders
OF THE NORTHWEST

Being the Narrative of PETER POND
and the Diaries of JOHN MACDONELL, ARCHIBALD N. MCLEOD,
HUGH FARIES, *and* THOMAS CONNOR

Edited by
CHARLES M. GATES

with an Introduction by
GRACE LEE NUTE

and a Foreword by
THEODORE C. BLEGEN

MINNESOTA HISTORICAL SOCIETY ST. PAUL
1965

FOREWORD AND SPECIAL CONTENTS © BY THE
MINNESOTA HISTORICAL SOCIETY, 1965

Second Printing, 1971

LIBRARY OF CONGRESS CATALOG CARD NUMBER: 65–63528

Foreword

Much has happened in the domain of fur-trade history since the narrative and diaries comprising this book were originally published in 1933. Grand Portage, the lively lakeside emporium of the eighteenth century, has become a United States national monument. Its palisaded trading post has been in part rebuilt; new excavations of the site are under way; and a fur-trade museum is being established. The underwater research program, begun by the Minnesota Historical Society in 1960, is recovering kettles, axes, spears, and other artifacts lost in turbulent streams when canoes capsized in the days of the singing voyageurs. Now, nearly four decades after Irving H. Hart published in *Minnesota History* a detailed and scholarly study of the old Northwest Company post on Sandy Lake, the society is using scuba divers to search the waters offshore from that important site. The ground where Thomas Connor, one of the diarists in this volume, built in 1804 a stockaded trading post on the Snake River near the present Pine City, Minnesota, has been identified and is being excavated in preparation for an eventual restoration by the society.

Through the more than three decades since 1933 not a few additional manuscript collections relating to the fur trade have been gathered up and are being preserved by historical societies and other agencies. Almost equally important for historical scholarship, manuscript materials which have been scattered in institutions throughout the world have been made accessible to students through photostats, microfilms, and other copying devices. Thus today's scholar has ready access to such extensive sources as the records of the American Fur Company in New York, the Hudson's Bay Company in London and elsewhere, and the Northwest Company in various Canadian institutions.

Drawing upon such manuscript sources, numerous books and

articles on the fur trade of Canada and the United States have been published since 1933. The Hudson's Bay Record Society of London, for instance, has brought out some two dozen publications of original records during these years; and the Champlain Society has continued its program of issuing fundamental sources such as W. Stewart Wallace's edition of *Documents Relating to the North West Company* (1934), and a volume containing *David Thompson's Narrative* (1962).

Not a few important histories have been published in new editions — Hiram M. Chittenden's *The American Fur Trade of the Far West* (2 vols., 1954) and *The Fur Trade in Canada* by Harold A. Innis (Toronto, 1956). Edwin E. Rich has written *The History of the Hudson's Bay Company, 1670–1870*, a two-volume work of careful scholarship (1958–59); Marjorie E. Campbell is the author of a new history of *The North West Company* (1957) — an earlier one by Gordon C. Davidson was published in 1918; Grace Lee Nute did notable service in editing a *Calendar of the American Fur Company's Papers* (2 vols., 1945–51), prefaced by a critical appraisal of the papers and their historical value. Useful bibliographies have been compiled by Stuart Cuthbertson and John C. Ewers (1939) and by Henry P. Beers (1957, 1964).

Scholars have also explored various aspects of the fur trade and related explorations and cartography. Routes of travel are set forth in Dr. Nute's *The Voyageur's Highway* (1941), J. Arnold Bolz's *Portage into the Past* (1960), and Eric W. Morse's *Canoe Routes of the Voyageurs* (1962). Leaders have been portrayed in such works as A. S. Morton's *Sir George Simpson* (1944), Marjorie E. Campbell's *McGillivray: Lord of the Northwest* (1962), in important books by Dale Morgan on Jedediah Smith (1954), and by Burt B. Barker on *The McLoughlin Empire and Its Rulers* (1959). W. Stewart Wallace has written a series of eleven interesting essays under the title *The Pedlars from Quebec and Other Papers on the Nor'Westers* (1954).

If a masterwork on the North American trade, recording and interpreting it in its full magnitude, has not yet appeared, honor must be accorded the late Paul C. Phillips for his two-volume study entitled *The Fur Trade* (1961). Unhappily he did not live to finish his *magnum opus*, and his researches, despite a lifetime of dedicated effort, had not taken him into all the fur-trade manuscript treasures of America and Europe. But he set himself a monumental task, saw the trade in its international sweep, and used many of the best fruits of international scholarship in his attempt to achieve a synthesis.

The foregoing titles are mentioned merely as examples. Many more could be added, and a vast number of articles could be listed. A cursory view is sufficient, however, to indicate that the subject has attracted much research, editing, and writing. It seems safe to predict that the field will continue to attract the attention of historians. In many areas of scholarly work, cultivation across the years and decades is inevitably uneven. Shifts of interest, with changing times, affect the course of historical research. Illustrations may be found in the concern of historians with the American frontier and its role in the nation's history, or in the Civil War, which has generated an avalanche of books in recent years. The changes in approaches, interpretations, and fashions may be traced in part to the compelling need of society to probe its experience afresh as new problems, or new aspects of old problems, emerge. The same need may throw light on the changes in direction that take place in the collecting of manuscripts and other sources, though now and then fortunate "finds" may stimulate new work. Whatever the underlying causes, there are undulations of scholarly interest, and they seem to be regional as well as national.

The publication in 1933 of *Five Fur Traders of the Northwest* came at a point of lively Minnesota interest in the fur trade and its sources, in exploration, and more generally in the transition from wilderness to settlement and civilization. There appears now to be a renewed interest in the business of furs and in the men of trade. No one supposes that the original sources have all been garnered. New aspects of the subject invite scholarly attention, and new techniques — such as underwater searches for artifacts — are being employed. Widespread institutional interest has developed in the United States and Canada in recent years in the interpretation of archaeological and historical materials. It is in such a general setting of increasing scholarly and public interest in the major industry of frontier North America, that the present volume is being reprinted by the Minnesota Historical Society. The institution is an appropriate one to undertake this task, for Minnesota occupied a central position in fur-trade activities of the eighteenth and nineteenth centuries, and its scholars have long been active in research on the history of that era.

No one can question the lasting value of these firsthand records of the fur traders. The Pond narrative and the Macdonell, McLeod, Faries, and Connor diaries — brought together as a volume in 1933 by the Minnesota Society of the Colonial Dames of America and published by the University of Minnesota Press — have lost none of their significance because of the passing of a few decades. Indeed, if anything, they have gained in value. They are authentic, dependable, vivid records from the late eighteenth century and the first years of the nineteenth. The lasting freshness of their impact comes not only from their contemporaneousness with the times and events they record, but also from the matter-of-fact, unpretentious way in which they were written.

Inevitably some questions have been raised with respect to the explanations and interpretations offered in 1933 by the original editors, Dr. Gates and Dr. Nute, but they do not lessen the enduring values in the documents. In most instances time supports conjectures offered in the book as originally edited; in a few others, errors seem to have been made, and these, where noted, have been corrected. The identity of the author of the diary attributed to Hugh Faries remains unresolved. Dr. Nute herself suggested the possibility that Thomas McMurray wrote the diary, but W. Stewart Wallace, the distinguished Canadian scholar, rules out McMurray because he was associated with the X. Y. Company and reached Rainy Lake only after the diary ended. Whoever its author may have been, his record is of value and interest.

Anyone working with the Canadian fur trade must be wary about such names as Fraser, Grant, McKenzie, McLeod. Wallace, in his *Documents Relating to the North West Company*, publishes as an appendix a biographical dictionary of the Nor'Westers in which he lists seven Frasers (four of them with the first name of Simon), fourteen Grants, fifteen Mackenzies or McKenzies (including five named Roderick), and seven McLeods — not to mention McTavishes and McGillivrays. Gates (p. 99) evidently confused an older and a younger Simon Fraser, and a suitable footnote change has been made. It seems highly probable, also, that he confused Archibald Norman McLeod with Normand McLeod (p. 123), and a few changes in the introductory note have been made to straighten out the identification. There is some question as to the identity of the Roderic Mackenzie, mentioned on page 198. Was he the first cousin of Sir Alexander Mackenzie, who had retired from active participation in the trade? Or was he another Roderick, a clerk who seems to have been at Lake Nipigon in 1804? Gates knew about both of these Rodericks, and he chose the more distinguished name. Wallace contends that Gates was mistaken, but cannot say more than that the Nipigon clerk probably was the McKenzie mentioned. Since no final proof seems to be available, the note by Gates (p. 198, n. 7) has been allowed to stand as he wrote it. Gates also identifies a certain Mr. Grant (p. 200) as probably Peter Grant, but the diary in which the reference occurs is from 1804, and Peter Grant returned to Montreal before that time; consequently Wallace may well be right in identifying the man as James Grant, who served as a clerk at Fond du Lac from 1805 to 1813. A reference to a trader named Black (p. 200) caused Gates to mention Samuel Black, a partner in the Northwest Company, without asserting that this was in fact the trader referred to; probably the Black of the diary was someone else, since Samuel Black was associated with the X. Y. Company.

x   FIVE FUR TRADERS OF THE NORTHWEST

Inevitably fur-trade literature includes controversial subjects. One of them is the role of the Connecticut Yankee, Peter Pond, whose narrative—the first of the documents in this book—is here presented in a new transcription of the original manuscript now owned by the library of Yale University (see page 17). To what extent were his ideas and maps basic to the achievements of the famed Alexander Mackenzie? Why did so many men of the Northwest Company, in which Pond was a creative figure, dislike him? Dr. Gates points out that Pond was irascible, and Professor Wallace has written an essay entitled "Was Peter Pond a Murderer?" His name was connected with two murders in 1782 and 1787. Wallace concludes that Pond was implicated in the first but was without any legal responsibility for the second. Ironically, it was the second that led to his retirement from the Northwest Company in 1790 and his ultimate return to Connecticut, where, seventeen years later, he died.

We know that a part of Pond's narrative was rescued from destruction in 1868 in the kitchen of a Connecticut governor named Pond. The manuscript was about to be destroyed as wastepaper, when, by good fortune, a lady interrupted the procedure. Happily for Minnesota history, what she saved included Pond's own account of his experiences as a fur trader in Minnesota just before the American Revolution. The narrative does not go beyond 1775. Pond had a career of major importance as fur trader, explorer, and cartographer during the decade and a half following that date, and then returned to Connecticut where, after the age of sixty, he wrote his recollections.

Many scholars, including Gates, the original editor of this volume, assumed that the detailed record of Pond's life after 1775 was fed into the kitchen stove. In 1955, however, the Yale University library published a booklet entitled *Peter Pond: Fur Trader and Explorer* in which Henry R. Wagner contends that probably not many pages of the manuscript were lost. He suggests that Pond himself broke off the story because 1775 synchronized with the beginnings of the American Revolution. Mr. Wagner offers a conjecture but no proof. No one knows how much, if any, of the manuscript now in the possession of Yale University was destroyed.

Because Pond's spelling is highly phonetic and echoes the twang of an unschooled colonial Yankee, it is too often quoted merely for its quaintness. The new version presented in this book, based upon the original manuscript, more faithfully preserves Pond's grotesqueries than the text of 1933 as prepared by Mrs. Nathan Gillett Pond for the *Connecticut Magazine.* Its quaintness is intensified by the extraordinary spelling, unorthodox capitalization, and meager punctuation. The narrative is unquestionably a documentary oddity, but it is also a substantial historical record written by a sagacious observer. Peter Pond, as disclosed in this account, was, as Wallace has said, "a man of inquiring and original mind." Gates detected a "sense of literary artistry" hidden beneath Pond's crudeness of form. The artistry, if it exists, is less apparent in the present version of the manuscript than it was in the text as transcribed by its original finder, Mrs. Pond. Yet Pond possessed an adequate vocabulary, and he related his early experiences with gusto, not infrequently with characteristic Yankee pungency and whimsicality.

The documents in this volume are important primarily for their historical value. They illustrate conditions of early travel and exploration. They record in realistic terms the Indian fur trade, the kinds of goods used in the barter of the traders with the natives, the building of trading posts and the activities they harbored, the problems of wind and weather. They illuminate the life and character of the voyageurs, Indian customs, and, more generally, the nature of the primitive Mississippi country and the American and Canadian wilderness west of Lake Superior. Much interest attaches to the portrayal offered of the strategic importance of Grand Portage, on the Superior shore, in a trade of international dimensions. Nor should one forget that, in the simplicity of these personal records, the hazards and daring of men stand starkly revealed, as well as the prosaic aspects of life in the wilderness long before the era of settlement.

The Minnesota Historical Society, I know, regards it as a

service to history to bring out this reprint of *Five Fur Traders of the Northwest*. It does so with appreciation of the interest taken by the Minnesota Society of the Colonial Dames of America in sponsoring such a book of basic sources, and by the University of Minnesota Press in publishing it in 1933. It is thankful for the careful editing done by the late Charles M. Gates and for the informing introduction by Dr. Nute (and also for her prefatory note to one of the diaries).

This work is certain to be of continuing value to historians and archaeologists, but I hope that it will be read also by many persons who lay no claim to specialization in history or archaeology. They will find these accounts absorbing in their human interest.

THEODORE C. BLEGEN

December 11, 1964
St. Paul, Minnesota

Contents

	Page
INTRODUCTION: THE FUR TRADE IN THE NORTHWEST	1
THE NARRATIVE OF PETER POND	9
THE DIARY OF JOHN MACDONELL	61
THE DIARY OF ARCHIBALD N. McLEOD	121
THE DIARY OF HUGH FARIES	187
THE DIARY OF THOMAS CONNOR	243
INDEX	279

MAPS

THE RAINY LAKE POST AND THE SURROUNDING AREA	70
FORT ALEXANDRIA AND NEIGHBORING POSTS	128
THE TRADING REGION OF THE ST. CROIX RIVER	254

INTRODUCTION
THE FUR TRADE IN THE NORTHWEST

Introduction

The Fur Trade in the Northwest

The fur trade has contributed much to the history of inland North America; it was responsible for the discovery of much of the region; it remained for many years the major industry of the continent, producing the first great monopolies; it developed in northern latitudes a class of men, the voyageurs, whose picturesqueness may be compared to that of the negro in the South. Finally, through the fur trade the white man wielded his influence, for good and for evil, upon the Indians of the region.

For almost exactly two centuries after two unknown Frenchmen reached the Green Bay region in 1654, the fur trader may be said to have held in almost undisputed possession the great stretch of territory between Lake Michigan and the Red River of the North. Until shortly after 1760, when the age-long rivalry between France and England terminated temporarily, the lilies of France floated above the bastions of numerous Minnesota forts, where titled adventurers, obscure soldiers, and devoted missionaries were opening the region for white men. The British colors waved for another half century, though illegally for more than half that time. It was during this period of the British régime that the fur trade of the Northwest reached the peak of its development, and that all the documents published in this volume were written. At the close of the War of 1812 the United States claimed the region for her own traders, as she might have done, had she been sufficiently interested, at any time after the ratification of the treaty of 1783.

By 1790 the trade had already been organized along the lines that were to be maintained until the industry declined as a result of advancing settlement. This organization was the product of many years of growth and experience. A system of restriction and privilege in the French period had given way, about 1767, to another system with almost no restrictions, which was attended by perhaps even greater evils. The result was a ruthlessness and competition to the death that could end only in such a union of rivals as the Northwest Company proved to be. This company began obscurely with its headquarters in Montreal just as the American Revolution broke. It soon began to challenge the Hudson's Bay Company of England, the oldest company in the trade, which had been apathetic in opening new areas distant from the Bay. Finally, in 1821, the Northwest Company and the Hudson's Bay Company were united, and the corporation thus formed has remained to this day.

In the period covered by this volume, the rivalry between these giants had not yet become bitter, and visits between the factors of the two companies in adjacent posts were still possible. It was rather between the X. Y. Company, an offshoot of the Northwest Company, and its parent organization that unfriendly relations prevailed. Many references to this rivalry are found in the diaries here published. These two factions of the great company were reunited in 1804.

Montreal, Three Rivers, and Quebec, located on tidewater at one end of the finest water highway to the heart of a continent that exists anywhere, naturally enough became the centers of the North American fur trade. But by the time Great Britain took possession of Canada at the end of the Seven Years' War, Montreal was the capital of the fur trade, its earlier rivals having lost much of their prestige. Montreal in 1763 already had a fur trade tradition, a class of trained executives, and a class of trained servants. Hence the new masters took over the personnel of the French trade almost without change, except in its two uppermost strata. For the nabobs of the French régime Scotch and English merchants were substituted, though the name of *bourgeois,* by which this class of stockholders was known, remained as long as the trade flourished in the region. In time the word seems to

THE FUR TRADE 5

have been slightly corrupted to mean any superior, whether clerk or partner in the company, though it was ordinarily used in the earlier sense. The executives in the field were now chosen from among the sons and relatives of the *bourgeois* and were generally called clerks, or *commis*. Next in the social scale were the guides, interpreters, and other experienced hands, whose long years on inland waterways and in Indian villages made them indispensable to those above them. Finally came men more humble but quite as indispensable — the voyageurs, or canoemen, whose uncanny mastery of birch canoe navigation was a revelation even to Indians.

By 1790 the trade was governed by rigid regulations. Bales of goods and other packages must be wrapped in certain approved ways and must weigh almost exactly ninety pounds. Engagements of voyageurs must be conducted in the hamlets on the lower St. Lawrence at certain seasons of the year, must be couched in the accepted language of the trade, must allow for certain privileges, and must terminate at given places and on given dates. The voyageurs even had their repertoire of songs, without which no brigade could have functioned satisfactorily.

A brigade of canoes leaving Montreal at the customary time in May followed a long-established route up the Ottawa River and down the French River. Many routes branched off the main transcontinental line after Lake Huron was reached. Those leading into the area with which these diaries are concerned started from Lake Michigan or Lake Superior. Hence the large post, Michilimackinac, located at the junction of these lakes, was of the greatest importance to all the traders of the region. It was, indeed, second only to Grand Portage, the great inland post of the Northwest Company's men until about 1804, when Fort William on Canadian soil became the principal rendezvous and storage place. Grand Portage was the point at which the Montreal canoes turned back, being unable to navigate on the small lakes and streams beyond. The men who paddled them were thus acquainted with only a small portion of the route, and were called "pork-eaters" (*mangeurs de lard*) in derision of their lack of experience. Those who passed on to the West were the winterers (*hivernants*), or "old hands."

The area covered in these documents contained many forts and was reached by several different routes. Peter Pond, the forceful though illiterate Yankee whose quaint reminiscences open this series of diaries, reveals that even before the outbreak of the Revolution the upper Mississippi and the valley of the Minnesota were haunts of a numerous class of traders. His account presents the region from the point of view of one entering it by the old and, to the early explorers, familiar route from Lake Michigan to the Mississippi by way of the portage between the Fox and Wisconsin rivers. This was not the main thoroughfare to the West. That route lay along the present northern boundary of Minnesota, where rock-bound lakes, short streams, and the beautiful, fertile valley of the Rainy River led the trader into the Lake of the Woods, thence to Lake Winnipeg, to the Churchill and the Peace rivers, and so to the Pacific. Of this route as far as Lake Winnipeg John Macdonell's diary, the second in the series, gives an admirable description. His account is thus closely linked with the next two narratives, those of Archibald N. McLeod and Hugh Faries, whose posts were reached by way of this main route, though one was situated on the headwaters of the Assiniboine River and the other at the exit of Rainy Lake.

Another favorite route into the region was that taken by Thomas Connor, the last of the diarists. His post in the St. Croix Valley, which was being built in the autumn covered by his diary, was reached from Grand Portage by way of Fond du Lac, at the extreme end of Lake Superior, the Bois Brûlé River, which emptied a few miles to the east in what is now Wisconsin, and the portage from that stream into the St. Croix. Near this post Connor was to spend almost a half century of his long life. Thus all parts of the region are represented and all but one of the major routes leading to it are

THE FUR TRADE 7

described in this volume. None of these diarists took the very popular canoe route from Fond du Lac up the St. Louis River and then by portage to Sandy Lake.

Once at his destination the trader must erect a fort, unless, of course, one had already been built. This task involved selecting a site, usually with the advice of local Indians, clearing the ground, felling trees, building houses, and erecting a palisade around the entire fort. No existing account, perhaps, is more valuable than Connor's diary in establishing the typical sequence of events in this highly interesting performance. The winterers at a post almost always had with them at least one clerk, and an important fort, such as Grand Portage, required a *bourgeois* as well.

Life in a fur trader's cabin was not humdrum, as all these diaries prove. Indians and their families came and went; births and deaths occurred with about normal frequency; petty jealousies, trade rivalries, balls and other forms of merrymaking, sickness, siege, heroic self-sacrifice, and murder, all are recorded in the more or less laconic style of the trader. The diarists themselves offer an interesting contrast in character: Pond, the clear-visioned blazer of western trails, whose eloquence is as remarkable as his spelling is quaint; Macdonell, the naïve but very game tenderfoot clerk making the first of many trips into the wilderness; McLeod, the efficient but rather blasé *bourgeois;* Connor, least ambitious of the five; and Faries, the experienced clerk with a penchant for details and a genuine interest in men, whether red or white. The normal life at typical forts in the wooded country is pictured vividly in Faries' and Connor's diaries. Macdonell's and McLeod's journals describe the life at prairie forts.

The differences between wooded country and prairie as the site of trading establishments in this region must be kept clearly in mind. Not only was the trader's life different in the two areas; the Indians also were different. Two great hostile tribes, the Chippewa and the Sioux, held the territory. A bitter feud had existed between them since the Chippewa, supplied with white men's firearms, in the middle of the seventeenth century began to drive the Sioux out of their homes along the upper Mississippi and St. Croix rivers into the prairie country beyond. After that the Chippewa tended to keep to the forests, the Sioux to the prairies — a fact of the greatest importance in many respects. Excellent interpreters and guides in one area might be of practically no use in the other, being unacquainted with the language and customs of the Indians. Voyageurs who took squaws from one tribe could not be sent into the country of the other without endangering everyone in the party. Everywhere in the region, traders had to reckon with the feud.

The fur trade flourished in the Northwest for approximately two centuries. By 1850 settlement was spreading rapidly and the natives and their former means of livelihood were doomed. The fur trader had been able to see the Indian as a human being. Few white persons who arrived after 1850 could recognize him as anything but an obstacle. *Land* had become the chief word in the vocabulary of the region, and *justice* had lost its force. The Indians rapidly became a degraded, shiftless people in comparison with the independent, high-minded race of the fur trader's day. Only in such documents as these diaries is it now possible, therefore, to behold the original Chippewa and Sioux. It is fortunate indeed that a few such records have survived the ravages of time.

GRACE LEE NUTE

Minnesota Historical Society
1933

THE NARRATIVE
OF PETER POND

The Narrative of Peter Pond

Introductory Note

Peter Pond, though known primarily for his explorations in western and northwestern Canada and for his part in the organization of the Northwest Company, was also an explorer and trader of the first rank in the Upper Mississippi country. This fact is proved by his narrative, which he wrote in the later years of his life, intending it to preserve for publication a detailed account of his life in the interior. It has survived the ravages of time only in part, the portion dealing with his exploits after 1775 having been destroyed as waste paper. Regrettable as this loss is, the narrative is not thereby robbed of its value; for it is the earlier years of Pond's life that have been veiled in obscurity, whereas there are other sources of information concerning the years not covered by the fragment of the journal that remains to us.

Peter Pond, as his narrative shows, was born in Milford, Connecticut, on January 18, 1740, grew up in New England, and appears to have been trained to the trade of a shoemaker. After his experiences as a provincial trooper in the French and Indian wars, which are described in detail in his narrative, he tried his fortunes at sea, but the death of his mother forced him to remain at home for several years.

About 1765 he began a trading career in the country about Detroit, which, nearly a decade later, took him to the upper Mississippi; from that time until 1788 his life was one of trading and exploration in the Northwest. The following sketch of the Canadian trade reveals how prominent a part was taken by Pond in that trade from 1775 until he "came out" for the last time in 1788.

In 1774 the Hudson's Bay Company took steps to penetrate into the interior, sending Samuel Hearne to establish a fort

(Cumberland House) at Sturgeon Lake on the Saskatchewan. The next year a group of the Canadian traders, including Joseph and Thomas Frobisher, Alexander Henry, Jean Baptiste Cadotte, and Peter Pond, gathered at Sturgeon Lake on their way to posts in the Indian country. Although Pond seems to have been an independent trader, and not party to any previous arrangements, his winter position at Lake Dauphin in 1775-76 may well have enabled him to intercept Indians taking furs to the Cumberland House from the south, whereas the other traders, wintering on the Saskatchewan, intercepted those coming in from the west.

Pond spent two winters on the Saskatchewan, but finding competition keen with the Hudson's Bay people, he decided to push farther to the north. In 1778 he was chosen to take four canoes, representing the pooled interests of several Canadian traders, northward into the Athabasca region, where a post was established near the site of Fort Chipewyan on Lake Athabasca. Trade in the north country far exceeded his expectations and he was forced to leave some of his peltries *en cache* because he had no canoes with which to take them down to the Grand Portage. As the trade developed, competition between the more powerful firms and the smaller traders grew more keen. Mutual hostility finally resulted in the death of Jean Etienne Waden, representative of the smaller traders, after which the two groups organized themselves into competing companies; Pond, who had represented the larger concerns, joined McTavish and Benjamin and Joseph Frobisher rather than Pangman, Ross, and Gregory, a concern composed of smaller traders.

Pond spent the year 1784-85 in Montreal and the United States. It was at this time that he presented to the Congress of the Confederation his map of northwestern Canada. Only a bare mention can be made here of the Pond maps and the influence they had on diplomatic affairs and on the course of exploration. If David Thompson, known for his blunt veracity, is to be regarded as trustworthy, it was Pond who furnished Benjamin Franklin with information about the geography of the Great Lakes area which, though faulty, enabled him to drive a sharp bargain with the British commissioners during the course of the boundary negotiations of 1782–83. Copies of a map dated 1785 were studied by officials of the trading companies and found their way into government archives. In fact, it is not improbable that this map, showing the upper waters of the Mississippi River to be some distance south of the Lake of the Woods, may account in part for the incorporation into Jay's Treaty of 1794 of Article IV providing for a reliable survey of the source of that river.

The geographical information and maps that Pond brought out with him from the interior became more significant with the publication of the accounts of Captain Cook's voyages along the northwest coast of Canada. The combined data of the two explorers seemed to indicate that only a narrow stretch of unknown territory remained to be crossed to make the long desired northwest passage a reality. Pond saw an added reason for exploration in the recent treaty with the United States, which, by opening to traders from the United States the canoe route via Grand Portage, the southern gateway to the Canadian Northwest, might encourage rivalry with the Canadians for the trade west and north of the Great Lakes. Pond, New Englander though he was, sent to Lieutenant Governor Hamilton of the province of Quebec a memorial dated March, 1785, urging that the British government aid the fur traders in establishing posts all the way to the Pacific coast.

He himself soon returned to the interior, determined to find some river communication between Lake Athabasca and the river that Cook reported as flowing into the Pacific from the northeast. Whether from conversations with Alexander Henry or because of explorations made in the years 1785–87, he seems to have come to the conclusion that the Mackenzie River, instead of falling northward into the Arctic Sea as he had indicated on his map of 1785, might well flow west into Cook's inlet.[1] It was not his good fortune, however, to enjoy the distinction of exploring the true course of the river; his plans to do so were interrupted in 1788 by the necessity of going to Montreal, and it was left to Mackenzie to carry them into execution. The young Scotchman received much of his information and inspiration from Pond during the winter of 1787–88 when the two were both in Athabasca.

In 1787, after two years of bitter rivalry, which resulted in the death of John Ross, the competing groups of Canadian traders agreed to join forces; the Northwest Company was organized, Peter Pond holding one of the twenty shares of stock.[2] The following year Pond returned to Montreal to urge once more the need for government aid in exploration projects. While he was there the news was received that Mackenzie had descended the river which then took his name, and had charted its course northward to the Arctic Sea. The result of this voyage, disproving as it did Pond's theories concerning the northwest passage, was to discredit the veteran trader despite his invaluable services. Pond sold out his share in the Northwest Company to William McGillivray for eight hundred pounds, and some time in 1790 or 1791 he returned to the United States, where he was commissioned a captain in the army, and served for a time as a special agent for Secretary of War Henry Knox. He was undoubtedly selected for this work because of his long experience as a fur trader. General St. Clair had been defeated by the Indians in November, 1791, and Knox, worried, wished for peace, yet anticipated further hostilities with the Miami and the Wabash tribes. He therefore sent Pond and William Steedman secretly to Niagara and Detroit to assume the character of traders and learn whatever they could from the Indians concerning their intentions for the coming year, and to ascertain how well they were supplied

[1] One of Pond's maps, clearly indicating his opinion, has been reproduced recently in *Minnesota History*, 14:81–84, accompanied by a brief explanatory article by Miss Grace Lee Nute.
[2] Ross represented the interests of the Pangman-Gregory group in Athabasca. Pond traded in that region in competition with him. In a scuffle between Ross's men and Pond's, Ross was accidentally shot.

with arms, ammunition, and provisions. While securing this information the two agents were to urge upon the Indians the humane disposition of the United States government, and to persuade them, if possible, to ask for peace.[3] The mission was a dangerous one requiring courage, tact, and a sharp eye. The fact that the task was intrusted to Pond is evidence that he still enjoyed the confidence of the government in his own country. The details of Pond's adventures are lost, and we cannot estimate the importance of his work in contributing to the Indian settlement of 1795. In fact, almost nothing is known of the man after 1790. Eventually he returned to New England, withdrew from active life, and spent his declining years reading Lahontan and Carver and other works on the Northwest, and writing his narrative. He died in poverty about 1807, a forgotten old man.

Peter Pond's autobiography, written when the author was over sixty years of age, does not, perhaps, portray in true colors the man as he was in earlier life. Some of his contemporaries found in him a volatile, at times an explosive, temperament, and have given the impression that he was an irascible person, given to outbursts of violence. The implication of Pond in the deaths of Waden and Ross has ordinarily been taken as evidence in support of such a characterization. Harold A. Innis in his study, *Peter Pond, Fur Trader and Adventurer* (Toronto, 1930), discounts much of this adverse criticism and finds the evidence slight that Pond was responsible for the death of either Waden or Ross. Proud and sensitive, sometimes impetuous and intractable, he may well have been a man who made enemies in a day when individual forcefulness was necessary to success and standards of conduct were none too high. Yet must there not have been in the active trader something of the whimsical good humor and the sense of literary artistry which, though hidden beneath a certain crudeness of form, characterize the memoirs here presented?

[3] See Instructions to Captain Peter Pond and William Steedman, January 9, 1792, from H. Knox, Secretary of War, *American State Papers, Indian Affairs*, 1: 227.

Whatever his personal faults, there can be no doubt that Peter Pond deserves a place among the stalwart Canadians who did so much to inject new vitality into the fur trade of the Northwest. As explorer he was the first to cross the Methye Portage into the Mackenzie River basin, and he laid the foundations for the later voyages down the Mackenzie and up the Peace rivers. As trader he was largely responsible for the building up of an efficient organization in the Athabasca department, the exploitation of which was to be indispensable to the development of the Northwest Company. Canada is deeply indebted to Peter Pond.

C. M. G.

A New Transcription

In the 1933 edition of this book, Pond's narrative was reprinted from the transcription evidently made by the manuscript's finder, Mrs. Nathan G. Pond, and first published in the Connecticut Magazine *(vol. 10, 1906). For this edition a completely new transcription from photographic copies of the original document, now in the library of Yale University, was prepared by three members of the Minnesota Historical Society's staff — June D. Holmquist, Anne A. Hage, and Lucile M. Kane — who also revised and expanded the footnotes. Their transcription differs in hundreds of details from other printed versions, corrects earlier misreadings, and includes portions of ten sentences omitted by Mrs. Pond. It is here printed with the permission of Yale University.*

The edges of the first and last pages of the manuscript have crumbled and are now missing. Bracketed words in italics in these sections are shown as they were transcribed by Mrs. Pond. The original handwriting is difficult to decipher, and where readings are uncertain, question marks have been placed in brackets. Pond's spelling, capitalization, punctuation, and paragraphing are preserved. In order to make reading somewhat easier, spaces have been inserted to indicate the ends of sentences. The trader frequently omitted words or failed to complete a word and these have occasionally been supplied in brackets. The following pages present an original document without editorial embellishment. The text is authentic Peter Pond, and the historically significant narrative may also prove of interest to students of past patterns in New England colloquial speech.

THEODORE C. BLEGEN

The Narrative

[*I was born in*] Milford in the countey of New Haven in Conn [*the 18 day*] of Jany 1740 and Lived thare under the Goverment and [*protec*]ton of my Pairans til the year 56 a Part of the British troops which Ascaped at Bradixis [Braddock's] Defeat on ye Bank of the Monagahaley in Rea the french fortafycation which is now Cald fort Pitmen Cam to at Milford toward Spring Goverment Bagan to Rase troops for the Insewing Campain aGanst Crounpoint under the Command of [*G*]enarel Winsloe[1] Beaing then Sixteen years of age I Gave my Parans to understand that I had a Strong Desire to be a Solge that I was Detarmend to Inlist under the Ofisers that was Going from Milford & joine the armey But thay for bid me and no wonder as my father had a Larg & young famerley I Just Began to be of Sum youse to him in his afairs Still the sam Inklanation & Sperit that my Ansesters Profest Run threw my Vanes it is well Knone that from fifth Gineration downward we ware all waryers [warriors] Ither by Sea or Land and In Dead Both So strong was the Popensatey for the arme that I [*c*]ould not with Stand its Temtatons One Eaveing in April [*the*] Drams an Instruments of Musick, ware all Imploid [*to th*]at Degrea that thay Charmd me I Repair to a Publick [*hou*]se whare Marth & Gollatrey was Highley Going on I found [*ma*]ney Lads of my Aquantans which Seamd Determined [*to*] Go in to the Sarvis I talkt with Capt Baldwin & ask him [*we*]ather he

---

[1] General Edward Braddock was defeated by the French when he attacked Fort Duquesne in 1755 at the beginning of the French and Indian War. When the fort was recaptured by the British three years later, it was named Fort Pitt. General John Winslow, a native of Massachusetts, was commander of the provincial troops in the unsuccessful campaign of 1756 against Ticonderoga and Crown Point which Pond describes.

THE NARRATIVE OF PETER POND   19

would take me in his Companey as he was the [*Recrui*]teing Offeser² he Readealey a gread & I seat my [*hand*] to the Orders My Parans was So Angrey that thay forb[*id me*] makeing my apearans at Home I taread [tarried] a bout the [*town*] among my fello Solgers and thought that I had made [*a profitable*] Exchange giting a Rigmintal Coate in Plase [*mss. torn*] llard Cloth at Length the time Came to Repo[*rt. Early in*] June we imbark on bord a Vasel to jion [*sic*] the [*Arme at*] the Randavuese [rendezvous.] We Sald from Milford to New Y[*ork proceeded up*] North r[*iver and arrived safe*] at A[*lbany*.] I came on Smartly as I had Sum of my Bountey Money with me I did not want for Ginger Bread and Small Bear and sun forgot that I had left my Pairans who was Exseadingley trubeld in Minde for my well fair after taring thare Sum weakes the Prinsabel Part of the armey got to Gather and we Proseaded up to the Halfmoon and thair Lay til the Hole of the armey from Differant [parts] of the hole Cuntray Got to Gather³ In the Mean time Parties & Teamsters war Imploid In forwarding Provishon from Post to Post & from Forte Eadward to the Head of Lake George⁴ it was suposed that we should Crose Lake George & make a Desant on ticandaroge. But befour that Could be aComplishead the Sumer Endead fall of ye Year Seat in and we went to work at the fort George which Lay on the Head of the Lake By that name In Novmber it Groed two Cold to Sleap in tents and the men began to Mutanise and Say that thay had Sarved thare times Out for which thay ware Inlisted and

---

² Captain David Baldwin was in command of the Seventh Company of the First Connecticut Regiment in 1756; Peter Pond is listed among the privates in the company. Connecticut Historical Collections, 9:105.

³ The Half-Moon was a place on the Hudson River, a short distance above Albany, where rapids interrupted navigation. Francis Parkman, *Montcalm and Wolfe*, 2:71 (Boston, 1906).

⁴ Fort Edward was situated on the Hudson River at the beginning of the carry to Lake George. The fort constructed at the head, or southern end, of the lake was William Henry; Pond calls it Fort George, perhaps confusing it with a fort of that name later built at the same location. Details of the campaign of 1756 are given in William H. Hill, *Old Fort Edward before 1800* (Fort Edward, New York, 1929), pp. 100–110.

would Return Home after Satisfying thim with Smooth words thay ware Provaild on them to Prolong the Campain a few Weakes and at the time Promest By the Gennarel the Camp Broke up and the troops Returned to thare Respecttive Plaiseis in all Parts of ye Cuntrey from whic[h] thay came But not without Leaveing a Grate Number Be Hind which Died with the Disentarey & other Dissaeses[?] whi[ch] Camps are subget to Aspesaley [especially] among Raw troops as the Amaracans ware at that time and thay Beaing Strangers to a Holsum Mod of Cookerarey it mad Grate Havock with them in makeing youse of Salt Provshans as thay did which was in a grat part Broyling & Drinking water with it to Exses

The year insewing which was 57 I taread at home with my Pairans So that I ascapet the Misfortins of a number of my Cuntrey men for Moncalm Came aganst Fort George & Captord it & as the amaracans ware Going of[f] for fort Eadward a Greabel to ye Capatalasion [capitulation] the Indans fel apon them & mad grate Havock[5] In ye year 58 the Safetey of British Amareaca Requird that a Large Arme should be Rased to act with the British troops a Ganst Cannaday and[?] under the Command of Gennarel Abeacrombea a Ganst ticanaroga[6] I found tareang at Home was two Inactive a Life for me tharefore [I] joind meney of my Old Companyans a secant time for the arme of the end of ye Campain under the Same Offisers and Same Reagimen[t] under the Cumand of Corll [Colonel] Nathan Whiteing[7] I[n] the Spring we Imbark to gine the armey at Albaney whare we arived Safe at the time apointed we ware

[5] During 1757, another unfortunate year for the British, General Montcalm captured Fort William Henry, and his Indian allies massacred many of the British prisoners while they were being escorted under parole to Fort Edward.

[6] General James Abercromby became commander in chief in 1758 when the British government decided to launch a vigorous offensive against the French. Abercromby's incapacity soon became apparent in his unnecessary defeat at Ticonderoga and he was immediately recalled; other British campaigns of 1758 were more successful.

[7] The Second Connecticut Regiment was commanded in 1758 by Colonel Nathan Whiting of New Haven. Captain David Baldwin was one of his officers. Connecticut Historical Collections, 10:37.

Inployde in forwarding Provishons to fort Eadward for ye youse of the Campain with a Grat Number of Other artickels for ye youse of the Sarvis when all so readey for us to Cross Lake George the armey Imbarked Consisting of Eighteen thousend British & Provensals in about twelve Hundred Battoes & a number of whaleboates floteing Battereys Gundaloes Rogalleyes & Gunboates the Next Day we arived at the North end of Lake George & Landed with Out Oposhion [opposition] the french that ware Incampt at that End of the Lake flead at our apearanc as far as Tiandarogeea & joind thair old Commander Moncalm and we ware Drawn up in Order & Devideed into Collams & Ordred to March to ward Moncalm in his Camp Befour the fort But unfortinnatly for us Moncalm Like a Ginnaral Dispateachd five Hundred to apose us in Our Landing Or at Least to Imbairis us in Our march til he mite Put his Camp in sum sort of Defens Befor Our armey Could arive & thay Did it Most Cumpleatly we had not Marcht more then a Mile & a Half Befoar we Meat the falon Hope for Such it Proved to be the British troops Kept [the] Rode [road] in One Collom the amaraCans Marcht threw ye Woods on thare Left on the ye Rite of the British was the Run of Water that Emteys from Lake George into Lake Champlain the British & french Meat in the Open Rode Verey Near Each Other Befour thay Discoverd the french On a Count of the Uneaveneas of the Ground Lord How held the sacond Plase in Cammand & Beaing at the Head of the British troops with a Small side arm in his Hand he Ordered the troopes to forme thare front to ye Left to atack the french But While this Was Dueing the french fird & His Lordship Recved a Ball & three Buck Shot threw the Senter of his Brest & Expird without Spekeing a word [8] But the french Pade Dear for this Bold atempt it was But a Short [time bef]oar thay ware Surounded By the Hole of the Amarecan

---

[8] General George Howe was an excellent soldier, and he was well liked by his troops. His death in this preliminary skirmish had much to do with the defeat which followed. He was an older brother of William and Richard Howe of Revolutionary War fame.

troops and those that Didnot Leape into the Raped Stream in Order to Regain thare Camp ware Made Prisners or Kild & those that Did went Doan with the Raped Curant & Was Droanded from the Best Information I Could Geat from ye french of that Partea was that thare Was But Seven men of ye five Hundred that Reacht the Campt But it answerd the Purpas Amaseingly this afair Hapend on thirsday the troops Beaing all Strangers to the Ground & Runing threw the woods after the Disparst frenchmen Night Came on and thay Got themSelves so Disparst that thay Could not find the way Back to thare Boates at the Landing that Nite the British Did Beatter haveing the Open Rod to Direct them thay Got to ye Lake Sid without trabel a Large Partey of ye amarecans Past the Nite within a Bout half a Mile of the french Lines with Out nowing whare thay ware til Morning I was not in this Partey I had wanderd in ye woods in the Nite with A Bout twelve Men of my aquantans finealey fel on the Rode a Bout a Mile North of ye Spot whare the first fire began Beaing in the Rode we Marched to ward Our boates at ye water Side But Beaing Dar[k] we Made But a Stumbling Pece of Bisness of it & So[o]n Coming a Mong the Dead Bodeyes which ware Strueed Quit thick on the Ground for Sum Lettle Distans we Stumbled over them for a while as Long as thay Lasted at Lengh we Got to the Boates just Before Day Lite in the Morn what Could be found of the troops Got in sum Order & Began our March a Bout two a Clock in ye afternoon Crossing the Raped Stream and Left it on Our Left the Rode on this Side was Good & we advans toward the french Camp as fars the Miles [Mills?] about a Mile from the Works & thare Past the Night Lying on our armes this Delay Gave the french what thay wanted time to Securea thare Camp which was well Executed the Next Day which was Satterday about Eleven we ware Seat in Mosin the British Leading the Van it was about thay ware Draun up Before Strang Brest Work But more in Extent then to Pormit four thousend five Hundred Acting we had no Cannon up to the works the

Intent was to March Over this work But thay found themSelves Sadley Mistakeen the french had Cut Doun a Grate number of Pinetrease in front of thar[e?] Camp at Sum Distans while Sum war Entrenching Others ware Imployed in Cuting of the Lims of the trease and Sharpen[in]g them at Both Ends for a Shevoe Dafrease [*chevaux de frise*] others Cuting of Larg Logs and Geting tham to the Brestwoork at Lengh thay ware Readey for Our Reseption abot twelve the Partes Bagan thare fire & the British Put thare Plan on fut to March Over the Works But the Limes & tops of the Trease on the Side for the Diek Stuck fast in the Ground and all Pointed at ye upper End that thay Could not Git threw them til thay ware at Last Oblige to Quit that Plan for three forths ware Kild in the atempt But the Grateer Part of the armey Lade in the Rear on thare faseis till nite while the British ware Batteling a Brestwork Nine Logs thick in Sum plaseis with [which?] was Dun with Out ye Help of Canan tho we had as fine an Aartilrey Just at Hand as Could be in an armey of fifteen thousend men but thay ware of no yous while thay ware Lying on thare faseisis. Just as the sun was Seating Abeacrumbea Came from left to Rite in the Rear of the troops ingaged and Ordread a Retreat Beat and we Left the Ground with a Bout two thousand two Hundred Loss as I was Informd By an Officer who Saw the Retans of ye Kild Wounded & Mising[9] we ware Ordered to Regain our Boates at the Lake Side which was Dun after traveling all Nite so Sloley that we fell a Sleape by the way A Bout Nine or tenn in the Morning we ware Ordred to Imbarke & Cross the Lake to the Head of Lake George But to Sea the Confusan thare was The Solgers Could not find thare thare One Botes But Imbarked Permiskenley [promiscuously] whar Ever thay Could Git in Expeting the french at thare Heales Eaverey mennet we ariveed at the Head of the Lake in a Short time took up our Old Incampment which was well fortefide after a few Day the

[9] Abercromby's defeat at Ticonderoga is described in Parkman, *Montcalm and Wolfe*, 2:289–320. As Reuben G. Thwaites pointed out when he printed Pond's

arme Began to Cum to themselves and found thay ware Safe for the hole of the french in that Part of the Cuntrey was not more then three thousend men and we a bout fortee[n] thousend we then Began to Git up Provshan from fort eadward to the Camp But the french ware so Bold as to Beseat our Scouting Partey Betwene the Camp and fort eadward & Cut of all the teames Destroy the Provshon Kill the Parties and all under thare aScort we Past the samer in that Maner & in the fall Verey Late the Camp Broke up and what Remand went into winter Qaters in Differant Parts of the Collannes thus Ended the Most Ridicklas Campane Eaver Hard of.

The year 59 an armey was Rased to go a ganst Niagaray to Be Cammanded By Ginaral Broduck [Prideaux][10] as the Connecticut troops ware not to Be Imploid in that Part of the armey I wen[t] to Long-Island and Engaged in that Sarvis In the Spring we Repaird to Alboney & Gind the armey as that was the Plase of Randevuse we ware Imploid In Geating forward Provisons to Oswago for the Sarvis of the Campain when we aSemeld at Osawago Corll Haldaman took Part of the troops under his Cummand & Incampt on the Ontarey Side [11] But the troop that ware Distanade [destined] to Go a ganst Niagarey Incampt on the Opaseat Side of the River under the Cummand of Genneral Broduck But the Companey I Belong to was not Ordred Over the Lake at all But Corll Johnsen who was in the Garsea [Jersey] Sarvis Sent for me In Partickler to Go Over the Lake I wated on him and Inquiard of him How he Came to take me the Ondley Man of the Companey Out to Go Over the Lake he sade He had a mind I should be with him I then ask him for as meney of the Companey as would make me a Seat of

---

narrative in 1908, the accuracy of Pond's description of this battle attests to the value of the document as a historical source. Wisconsin Historical Collections, 18:320n.

[10] General John Prideaux was the British officer who led the assault on Fort Niagara and was killed in action there.

[11] Colonel Frederick Haldimand and nearly half of the force were left at Oswego to rebuild Fort Ontario, which had been destroyed by the French in 1756.

THE NARRATIVE OF PETER POND 25

tent mate he sun Complid & we went & Incampt with the troop for that Sarvis Capt Vanvaeter Commanded the Company we joind [12] we Sun Imbarkd and Arived at Nagarey In a fue Days when all was Landead I was Sent By the Agatint Mr Bull as Orderley Sarjant to Gennaral Broduck I was Keept So Close to my Dutey that I Got nither Sleape nor Rest for the armey was up Befoar the works at the fort & the Gennarel was Doan at Johnsons Landing four Miles from the acting part of the armey I wa[s] forsed to Run Back & forth four miles Nite & Day til I Could not Sarve Eney Longer I sent to Mr Bull to Releve me by Sending another Sargint In my Plase which was Dun & I Gind my frends a Gane and shot[?] In the trenchis a Ganst the fort Befoar we had Capterd the fort the Gennaral had gind the arme and himSelf & my frend Corll Johnsen ware Both Kild in One Day and Corll Shaday [Thodey] of the New York troops shot threw the Leag this was a Loss to Our Small armey three Brave Offesares in One Day we Continud the Seage with Spereat under the Command of Sir William Johnson who it fel to after the D[e]ath of Braduck [13] I was faverd I Got But One Slite wound Dureing the Seage at the End of Twenty five Days the fort Capatalateed to leave the works with the honners of ware & lay doan thare Armes on the Beach whare thay ware to Imbarke in Boates for Schanackaday [Schenectady] under an ascort after apointing troop to Garsen the fort we

[12] Colonel John Johnstone of Perth Amboy, New Jersey, served as colonel of the New York regiment in 1759 and was second in command of the western army. Vanvaeter was probably Captain Dirck Van Veghte of New Brunswick, New Jersey. Wisconsin Historical Collections, 18:321n., 322n.

[13] Colonel Shaday has been identified as Colonel Michael Thodey, a merchant of New York City who had enlisted in the provincial troops in 1755. His wound did not disable him, and he served as colonel of the New York regiment during the years 1761–63. Wisconsin Historical Collections, 18:322n. Sir William Johnson was an important landed proprietor in the Mohawk Valley and an influential figure among the Indians. He had been active in frontier defense for some years and was given command of the attack on Niagara after the death of Prideaux. On July 28, 1759, Johnson made the following entry in his diary: "Buried Brigadier General Prideaux in the chapel, and Colonel Johnson with a great deal of form. I was chief mourner." See "Private Diary Kept by Sir William Johnson at Niagara and Oswego, 1759," in Captain John Knox, *Histori-*

Returnd to Osawago and Bilt a fort Cald fort Erey [14] at the Close of the Campain what was a live Returnd Home to thare Native Plaseis But we had Left a number Behind who was in thare Life Brave men. On my arival I at Milford I found Meney of the Prisners I had Bin So Indastresley In Captering was Billeated in the toun I Past the winter among them & in 1760 I Recved a Commision and Enterd a forth time in the armey we then Gind the Armey at the Old Plase of Randavuese and after lying thare a fue weakes in Camp Duing Rigmentals Dutey Ganeral Amarst [Amherst] Seat of in fourteen [boats] to Carrea thir Bageage to Osswago whare Part of the armey Had allready arived I was Ordred on this Command four Offeser & Eightey Men On Our arival at Osswago the Ginneral Gave the Other three Offercers as Meney Men as would Man One Boate & Ordred them Return to thare Regment Me He Ordred to Incamp with my men in the Rear of his fammaley til farther Orders with Seventey Men til Just Befour the armey Imbark for Swagochea [Oswegatchie] and then Gind my Rigment [15] Sun after thare was apointed a Lite infantrey Cumpaney to Be Pick Out of Each Rigment Hats Cut Small that thay mite be youneform I was apointed to this Cumpaney when Orders was giveen the arme A Bout Nine thousend Imbark in a Number

cal Journal of the Campaigns in North America for the Years 1757, 1758, 1759, and 1760 (edited by Arthur G. Doughty, Publications of the Champlain Society, Vol. 10, Toronto, 1916), p. 189. The most important military event of 1759 was General James Wolfe's capture of Quebec in September.

[14] Pond is speaking here again of Fort Ontario, located on Lake Ontario near Oswego. (Fort Erie was situated at the lower end of Lake Erie.) After Fort Ontario was rebuilt, it became a camp of some ten thousand men. From this point General Jeffrey Amherst set out down the St. Lawrence River in 1760 on the expedition Pond describes below, which resulted in the fall of Montreal and New France. Herbert L. Osgood, *American Colonies in the Eighteenth Century* (New York, 1924), 4:383–384; George M. Wrong, *The Fall of Canada* (Oxford, 1914), pp. 212–216. Sir William Johnson supervised the work of reconstructing the fort, and some details concerning it are to be found in his "Private Diary." See note 13, above.

[15] Oswegatchie was the site of a mission named La Présentation which was located on the St. Lawrence River at the mouth of the Oswegatchie River. The military objective was Fort Lévis, built on an island in the river opposite La Présentation.

of Boates & went on the Lake toward Swagochea whare we aRived safe thare we found Poshoe [Pouchot] that had Bin taken at Niagarey the sumer Before Cummanding the fort and Seme to Be Detarmenad to Dispute us & Give us all the trubel he Could But after Eight or a fue more Days he was ablige to Compley with the tarmes of Our Victoras armey a seacand time in les then One year[16] we then Left a Garrson and desonded the River til we Reacht Montreal the Ondlay Plase the french Had In Prosesion in Cannaday hear we lay one Night on Our Armes the nex Day the toun Seranderd to Gineral Amharst in thre[e] years while I was in the armey all Cannaday was in the Hands of the British Nor have thay [the French] Had aney Part of it Sins all Cannaday subdued I thought thare was no bisnes left for me and turnd my atenshan to the Seas thinking to make it my Profesion and in Sixtey one I went a Voige to the Islands in the West Indens and Returnd Safe but found that my father Had gon a trading Voig to Detroit and my Mother falling Sick with a feaver Dide Before his Return I was Oblige to Give up the Iedea of going to Sea at that time and take Charge of a young fammaley til my father Returnd after which I Bent my Mind aftor Differant Objects and taread in Milford three years which was the Ondlay three years of my Life I was three years in One Plase Sins I was Sixteen years old up to Sixtey at ye End of the three years I went into Trade first at Detroit I Continued in trade for Six years in Differant Parts of that Cuntrey But Beaing Exposed to all Sorts of Cumpaney it Hapend that a parson [person] who was in trade himSilf to Abuese me in a Shamefull manner Knowing that if I Resontd he Could Shake me in Peaceis at same tim Supposeing that I Dair not Sea him at the Pints or at Leas I would not But the

[16] Captain Francois Pouchot had been in command at Niagara in 1759 when it was captured by Sir William Johnson. He was taken as a prisoner to Albany but was soon exchanged and sent to defend Fort Lévis. Wisconsin Historical Collections, 18:211n., 323n. An account of the action at Fort Lévis is found in P. S. Garrand, *History of the City of Ogdensburg* (Ogdensburg, New York, 1927), pp. 139-145.

Abuse was two Grate we met the Next Morning Eairley and Discharged Pistels in which the Pore fellow was unfortennt I then Came Doan the Cuntrey & Declard the fact But thare was none to Prosacute me I then Made a ture to ye West indaes and on my Return Home I Recved a Leatter from a Gentelman in New York to Cum Doan and Sea him for he was Desiaras to Go into Partner Ship with me in trade I Cumplyed and we Lade in a cargo to the amount of four thousand Six Hundred Pounds & I went into the Entearor Part of the Cuntrey first to Mishlemackenack from thenst to the Masseppay and up Sant Peters [Minnesota] River and into the Plains Betwene the Misseppey & the Miseeurea and Past my winter a mong the NattawaySease [Sioux] on Such food as thay mad youse of them Selves which was Verey darteyaly [dirtily] Cooked.[17]

The Next is to Show the Way of Convance [conveyance] of these Goods to the Most Remot Parts of ye Cuntrey for that year or Season In the first Plase thay ware Shipt at New-York for allbaney from thens thay ware takeen to fooreteen Miles By Land to Sconacaday in wagens then Shipt on Bord Battoes & takeen up the Mohawk River to fort Stanwex thare Carread a Mile By Land with the Boates and Put in to Woodcrick & from thens threw the Onida Lake & Doun them waters to Lake Ontarey & Coasted aLong the South Side of that Lake till thay Came to Nagarey & from the Landing Plase a fue Miles South of that fort thay ware with the Battoese Caread a Cross that Caring Plase about Nine Miles then Put into the waters that Coms out of Lake Erey into Lake Ontarey at a Plase Cald fort Slosser [18] from that in thos Boates ware takeen to a Small fort Cald fort Erey on the north Side of Lake Earey then Coasting a long the North Side of that Lake til thay Cam to the

[17] Pond is here summarizing his travels as recounted in the remaining pages of the journal; he is not referring to a separate expedition.

[18] Fort Schlosser was a British fort situated at the upper end of the Niagara portage about two miles above the falls. See "Diary of Ralph Izard, 1765," in Frank H. Severance, *Studies of the Niagara Frontier* (Buffalo Historical Society Publications, Vol. 15, Buffalo, 1911), p. 342. See also Severance, *An Old Frontier of France* (New York, 1917), 2:305, 331, 346.

THE NARRATIVE OF PETER POND 29

Mouth of the River then up to De[t]roit from thens up them waters to Lake St Clair a Small one aBout fourteen Miles Long. from thens Proseaving these waters which Cum out of Lake Huron you com to that Lake & Coasting a Long the West Sid of it aBout five Hundread Miles thay Cam to Mishlamacneck that Lay at that on the South Side of a Strate Betwene Lake Huran & Mishagon thare was a British Garason whare all the traders aSembel yearley to arang thare afairs for the InSewing Winter But I Didnot A Cumpany My Goods mySelf Left that Part to my Partner Mr Graham [19] I wanted Sum Small artickels in the Indan way to Cumpleat my asortment which was not to be had in New York I tharefour took my Boat threw Lake George & threw Lake Champlain to Montreal whare I found all I wanted this was in the Spring 1773 thare was a number of Canues fiting for Mishlamacanac I a Gread with Isac Tod [Todd] aSqur. to take my Good in His Canneues an fraight and Imbark with him & James McGill Esqr in one of his Canues and Seat of from Lashean [Lachine] for Mackenac By way of the Grand [Ottawa] River [20] as you Pass the End

---

[19] Pond's associate was Felix Graham, a merchant who was trading at the time from New York to Mackinac but who seems to have removed to Montreal during the next few years. An invoice of the goods belonging to the partnership in June, 1773, valued them at £1,244, 13s, 11 1/2d. The partnership began in 1771 and was renewed in 1773. Harold A. Innis, *Peter Pond, Fur Trader and Adventurer* (Toronto, 1930), pp. 20, 67, 150.

[20] Isaac Todd and James McGill were Montreal merchants who built up a profitable business in furnishing goods and supplies for the Indian trade and disposing of the furs in English and European markets. They were active as early as 1767, and by 1773 they had formed the firm of Todd and McGill, which was to remain a force in the fur trade for more than twenty years. In 1775 McGill, Benjamin Frobisher, and Maurice Blondeau sent out twelve canoes, three guides, and seventy-five men, together with a shipment of goods which marked the beginning of extensive trade in the Northwest by Canadian traders. The business grew until in 1786 the McGill and Frobisher concerns gave security for thirty canoes, three hundred men, and goods to the amount of £3,000. McGill gained for himself a position of considerable prestige, taking an active part not only in the commercial life of Canada but in its political life as well. He died in 1813. McGill University was established as a result of a large bequest by this Canadian merchant. The following works give biographical material: Robert Campbell, *History of the Scotch Presbyterian Church, St.*

of the Island of Montreall to Go in a Small Lake Cald the Lake of the Two Mountans thare Stans a Small Roman Church Aganst a Small Rapead this Church is Dedacateed to St Ann who Protescts all Voigeers[21] heare is a Small Box with a Hole in the top for ye Reseption of a Lettle Muney for the Hole father to Say a Small Mass for those who Put a small Sum in the Box Scars a Voigeer but Stops Hear and Puts in his mite and By that Meanes thay Suppose thay are Protacted while absant the C[h]urch is not Locked But the Munney Box is well Sacured from theaves after the Saremoney of Crossing them Selves and Rapeting[?] a Short Prayer we Crost the Lake and Entard the Grand River so Calld which Lead us to the waters which Cams in to that River from the Southwest we a Sended these waters & Makeing Sum Caring Plaseis we Came to a Small Lake Cald Nipasank [Nipissing] whos waters fall into Lake Huron By the french River we Desended that River and Coasted a Long the North Side of that Lake til we Came Oppaseat to Mackenac then Crost the Strat to the Garreason whare I found my Goods from New York Had A Rived Safe Hear I Met with a Grate meney Hundred People of all Denomanatons Sum trading with the tribes that Came a Grate Distans with thare furs Skins & Mapel Suge[r] &c to Marke[t] to these May Be adead Dride Venson Bares Greas and the Like which is a Considerabel Part of trade Others ware Imployd in Makeing up thare Ecipments for to Send in to the Differant Parts of the Cuntrey to Pas the winter among ye Indan tribes and trade what thay Git from the Hunt of ye winter Insowing I was one of this Discription I Devided my Good in to twelve Parts and fited out twelve Large Canues for Differant Part of the Massasippey River Each can-

Gabriel Street, Montreal (Montreal, 1887); Gordon C. Davidson, *The North West Company* (University of California Publications in History, Vol. 7, Berkeley, 1918); Wayne E. Stevens, *Northwest Fur Trade, 1763–1800* (Urbana, 1928); Harold A. Innis, *The Fur Trade in Canada* (Toronto, 1956).

[21] The Church of Ste. Anne, located at the western end of the island of Montreal, was a customary stopping place for fur brigades on their way to the interior. It is mentioned by many traders, including other diarists in this volume.

new was mad of Burch Bark & white Seader [cedar] thay would Carry Seven Thousand wate; A Discripion of Macenac this Plase is Kept up By a Capts Cummand of British which are Lodge in Good Baracks with in the Stockades whare thare is Sum french Bildings and a Commouds [commodious] Roman Church whare the french Inhabatans & InGasheas [*engagés*] Go to Mass Befour it was giveen up to the British thare was a french Mishenerae aStableshed hear who Resideed for a number of years hear [22] while I was hear thare was[?] None But traveling One who Cams sumtimes to make the a Short [stay] But all way in the Spring when the People ware ye Most numeras — then the Engasheas oftan went to Confes & Git absalution I Had the next winter with me [one] who was aDicted to theaveing he took from me in Silver trinkets to the amount of ten Pound But I Got them agane to a trifel In the Spring we found one of those Preast at Mackenac who was Duing wonder among the People My Young Man Babtest who had Cumited the theft Heard of it from his Cumrads who had Bin to Confess his Consans [conscience] Smit Him & He Seat of to Confess but Could not Git absalution he went a seacant tim with out suckses But Was Informd By his Bennadict that Sumthing was wanting He Came to me Desireing me to leat him Have Two Otter Skins Promising that he would Be Bater in futer and sarve well I Leat him Have them he went of In a fue Minnets after or a Short time he Returnd I askt him what Suckses O, sade he the farther sais my Case is a Bad one But if I Bring two Otter more He will take my Case on him Self and Discharge me I let him Have them & in a Short time he Returnd as full of thanks as he Could Expres and Sarved me well after the InHabetans of this Plase trade with the natives and

[22] The register of marriages at Mackinac indicates that Father Pierre du Jaunay and Father Marie Louis le Franc were missionaries at Mackinac during several years preceding 1761. Father du Jaunay continued his ministrations until 1765, but no priest seems to have been there from 1765 to 1768. Father Pierre Gibault, vicar-general of the Illinois, visited the post in 1768 on his way to the Illinois country, and entries also appear in the register over his name in 1773 and 1775. Wisconsin Historical Collections, 18:292, 469–490.

thay Go out with ye Indans in the fall and winter and winter with them Men, woman & Childran   Moste of the frenchmans wives ar white woman   in the Spring thay make a Grat Quantatey of Mapel Suger for the youse of thare famelies & for Sale sum of them [23]   the Land about Macenac is Varey Baran a mear Sand Bank But the Gareson By Manure Rase Good Protaters and Sum Vegatabels   the British Cut Hay anuf for thare Stock a fue Miles Distans from the Gareson & Bring hom on Boates Others Cut the Gras & Stack it on the Spot & Slead it on the Ice thirtey Miles in ye winter   thare is Sum Injan Villeges twentey or thirtey Miles from this Plase whare the Natives Improve Verey Go[o]d Ground   thay rase Corn Beens and meney artickels which thay youse in Part them Salves and Bring the Remander to Marke[t]   the Nearest tribe is the Atauwas [Ottawa] and the most Sivalised in these Part But Drink to Exses   often in the winter thay Go out on a Hunting Partey   in ye Spring thay Return to thare Villeag and Imploy the Sumer in Rasein thing for food as yousal   But this is to Be understud to Belong to the Women   the men Never Meadel with Part of thar basnes is Confind to the feamales Onidley   Men are Imploid in Hunting fishing & fouling War Partis &c   these Wood aford Partreages Hairs Vensen foxis & Rackcones Sum Wild Pigins   this Lake or Strate abounds in all sorts of fine fish   I have Wade a trout takeen in By Mr Campo with a Hoock & lind under the Ice in March Sixtey Six Pounds wait   I was Present   the water was fifteen fatham Deape; the white fish are another Exqiuseat fine fish   thay will way from 2 1/2 to 9 & 10 Pound wt   Baran La

---

[23] Sugar was a delicacy highly prized in the wilderness, and each spring saw the women tapping the maple trees, inserting spouts of basswood, and collecting the sap in birch bark containers. After cooking for the required time, the syrup was taken from the fire and stirred with a long paddle until it thickened into a sugar that might be packed into containers. For the purpose of storing, makuks of birch bark, holding from thirty to eighty pounds, were used. For a description of sugaring as it was done in 1820 see Elizabeth T. Baird, "Reminiscences of Early Days on Mackinac Island," Wisconsin Historical Collections, 14:28–34. See also "Uses of Plants by the Chippewa Indians," in Forty-fourth Annual Report of the Bureau of American Ethnology (Washington, 1928), pp. 308–313.

THE NARRATIVE OF PETER POND   33

Huntan[24] who was the first that made an Excirtion from Mackanac Into the Masecipey By the Rout of the fox River, tho his Ideas ware Rong in Sum things as I have Proved Sins his say that Buter spild the flave[r] of white fish was Right the Sturge[on] are the Best in these Lakes & the Harens [herring] Exsead in flaver the waters are transParant and fine I return to my one [own business.] In Septr I Had my Small fleat Readey to Cross Lake Mishegon on my way to Grean Bay at the Mouth of the fox River I Engaged Nine Clarks for Differant Parts of the Sourthan & Westarn Cantrey and Beaing Mand we Imbarkt & Crost the Lake without Seaing an Indan or Eney Parson Except our Ome [own][25] in three or four Days we arive at the Mouth of the Bay which is two or three Miles Brod in the Mouth is Sum Islands which we follow in Crosing to the South west Sid, and then follow ye shore to the Bottom which is Seventey Miles whare the fox River Emtey in to the Bay, we went a Short Distans up the River whare is a Small french villege and thare Incampt for two Days this Land is Exalent, the InHabatans Rase fine Corn and Sum Artickels for fammaley youse in thare Gardens, Thay Have Sum trad with ye Indans which Pas that way on the North Part of this Bay is a Small Villeag of Indans Cald the Mannamaneas [Menominees] who Live By Hunting Chefely thay Have anothe[r] Resors [resource] the Bottom of the Bay Produsus a Large Quantity of Wilde Rice which thay Geather in Septr for food I ort to have Menshand that the french at ye Villeg whare we Incamt Rase fine Black

[24] Lahontan was supposed to have made his voyage during the winter of 1688–89. The authenticity of his account of the expedition has been contested, and the view has been expressed that the French baron probably did not reach the Mississippi, but may have spent the winter months in Indian villages and hunting camps in the Fox River region. For a discussion of this question see Thwaites's introduction to Lahontan's *New Voyages to North America* (Chicago, 1905). Louise P. Kellogg, in her work on the *French Régime in Wisconsin and the Northwest* (Madison, 1925), p. 239, defends the accuracy of Lahontan's description of eastern Wisconsin.

[25] Pond's clerks were subordinates in the trade who were hired and stationed on the different rivers tributary to the Mississippi, where they collected furs

Cattel & Horseis with Sum Swine at the End of two Days we
aSended the fox River til we Came to a Villige which Lises on
the East End of a Small Lake that Eties [empties] in to the fox
River these People are Cald Pewans [Puans] & the Lake By the
Same Name these People are Singelir from the Rest of thare
Nighbors thay Speake a Hard un Corth [uncouth] Langwige
Scarst to be Larnt By Eney People thay will not aSosheat with
or Convars with the other tribes Nor Intermarey among them I
Enquird in to the Natral Histrey of these People when I was at
Detroit of the Oldest and Most Entelaget french men Who had
Bin aquanted with them for Meney Years the Information
amounted to this that thay formely Lived west of ye Miseiarey
[Missouri] River that thay Had Entarnal Disputes among
themsel[ves] and Dispute with the Nations about them at
Length thiare Nighber In Grat Numbers fel apon them and
what was Saved flead acros the Misesurea to ye [e]astward and
Over the Massappey and on to this Lake whare thay now live
thare thay met with a tribe of Indans Who Suferd them to Seat
Doun in it was as is Suposed the fox Nation who leved Near
them the foxis was Drove from Detroit for thare Misbehaver
which ware a proper People to aSist tham in thare flite I Beleve most of it thay are Insalent to this Day and Inclineing
Cheaterey thay will if thay Can Git Creadeat from the trader
in the fall of ye Year to Pay in the Spring after thay Have made
thare Hunt But When you mete them in Spring and Know
them Parseneley ask for your Pay and thay will Speake in thare
one Langwege if thay Speake at all Which is not to be understud or Other wase thay will Look Sulkey and Make you no
answer and you lous your Dept [debt?] I was at Mackenac
when Capt George Turnbull Cumanded Preaves to the aMarecan Reverlution and thare Came in a Cheafe with a Small Band

from the Indians. A rendezvous was arranged at Prairie du Chien. For a further
explanation of the various ranks of traders as they developed in later years see
below, page 67n.

of these [26] he Held a Counsel with them But he Could[not] Git an Intarpreter in the Plase that UndarStud them at Length the Captn Said that he Had a mind to sand for an Old Highland Solger that Spoke Leatels But the Hars[h] Langwege Perhaps he mite understand for it Sounded Much Like it the Land about them on the Lake is Exalant thar women Rase Corn & Beens Punkpins &c But the Lake aford no Varietey of fish thare wood Produse Sum Rabits & Partrageis a Small Quantatey of Vensen thay Live in a Close Connection among them selves We made But a Small Stay Hear and Past a Small Distans on this Lake and Entard the fox River a gane Which Leads up to the Cairing Plase of Ouiconstan [Wisconsin] we asendead that River til we Cam to a High Pece of Groand Whare that Nation yous to Entair thar Dead whin thay Lived in that Part [27] we stopt hear a while finding Sum of that Nation on the Spot who Came thare to Pay yare Resepct to thar Departed frend thay Had a small Cag of Rum and seat Around the Grave thay fild thar Callemeat [calumet] and Began thare Saremony By Pinting the Stem of the Pipe upward then giveing it a turn in thare and then toward ye head of the Grave then East & West North & South after which thay smoake it out and fild it a Gane & Lade [it] By then thay toock Sum Rum Out of the Cag in a Small Bark Vessel and Pord it on the Head of the Grave By Way of giveing it to thare Departed Brother then thay all Drank them Selves Lit the Pipe Smokd and seam to Injoie themselves Verey well thay Repeated this till thay the Sperit Began to Operrate and thare harts Began to Soffon then thay

[26] The period of Captain Turnbull's service as commandant of the post at Mackinac is not clear. He was sent to Detroit in 1766, where he remained in charge for three years, and apparently went from Detroit to Mackinac. Wisconsin Historical Collections, 18:312n.

[27] In the latter years of the seventeenth century the Fox Indians left their home on the upper Wolf River and built a village at this spot, near the site of the present Butte des Morts, Wisconsin. It is believed that the great mound found there was erected to cover the warriors, Foxes and Sauks, who were slain in the Battle of Butte des Morts (1733), an important engagement of the Second Fox War. Kellogg, *French Régime*, pp. 205, 332.

Began to Sing a Song or two But at the End of Everey Song thay Soffend the Clay after Sum tim Had Relapst the Cag hat Bin Blead often thay Began to Repete the Saisfaction thay had with that frind while he was with them and How fond he was of his frinds while he Could Git a Cag of Rum and how thay youst to Injoy it togather thay amused them selves in this manner til thay all fell a Crying and a woful Nois thay Mad for a while til thay thought wiseley that thay Could not Bring him Back and it would not Due to Greve two much that an application to the Cag was the Best way to Dround Sorrow & Wash away Greafe The Moshan was sun Put in Execution and all Began to be marey as a Partey Could Bea thay Contineued til Near Nite Rite wen thay ware More then Half Drunk the men began to aproach the femals and Chat frelay and apearantly frindley at Length thay Begin to Lean on Each other Cis & apeard Virey amoras at Length two would Steapt a Sid in ye Eag [edge] of the Bushis Prasently two more would Steap of But I Could Obsarve Clearley this Bisnes was first Pusht on By the women who mad thare Viseat to the Dead a Verey Pleaseing one in thare way Wone of them who was Quit Drunk as I was By [my] Self Seating on the Ground obsarveing thare Saremones Came to me and ask me to take Share of Her Bountey in the Eag of the Bushis But I thought it was time to Quit and went about Half a mile up the Rive[r] to my Caneuees whare My men was Incampt But the Indans Neaver Came Nigh us thar the Men Menshan that thre[e] of the Women had bin at the Camp In the Night In Quest of Imploy; the nest Morning we Praseaded up the River which was Verey Sarpentine indea [indeed] till we Came to a Shallo Lake whare you Could Sea no water But Just in the Caneu track the Wild Oates was so thick that the Indans Could Scarse Git one of thare Small Canues into it to Geather it and the Wild Ducks Whe[n] thay Ris Maed a nois like thund[er] we Got as meney of them as we Chose fat and Good we Incampt hear would not undertake to Cros til Morning the water was two Deap to wade and ye Bot-

THE NARRATIVE OF PETER POND 37

tom Soft the Rode narrow that it toock the Most of ye next Day to get about three Miles With our Large Cannewes the track was so nare Near nite we Got to Warm Ground whare we Incampt and Rest[?] Well after the fateages [fatigues] of the Day the Next Day we Proseaded up the River which was Slack water But Verey Sarpentine ye Have to go two Miles with out Geating fiftey yards ahead so winding But Just at nite we reacht within Site of ye Caring [carrying] plas and Incampt Next morning Near non we arived and unLoded our Caneues & toock them out of the water to Dry that thay mite be liter on the Caring Plase— An acount of the fox River and its Neghbering Cuntrey A Long its Shores from the Moath to the Peuans Lake is A good Navagation One or two Small Rapeds from that Lake the Water up to the Caring plase is Verey Gental But Varey Sarpentine In Meney Parts In Going three Miles you due not advans one the Bank is all most Leavel With the Water and the Madoes on Each Side are Clear of wood to a Grate Distans and Cloth with a Good Sort of Grass the Ope[n]ings of this River W[h]ich are Cald Lakes But thay are no more than Large Opening [In] these Plaseis the water is aboat four or five feet deap with a Soft Bottom these Plaseis Produseis the Grateest Qantateys of Wild Rise of which the Natives Geather Grat Qantaties and Eat what thay Have Ocation for & Dispose of the Remainder to People that Pas & Repass on thare trad this Grane Looks in its Groth & Stock & Ears Like Ry and the Grane is of the Same Culler But Larger and Slimer when it is Cleand fit for youse thay Boile it as we Due Rise and Eat [it] with Bairs Greas and Suger But the Greas thay ad as it is Bileing which Helps to Soffen it and make it Brake in the Same maner as Rise when thay take it out of thare Cittels [kettles] for yous thay ad a Lettle suger and it [is] Eaten with fres Vonsen or fowls we yoused it in the Room of Rise and it Did verey well as a Substatute for that Grane as it Busts it tarns Out Parfectly White as Rise Back from this River the Lands are as Good as Can be Conseaved and Good timber But not

Overthick it is Proverbel that the fires Which Ran th[r]ew these woo[d]s and Meadoes Stops the Groth of ye wood and Destroise Small wood I Have Menshand the Vast Numbers of Wild Ducks which faten on ye Wild Rise Eaverey fall it would Sound two much Like a travelers Storey to Say What I Rearley Beleve from what I Have Sean you Can Parchis them Verey Cheape at the Rate of two Pens Per pese if you Par[fer] Shuteing them your Self you may Kill what you Plese— An acound of the Portage of Osisconstan the South End of this Caring plase is Verey Leavel But in wet wather it is Bad On acount of the Mud & Water which is two thirds of a Mile and then the Ground Riseis to a Considerabel Hith and Cloth with fine Open Wood & a Hansum Varder [verdure] this Spot is Abot the Senter of ye Portage and take up about a Quorter Part of it the North End is Low flat and Subject to Weat it was on this Spot that Old Pinneshon a french Man Imposed apon Carve[r] Respecting the Indan haveing a Rattel Snake at His Call which the Indand Could order into a Box for that Purpas as a Peat [pet][28] this frenchman was a Solder in the troops that ware stasond at the Elenoas [Illinois] he was a Sentanal A[t] the Mageasean of Pouder he Desorted His Post & toock his Boat up the Miseeurea among the Indans and Spant Maney years among them he Larnt Meney Langeweg and from Steap to Step He Got among the Mondans [Mandans] whare he found Sum french traders who Belongd to the french facterey at fort Lorain on the Read River[29] this facterey Belong to the

[28] Jonathan Carver is chiefly deserving of note as the author of a book that aroused tremendous interest in America among European readers and writers. This work, *Travels through the Interior Parts of North America*, describing his journeys of 1766–67 and his winter among the Sioux on the St. Peter's (Minnesota) River, was first published in 1778, and in numerous editions thereafter. Carver's Journal of the expedition is in the British Museum. The Minnesota Historical Society has a photostatic copy. "Old Pinnashon," in Thwaites's opinion, was Pennesha George, a trader. See Wisconsin Historical Collections, 1:41; 3:261–263.

[29] Fort la Reine, mentioned also by Macdonell, was built in 1738 by La Vérendrye. Situated at Portage la Prairie on the Assiniboine River, it served as

THE NARRATIVE OF PETER POND 39

french traders of Cannaday those People toock Pinneshon to the facterey with them and the Concarn took him into thare Sarvis til the Hole Cuntrey Was Giveen up to the English and he then Came in to thare Sarvis the french Strove to take him afor His Desarson But fald However thay Ordred him to be Hung in Efagea [effigy] Which was Dun; this is the a Count he Gives of himselvef I Have Hurd it from his one Lips Meney times as he has bin Relateing his advant[ure]s to Others He found Carver on this Spot Going on Dissoverey in an Obscur[?] Mananer without undirstanding orther [either] french or Indan & full of Enquirey threw his Man who Sarved him as an Enterprar thought it a Proper Opertunetey to ad Sumthing more to his adventers and Make his Bost of it after which I have Haird Menea times it hirt Cairver much hearing such things & Puting Confadens in them While he is Coruect [correct?] He Give a Good a Count of the Small Part of the Westarn Cuntrey he Saw But when he a Leude to Hearsase he flies from factes in two meney Instansis— After Two Day Hard Laber We Gits Our Canues over the Caring Plase with all our Goods and Incamp on the Bank of the River Oisconston & Gumd Our Canues fit to Desend that Rive[r]—[30] A Bout Midday we Imbark the River is a Gentel Glideing Stream and a Considabel Distans to the first Villeag which Lise on the Side North the River Runs near west from the Portag to the Misseppey its a Gentel Glideing Stream, as we Desended it we Saw Meneey Rattel Snakes Swiming a Cross it and Kild them, the Next Day we aRived at the Villeag whare we tarread two Days [31] this Beaing the Last Part of Septr these People had Eavery artickel of Eating in thare way In abandans—

an outpost from which expeditions reached the Mandan country on the Missouri. See Lawrence J. Burpee, ed., *Journals and Letters of Pierre Gaultier de Varennes de la Vérendrye and His Sons* (Publications of the Champlain Society, Vol. 16, Toronto, 1927), p. 10.

[30] The fur trader's canoe was made of large pieces of birch bark stretched over a frame of cedar. The seams were stitched with wattap or spruce roots and rendered watertight by a generous application of gum, a resinous substance made

I Shall Give Sum acount of these People and the Cuntrey—these People are Cald Saukeas thay are of a Good Sise and Well Dispost Les Inclind to tricks and Bad mannars then thare Nighbers thay will take of the traders Goods on Creadeat in the fall for thare youse In winter and Exept [for] Axedant thay Pay the Deapt [debt] verey well for Indans I mite Have Sade Inliteand Or Sivelisd Indans which are in General Made wors By the Opration thare Villeage is Bilt Cheafely with Plank thay Hugh of [o]ut of wood that is ye uprite the top is Caseh [cased?] Over with Strong Sapplens Suffisant to Suport the Ruf and Coverd with Barks which Makes them a tite ruf Sum of thare Huts are Sixtey feet Long and Contanes Saverl fammalyes thay Rase a Platform on Each Side of thare Huts a Bout two feet High & about five feet Brod on which thay Seat & Sleap thay have no flores But Bild thar fire on the Ground in the Midel of the Hut and have a Hole threw the Ruf for the Smoke to Pas In the fall of ye Year thay Leave these Huts and Go into the Woods in Quest of Game and Return in the Spring to thare Huts befou[r] Planting tim the women Rase Grat Crop of Corn Been Pumkens—Potatoes Millans and artickels the Land is E[x]alant & Clear of wood Sum Distans from the Villeage thare [are] Sum Hundreds of InHabbatan thare amusements are Singing Daning Smokeing matches Gameing and Feasting Drinking Playing the Slite of Hand Hunting & thay are famas in Mageack Thay are Not Verey Gellas [jealous] of thare women In Genaral the women find Meanes to

from pine pitch. The canoes received very hard usage and required gumming at frequent intervals.

[31] Carver reports this Sauk village as the largest Indian town he ever saw. Boasting a population of three hundred warriors, the settlement contained eighty large buildings besides a number of farmhouses in the fields for the convenience of the squaws. The town was situated on the north side of the Wisconsin River about forty miles below the end of the portage. It was built in the decade between 1740 and 1750, and was occupied until the end of the Revolutionary period, when a fear of the Chippewa drove the inhabitants to other homes near the Mississippi. Carver's Journal; Louise P. Kellogg in Wisconsin Historical Society Proceedings, 1907, pp. 143, 181; Wisconsin Historical Collections, 12:80.

Grattafy themSelves with out Censent of the men the Men
often jion war parteies with Other nations and Go aganst the
Indans on the Miseeure and west of that Sume time thay Go
Near St Fee [Santa Fe] in New Maxeco and Bring with them
Spanish Horseis; I have Sean Meney of them the River aford
But a fue fish thare woods aford Partragis a fue Rabeat Bairs &
Deear are Plentey In thare Seasons, wild foul thay have But
fue thar Religan is Like Most of the tribes thay a Low thare
is two Sperits One Goods Who Dwelve a Bove the Clouds Su-
perintends over all and helps to all the Good things we have
and Can Bring Sicknes on us if He pleaseis and another Bad
one who dwelves in the fire and air Eaverey whare among
m[en] & Sumtimes Dose Mischef to Mankind Cortship & Mare-
ages—[*two words illegible*] At Night when these People are
Seating Round thare fiuer [fire] the Elderly one will be teling
what thay Have Sean and Hard or Perhaps thay may be on Sum
Intrest[ing] Subg[ec]t the famley are lis[ten]ing if thare be
aney Young Garle in this Lodg or hut that any Man of a Dif-
feran Hut Has a Likeing for he will Seat among the Parson
of his Arrant [errand] Being Prasent hea will watch an Opertunety & through [throw] a Small Stick at Hair if She Looks
up with a Smile it is a Good Omen he Repets a Sacond tim
Perhaps ye Garle will Return the Stick the Simtam [symp-
toms] ar Still Groing Stronger and when thay think Proper to
Ly Doun to Slepe Each Parson Raps himself up in his One
Blanket he takes Notis whar the Garl Seats for thare [she]
sleep when all the famaley are Qui[e]t and Perhaps a Sleap he
Slips Soffely in to Hut and Seats himself Down By her Side
PresantLey he will Begin to Lift Her Blanket in a Soft maner
Perhaps she may twish it Out of his hand with a Sort of a Sie
& Snore to Gather But this is no Kiling Matter he Seats a while
and Makes a Sacond Atempt She May Perhaps Hold the Blan-
kead Doun Slitely at Length She turns Over with a Sith and
Quits the Hold of the Blanket He then Creapes under and
Geats as Close as he Can til allmost and than of[f] to his one

Hut this Meathard [method] is Practest a Short [time] and then ye yong Indan will Go ahanting and [if] he is Luckey to Git meat he Cums and Informs the famely of it and whare it is he Brengs the tung and hart with him and thay Seat of after the Meat and Bring it Home this Plesis [pleases] and he Begins to Gro Bold in the famerly the Garl after that will not Refuse him under the Blanket he Will then Perhaps Stay about the famerley a Year and Hunt for the Old father But in this Intram he Gives his Consent that thay may Sleap toogther and when thay Begin to have Children thay Save what thay Can git for thare One youse and Perhaps Live In a Hut apart afte[r] I had Giveen them a number of Cradeat to Recve Payment the Next Spring I Desended to the fox Villeage On the Same River and Same Sid about fiftey Miles Distans hear I meat a Differant Sort of People Who was Bread at Detroit under the french Goverment and Clarge [clergy]; till thay By Chrisanissing Grew so Bad thay ware Oblige to Go to war a Ganst them, tho thay Lived within thre Miles of the Gairsean and among the Inhabatans; thay Was Obligd To fite them and killd Grate Numbers of them, the Remander flead to the fox River whare thay made a Stand and treated the traders Going to the Misseappey Verey Ill, and Pilleaged them; at Lengh thay went a Stronge Partey aganst them and Beat them back to whare thay Now are But in Sad Sarkamstanis [circumstances] to what thay ware Before thay took So much on themSelves—[32] As I Aprocht the Banks of the Villeage I Perseaved a number of Long Pa[i]nted Poles on which Hung a Number of Artickels Sum Panted Dogs and a Grate Number of Wampum Belts with a Number of Silver Braslets and Other artickels in the Indan way I Inquird the Cause thay told me thay Had a Shorte time Before had a Sweaping Sicknes among them which Had Caread of

---

[32] Carver's Journal also gives a description of the unhappy condition of these Indians. The Fox village is stated to have been about eighty miles below the Sauk village on the northern bank. It consisted of more than fifty buildings. Thwaites suggests that Pond is here summarizing the Fox wars. Wisconsin Historical Collections, 18:337n.

THE NARRATIVE OF PETER POND 43

Grate Numbers of Inhabetans & thay had offerd Up these Sacrafisces to Apease that Beaing who was Angrey with them and Sent the Sicknes that it was Much Abateed tho thar was Sum Sick Still I told them thay had Dun Right and to take Cair that thay Did not Ofend him agane for fear a Grater Eavel myte befall them thare V[i]lleag was Bilt in the Sam form & ye Same Like Matearls [materials] as the Saukeas Prodes o [produce of?] the Ground the Same & Bote [brought?] in the Same By the Women But [not] in So Grate plentey as the former one on act [account] of thare Late sickness I taread hear One Day after Suplying mySelfe with Such artickels as I wanted and thay Had to Spare I Gave them Sum Cradeat and Desended the River to the Mouth which Enteys into the Masseeippey and Crost that River and Incampt the Land a long the River as you desend apears to be E[x]alant Just at night as we ware In Campt we Perseaved Large fish Cuming on the Sarfes of the water I had then a Diferant trader with me who had a number of Men with him, We ware Incampt near Each other We Put our Hoock and Lines in to the water & Leat them Ly all nite In the Morning we Perseaved thare was fish at the Hoocks and went to the water Eag and halld on our line thay Came Heavey at Lingh we hald one a Shore that wade a Hundred and four Pounds a Seacond that was One Hundred Wate a third of Seventey five Pounds the Men was Glad to Sea this for thay Hadnot Eeat mete for Sum Days nor fish for a long time we askd our men How meney Men the Largest would Give a Meale Sum of the Largest Eaters Sade twelve men Would Eat it at a Meal We a Gread to Give ye fish if thay would find twelve men that would undertake it thay Sun found them thay Began to Dres it the fish was what was Cald the Catfish it Had a large flat Head Sixteen Inchis Betwene the Eisse thay Skind it Cut it up it in three larg Coper k[ettles] Such as we have for the Youse of our men after it was well Boild thay Sarved it up and all Got Round it without [butter?] or Sas thay Began and Eat the hole with out the least thing with it—But Salt and

Sum of them Drank of the Licker it was Boild in the Other two was Sarved out to the Remainder of the People who finished them in a Short time thay all Declard thay felt the Beator of thare Meale Nor did I Perseave that Eney of them ware Sick or Cumplaind Nex Morning we Recrost ye River which was a bout a mile Brod and Mounted it a bout three Miles til we Came to the Planes of the Dogs [Prairie du Chien] So Cald the Grate Plase of Randavues for the traders and Indans Before thay Dispars for thare wintering Grounds Hear we Meat with a Larg Number of french & Indans Makeing out thare arangments for the InSewing winter and Sending of thare canues to Differant Parts Like wise Giveing Creadets to the Indans who ware all to Randavese thare in Spring I Stayd ten days Sending of my Men to Differant Parts I had Nine Clarks which I Imploid in Differant Rivers that fel into the River, When I had finished my Matters Hear in Octtober I Seat of with two traders in Cumpany for St Peters River which was a Hundred Leags up the River; But the Season was faverabel & we wen on Sloley to Leat the Nottawaseas [Sioux] Git Into the Plain that we Mite not be trubeld with them for Creadit as thay are Bad Pay Marsters in Going up the River we had Plenty of fat Gease and Duks with Venson Baires Meat In a Bantans [abundance] so that we Lived as well as hart Could Wish on Such food & Plentey of flower tea Coffea Suger and Buter Spirits and Wine that we faird well as Voigeers the Banks of ye River aforded us Plentey of Crab Apels which was Verey Good when the frost Had tuch them at a Sutabel tim we Enter St Peters River and Preseaded up it as far as we thought Best with out Seaing an Indan Except what we toock with us, we Incampt on a High Bank of the River that we mite not Be Overflone in the Spring, at the Brakeing up of the Ice, and Bilt us Cumfortbel Houseis for the Winter and trade Dureing the Winter & Got our Goods under Cover— To be Intelagabel I Go back to the Planes of the Dogs this Plain is A Verey Hansum one which on the East Side of the River on the Pint of Land

Betwene the Mouth of Oesconstan whare it Emties in to the Masseppey; & the Last River, the Plane is Very Smoth hear all the traders that Youseis [uses] that Part of the Cuntrey & all the Indans of Saveral tribes Meat fall & Spring whare the Grateist Games Are Plaid Both By french & Indans the french Practis Billeard ye latter Ball; Hear the Botes from New Orleans Cum thay are navagateed By thirty Six men who rose as meney oarse thay Bring in a Boate Sixtey Hogseats of wine on one flate[?] Besides Ham Chese &c all to trad with the french & Indans, thay Cum Up the River Eight Hundred Leages these amusements Last three or four weakes in the Spring of the Year; as we Proseaded up the River we found the Land & timber to be Exsalant fit for Eney Improvement as we Past up St Peters River a Bout fourtee[n] miles We Stopt to Sea Carvers Hut whare he Past his Winter when in that Cuntrey it was a Log House about Sixteen feet Long Coverd with Bark with a fireplase But One Room and No flore, this was the Exstent of his travels his Hole toure; I with One Canew Well mand Could make in Six weekes we Go forward to the Goods we made Our Selves Cumfortbel for the winter In Desember the Indanes Sent Sum Young men from the Planes a Long the River to Look for traders & thay found us after Staying a fue day to Rest them thay Departed with the Information to thare frends In Jany thay Began to Aproach us & Brot with them Drid & Grean Meet Bever Otter Dear fox Woolves Raccone & other Skins; to trade thay ware Welcom and we Did Our Bisnes to advantage threw the Winter I had a frenchman for my Nighber who had winter among the Nottawaseis Saverl winters in this River well Knone By the Differant Bands I perseaved that he Seamd to have a Prefran & Got More trade then my Self we ware Good frends I told him he Got mor then his Share of trade But Obsarvd at ye Same time it was not to be Wondread at as he had Bin Long a Quantead He Sade I hadnot Hit on ye Rite Eidea he Sade that the Indand of that Quorter was Giveen to Stealing and a Spacherley the women in Order to Draw Custam he Left a fue Brass Rings for the finger on the Counter Sum neadels & Alls which Cost But a trifel Leattle, Small Knives—Hakes[?] Bell & such trifels for the Sake of Stealing these trifels thay Came to Sea him and what thay Had for trad he Got I Beleved what he Sade and trid the Expereamant found it to Prove well; after which I Kept up Sides well thare was not Eney thing Extrodnerey Hapend Duering the winter we Prosude our trad with ease & Profet till Spring at the Brakeing up of the Ice In the River in Spring the water Rose twentey Six feat from its Common Surfes & Made Sad Work with its Banks at the yousal time We prepard to Desend to the Planes of the Dogs—I Shall not Make Eney Observatons aPon these People Nor Planes til the Insewing Year when I had a fair Opertunety the waters Sun went of or fell and we Imbark & Drifted Down with the Currant till we Came to the Plane whare we Saw a Large Colection from Everey Part of the Misseppey who had arived Beforur Us Even from Orleans Eight Hundred Leages Beloue us the Indans Camp Exeaded a Mile & a half in Length hear was Sport of All Sorts we went to Colecting the furs and Skins [*word illegible*] By the Differant tribes with Sucksess the french ware Verey Numarel [numerous] thare was Not Les then One Hundred and thirtey Canues which Came form Mackenaw Caring from Sixtey to Eightey Hundred wate Apease all Made of Barch Bark & white Seader, for the Ribs, those Boates from Orleans & Ilenoa and other Parts ware Newmares But the natives I[ndi]an have no true Iedea of thair Numbers the Number of Pack of Peltrey of Differant Sorts was Cald fifteen Hundred of a Hundred wt Each which went to Mackena all my Outfits had Dun well; I had a grate Share for my Part a[s] I furnish Much the Largest Cargo on the River after all the Bisness Was Dun & People Began to Gro tirde of Sport, thay Begin to Draw of for thare Differant Deprtment; and Prepare for the Insewing winter In July I arived at Mackenaw whare I found my Partner Mr Graham from New York with a Large

Cargo I had Dun So well that I proposd to bye him Out of ye Consarn & take it on my Self he Excepted and I Paid of the first Cargo and well on toward the One he had Brot me; Nothing Extrodnerey worth Notis Hapend hear Dureing my Stay I Apleyd my Self Closeley toward fiting Out a Cargo for the Same Part of the Cuntrey hear was a Grate Concors of People from all Quorters Sum Propareing to take thair furs to Cannaday others to Albaney & new York others for thare Intendead wintering grouns Other tradein[g] with the Indans that Came from Differant [parts] with thare furs Skins Suger Grease taller &c while Others ware amuseing themselves in Good Cumpany at Billards Drinking fresh Punch Wine & Eney thing thay Please to Call for while the Mo[re] valgear Ware fiteing Each other feasting was Much atended to Dansing at Nite with Respcttabel Parsons Not withstanding the fateages of the Industress the time Past of agrealay for two Months when the Grateer Part ware Read[y] to Leave the Plase for thar Differant Wintering Ground I had now a Large & Rich Cargo— But about the fi[r]st of august thare arived a trader from Lake Superier with the Disagreabel News that the Nawasease & Ochpowase [Ojibway] had Bin Killing Each other and Made it Dangres for the traders to Go in to the Cuntrey Except the Cummander whuld Interfare And Indaver to Reconsile the Parteas and a Counsel Was Cald of all the traders and the Cummander Laid his InferMation Befour the Counsel and told them it was O[u]t of his Power to Bring the Goverment Into Eney Expens in Sending to thise But Desird that we would fall on wase & Means among Ourselves and he would Indaver to youse his Enfluans as CumMandin[g] Ooffiser[33] W[e] heard and thanked Him We then Proseaded to Contrebute towards Makeing Six Large Belts of Wampam thre for the NotewaySease and three for the Ochpwase thay ware Cumpleated under the Gidans of the Cumander and Speachis Rote to Both

[33] Captain Arent Schuyler de Peyster of New York was commandant at Mackinac from 1774 to 1779. Michigan Pioneer and Historical Collections, 3:16.

Nations; I was Bound to the Senter of the Nottawaseis Cuntrey Up St Peters River the Counsel with ye Cumander thaught Proper to Give me ye Charge of thre Belts With the Speachis and the traders of Lake Superer Ware Charged with the Others the Import of the Bisnes was that I Should Send out Currears [couriers] into the Planes and avart [alert] all the Chefes to Repare to my tradeing House on the Bank of St Peters Rive[r] in the Spring and thare to Hear & Obsarve the Contents of the Offesers Speach and Look at the Belts and understand thare Meaning Likewise to Imbark and A Campaney me to Mackenaw those in Superea [Superior] Had the Same Orders I Cumplide on my Part to Grate advantage and aSembel Eleve[n] Chefe wh[o] went with me Beside A Number of Considerd Men; By the Intarpiter I had the Speach ExPland and the Intenshan of the Belts and after we had Got Readey for Saleing we all Imbark and went doun the River to its Mouth whare we found Sum traders who had Cam from Near The Head of the Misseppey with Sum Ochipawa Chefes with them I was Much Surprised to Sea them So Ventersum among the Peaple I had with me for the Blad [blood] was Scairs Cald the Wound was yet fresh But while we Stade thare a Young Smart Looking Chef Contineued Singing the Death Song as if He Dispised thare threats or torments after we had Made a Short Stay hea[r] we Imbark for the Plains of the Dogs whare we jond the a Vast Number of People of a[ll?] Description wateing for me to Cum doun and Go to Macanac to Counsel for these People had never Bin thare or Out of thare Cuntrey Exsept on a wor Partey it Excited the Careasatay of Sum part [of] Everey Nation South of the Lake of the woods and from that was a number of Chefes which was More then two thousand Miles Indead the Matter was Intresting to all Partes aspeshaley to the trading Partey for the following Reson Each of these Nations are as Much Larger then Eney of thare Negberng Nations as the Inhabatans of a Sittey is to a Villeage and when thay are at Varans [variance] Propertey is not Safe Even traveling threw thair Cuntrees when we Left the Plains of the Dogs Every Canue[?] Made the Best of thare way up Osconsen [Wisconsin] to the Portage and Got over as fast a[s] we Could and Got over the Portag while we ware on the Portage one of my men Informd me that thare was an Indan from St Peters River that was In Morneing for his Departead frind and Wishd me to take of the Mornein[g] for He Had worn it long anuf I Desird he mite Cum to me which was Dun He was Blacked with Cole from the fire Hand & face His Haire was Hanging Over His Eyes I ask what I Should Due for Him he Desird that his Hair Mite Be Pluckt out to the Croun of his Head his fase & Hands washt and a white Shirt Put on him I Cumplid with the Re quest and Seat him on the Ground Seat a Cupel of Men to work and with the asistans of a Leattel Ashis [ashes] to Provent thare fingers Sliping thay Sun had his head as Smooth as a Bottle he washd up & I Put a white Shirt on him which Mad the fellow So thankfull to think that He Could Apear in a Deasant Maner that he Could Scairs Cantain himselvef we Desended the fox River to th[e] Batam of Grean Bay So cald and thare joind the Hole of ye Canues Bound to Mackenaw the way ther was fair and Plesant we all Proseaded to gather Across Lake Misheagon at the End of two Days we all apeard on the Lake, about five Miles from Mecanac, and aproach it in Order We had flags on the Masts of our Canewes Eaverey Cheafe his flock My Canew Beaing the Largest in that Part of the Cuntrey and haveing a larg[e] Youan [Union] flage I Histed it, and when within a Mile & a half I took ye lead and the Indans followed Close behind, the flag in the fort was histed the ye Cannen of the Garresen Began to Play Smartley the Shores was lind with Peaple of all sorts, who Seat up Such a Crey and hooping which Seat the Tribes in the fleat a Going to that Degrea that you Could not Hear a Parson Speak, at Length we Reacht ye Shore and the Cannen Seast I then toock My Partey to the Cummander [De Peyster] who treated us verey well I Seat with them an Our and Relateed the afare and what I had

Dun & what Past Dureing the Winter, after Interreduseing the Chefe I Went to my one House whare I found a nunter [number] of Old frind, [with] whom I spent the Remander of the Day, the People from Lake Superor Had arived Befour us and Next Day the Grand Counsel was Held Before Cumander in the Grate Counsel Chamber, Befour a Vast Numper of Spectaters whare the artickels of Pece ware Concludeed and Grate Promises ware Mad on Both Sides for abideing and adhearing Closely to the artickels to Provent farthar BludShead the Prinsabel of which was that the Notawases Should Not Cross the Missacipey to the East Side, to Hunt on thare Nighbers Ground to Hunt Nor bread Eney Distarbans on the Chipawase [Chippewa] Ground, thay Should Live By the Side of Each other as frinds and Nighbors The Chipewase Likewise Promis On thare Part Strickley to Obsareve the Same Reagulations on thare Part toward ye Nattawasis that thay will not Cross the River to harm on the west Side to Hant, after all the artickels ware Draun up thay all Sind them; the Cummander then Made A Preasent of a Cag of Rum to Each nation and thay left the fort and went to thare Camp whare thay Seat Dound and Ingoied thare Present Sung a fue Songs and went to Rest in a Verey Sevel Manner the Next Day thare was a Large fat Ox Kild and Coked By the Solgers; all of these nations ware Biden to the feast thay Dined to Geather in Harmoney and finished the Day in Drinking Moderately—Smokeing to Gather Singing & Briteing the Chane of frindShip in a Verey Deasant way, this was Kept up for four Days when the Offiser Mad them Each a Present and thay all Imbark for thare One Part of thair Cuntrey

I now Go back to the Planes of the Dogs and St Peters River to Give A nar[ra]tive of Sum thing that I Have Om[i]ted in the foregoing work As foloues—

I Perseved that the Indans ware Uneasey In thare Minds about Sumthing I Enquird of them what Had Befel Thay Gave me to understand thare was a Parson at that Plase that Had an Eevel Sperit he Did things Beand [beyond] thare Conseption I wish to Sea him and Beaing Informd who he was I ask him Meney Questions I found him to be a french man who Had Bin Long among the Nations on the Misurea that Came that Spring from the Ilenoas to the Planes of the Dogs he Had the Slite of Hand Cumpleatly and Had Such A Swa[y] Over the tribes with whom he was Aquanted that thay Cunsendead to Moste of His Requests thay Gave him the Name of Minneto [Manitou] Which is a Sperite In thare Langueg as he was Standing Among Sum People thare Cume an Indan up to them with A Stone Pipe or Callemeat Cureesley Rought and which he Seat Grate Store By Minneto ask ye Indan to Leat him Look at it and he Did so he wished to Purchis it from the Indan But he would not Part with it Minneto then Put it into his Mouth as the Indan Supposed and Swallod it the Poor Indan Stud A Stonished Minneto told him Not to trubel him Self a bout it he Should have His Pipe agane In two or three Days it Must firs pass threw him at the time Seat the Pipe was Prosented to the Indan he Lookd apon it as if he Could not Bair to Part with it But would not Put his Hand apon it and Minneto Kept the Pipe for Nothing it was three times *Biger*[34] than Minetoes Mouth It was Made of the Read Stone of St Peters River so Much asteamd among the Eastarn & Southern Nations[35] I then Embarkt *and went up the River* the Thirteanth Day I arived and put my Goods into the Same House I Had Winterd In ye year before two Days *after* I Heard By Sum Indans who had thare was a Large Band of the Natives Incampt on the Banks of the River about Two Hundred Miles above me Which Wanted to Sea A trader I Conkluded ameatly [immediately] to Put a Small a Sortment of Goods Into a Canue and Go up to them a thing that neaver was atempted Before By the Oldest trader on Acount of the Rudnes of those People who was Natta-

[34] Italicized words here and in the three sentences that follow appear on the one page of Pond's original manuscript which he copied over. In copying he apparently omitted these words.

[35] The catlinite or pipestone found in what is now Pipestone National Monument in Minnesota was much used by the Sioux in fashioning calumets, which were held to be sacred among them.

wasease By Nation But the Band was Cald Yantonoes[36] the
Cheafe of the Band allwase Lead them on the Plaines as I was
about to Imbark; the Cheafe arived to Give me an Invatation
to Cum up and trade with them I agread and we Seat of to
Gather I By water & he by Land I was Nine Days Giting up
to thare Camp the Cheafe arived Befour m[e] his Roat was
Shorter then Mine By Cuting aCross the Planes When I arived
within three Miles of ye Camp it Beaing weat wather & Cold I
Incampt and Turnd up my Canew which Made us a good Shel-
ter; at Night it Begon to Snow & frease & Bloue Har[d.] we
ware then on a Large Sand flat By the River Side Earley In the
Morn[?] the wind toock the Canew up in the Air Leat hir fall
on the frosen flat & Broke Hir in Peceis I was then in a Sad
Sittuation aBout Noon I Perseved a Number of the Natives on
ye Opaset Sid of the River—Apraching me Sum on Horsback
Others on foot; When thay Come Near finding the Sittuation
we ware In thay fordead the River and offard me thare Asistans
to take my Goods up to thare Camp; I was Glad & Exeptd
thare offer; we Marcht on with Our Lodead Horseis and Cum-
ing Near the Camp Mad a Stop & Seat Down on the Ground,
I Perseved five Parsons from the Camp Aproching four was
Imployd in Caring a Bever Blanket finely Panted the Other
Held in His Hand a Callemeat or Pipe of Pece Verey finely
Drest with Differant feathers with Panted Hair; thay all Seat
By me Except one who Held the Pipe; thay Ordred the Pipe
Lit, With a Grate dele of Sarremoney after Smoking a fue
Whifs the Stem was Pinted East and West then North & South

[36] The Yankton branch was one of the seven principal divisions of the Dakota, being called by Le Sueur the Hinhanetons, "the village of the red stone
quarry." Lewis and Clark encountered the Yankton during the course of their
expedition up the Missouri in 1804 and found them to be of a more friendly
disposition than other bands of the Dakotas. According to the reports of the
American explorers, the Yankton roamed over the regions of the James, Big
Sioux, and Des Moines rivers. Pond was apparently one of the earliest English-
men to trade with them. See Frederick W. Hodge, ed., *Handbook of American
Indians North of Mexico* (United States Bureau of American Ethnology Bulletin
30, Washington, 1910), Part 2, p. 988.

then upward toward the Skies, then to ye Earth after which we all Smoked in turn and Apeard Verey frendly I Coul[d] not understand one word thay Said But from thare actions I Supposed it to be all frindship after smokeing thay toock of my Shoes and Put on me a pair of fine Mockasans or Leather Shoes of thare one make Raught in a Cureas Manner then thay Lade me Doun on the Blanket One [got] Hold of Each Corner and Cared me to the Campt In a Lodg a Mong a Verey Vennarabel ASembley of Old men I was Plas a[t] the Bottam or Back part which is A Steamd the Highist Plase afte[r] Smokeing an Old man Rose up on his feet with as much Gravatey as Can be Conseaved of the[n] Came to me Laid his Hands on my Head and Grond out I I I three times then draud his Rite Hand Doun on my Armes, faneing a Sort of a Crey [cry] as if he Shead tears then Sit Doun the Hole follode the Same Exampel which was twelve in Numb[er] [37] thare was in the Midel of the Lodg a Rased Pece of Ground a Bout fiv[e] Inchis in Hight five feet Long two & a Half Brod on which was a fire & Over that Hung three Brass Kettles fild with Meete Boiling for a feast while we ware Imployd in this Saremoney thare was wateing at the Dore four Men to take me up and Carre me to another feast at Lengh an Old man toock up Sum of the Vittels out of one of Kettles which apeard to Be a Sort of Soope thickend with Pounded Corn Mele he fead me with three Sponfuls first and then Gave me the Dish which was Bark & the Spoon Made out of a Buffeloes Horn to fead mySelf— as I had got a Good apatite from the fateages of the Day I Eat Hartey as Sun as I had Got threw with my Part of ye feast I was Desird to Steap Out the Dore which I Did the People in Wateing then toock me and Laid me on another Skin & Cairead me to another Lodg whare I went threw the same Sarremoney thare was not a Woman Among them Then to a third after which I was takeen to A Large [lodge] Prepaird for me in which thay Had Put my

[37] This custom, long practiced by the Sioux, is noted by Father Hennepin in *A New Discovery of a Vast Country in America* (London, 1699), p. 161.

People & Goods with a Large Pile of Wood and Six of thare Men With Spears to Gard it from the Croud At four Oclock I Cummenst a trade with them But ye Croud was So Grate that the Chefe was Oblige to Dubel His Gard and I went on with my trade In Safetey Seventey five Loges at Least teen Parsons in Each Will Make Seven Hundred & fiftey my People ware By Standers Not a Word to Say nor Acte The Cheafe who Came Doun the River to Envite me up to trade with them Gave me to understand that my trade was to begin at Sundoun But he was a[b]sent When thay Campeld me to Begin Before the time he lekewise told me if [I] was to Contend with them thay Mite take all that I had I was in a bad Sittuation But at Sundoun the Chefe arived and seeing the Croud Grate he Put to the Gard Six men more and toock the Charge on himselvef he was as well Obade & Kept up as Smart Dissapline as I Ever Saw One of ye Band was More then commanly Dairing he [the chief] Orderead One of the Gard to throw his Lans threw him I[n] Case he Persisted in His Imperdens the fellow Came aGane the Sentanal threw his Lans & it went threw his Close and Draud a Leattle Blud But he naver atempted AGane I Continued my Trad Till Near Morning By that time thare fars ware Gon thay Prepard to March of as thay had Lane on the Spot Sum time Befour my arival thay had Got Out of Provshon I was not in a Sittation to Asist them Beaing Destatute my Self By Day Lite I Could Not Sea One But the Cheafe who Cept Close By me till the Last to Provent aney Insalt which Mite arise as thay ware G[o]ing of, the reson of the Behaveer of these People is thay naver Saw a trader Before On thare One Ground or at Least Saw a Bale of Goods Opend Sum traders Long Befoar Sent thare Goods Into the Planes with thare Men to trade with these People thay Often would have them Cheaper then the french men Could sell them; these People would fall on them and take ye Goods from them at thair One Price till thay Could not Git eney I was the first that atempted to go t[h]are With a Bale of Goods these People are in thare

Sentaments Verey Averishas But in this Instans thay Made not the Least Demand for all thare Sarvis Late in the Morning[?] the Chefe Left me I went to work Bundling or Packing my furs wh[ich I *mss. torn*] Got from them I was now Destatute of frinds or asistans Except my o[wn men *mss. torn*] and thay Could [not] aford me aney A Sistans in the Provshon Line of Which I Was Much in want Nigherer Could thay A Sist me in the transPortation of My furs I then Concluded to Leave a Boy to take Care of them until we Could Retarn with Sum provishon the Pour fellow Seamd Willing to Stay By him Self and all we Could aford him was three Handfulls of Corn In Case of want I Left Him two Bever Skins which Had Sum Meat on them & Wone Bair Skin which he Could Singe the haire of and Roste in the fire that he Mite Live in Cas we ware Gon Longer then we Calkalateed The firs ware In a Good Lodg that he Mite Keep himself warm we Left him in that Sittauation and Got Back to the House whare we had Left the Goods By Crossing the Plains I found all Safe and the Clark had Colected a Lattle Provshon But the Provshons Could not Be Sent to the Boy on acct [account] of the wather [weather] Seating in So Bad that the men would not undertak to Go a Cross the Plane Sum days after it Grode More Modret and thay Seat of five In Number and Reacht him in fiften Days from the time we Left Him thay found him well But fab[le.] thay Gave him to Eat Moderately at firs and he Gand Strength thay wen to work & Put the furs on a Scaffel out of the way of Wool[ves] or Eney Varment and all Seat of for home The Day Befour thay arived thay ware Overtakeen By a Snow Storm on the Planes & Could not Sea thare way Near Night thay Seat Doan on the Plan[e] thare Beaing No wood Nigh and Leat the Snow Cover them Ove[r] H[ead? *mss. torn*] thay Had thare Blankets about them thay ware in the Morn[ing] it was Clear with ye Wind Nowest [northwest] and freaseing hard thay Dug out of the Snow and Being Weat in Sum of thare feet thay was Badley frosted tho Not More then teen Miles to Walk the Boy acapt as well as

Eney of [them] I Beleve the Best I had a long Job to Heal them But without the Loss of a Limb the Natives Had found out whare we ware and Came in with Meet and fur to trade while I was up the River among the Band I Informd the Chefe of the Belts I had with me and ye Cumanding offisers Speach and the Belts I had with me and Desird him to Make a Speach Befour thay Decampt this Chefes name was Arechea the Cheafe that Came to me first He Had a Smattran [smattering] of the Ochipway tung So much that we [understood] Each Other at Least Suffisantly to Convarse or Convea our IDease he Made a Long Speach By the yousal [usual] Sine of a Shout threw the Camp, thay ware willing to Cumply In the Spring; I sent my People after the fars thay Had Put on a Scaffel in the Winter, thay Had an Indan Hunter with them who Kild them Sum Buffeloes the men Cut Down Small Saplens and Made the frames of two Boates Sowed the Skins to Gather and Made Bottoms to thare frames Rubd them Over with Tallow which Made them tite anuf to Bring the fars Down to me whare I had Canues to Recve them —

On acount of the fase of the Cuntrey & Soile the Entervales of the River St Peter is Exsaland & Sum Good timber the Banks Bend the Intervals are High and the Soile thin & lite the River is Destatute of fish But the Woods & Meaddoues afords abundans of annamels Sum turkeas Buffeloes are Verey Plentey the Common Dear are Plentey and Larg the Read & Moose Dear are Plentey hear Esesly [especially] the former I have sean fortey Kild in One Our By Surounding a Drove on a Low Spot By the River side in the Winter season, Raccoons are Verey Large, no Snakes But Small ones which is not Pisenes Woolves are Plentey thay follow the Buffeloes and often Destroy thare yoang & Olde Ones in winter the Natives near the Mouth of the River Rase Plentey of Corn for thare one Concumtion — The Manners and Custams of ye Yantonose The Band I Saw up the River are Notawases By Nation But By Sum Intornal Disputes thay ware Seaperated into Six Differant Bands Each Band

THE NARRATIVE OF PETER POND 57

Lead By Cheafes of thare One Chois, the Names of Each tribe, the 1 Yantonoes 2 the Band of the Leaves 3 the Band of th[e] wes[t] 4 the Band of the Stone House; the Other two Bands are North one Cald asneboins [Assiniboines] the other Dog Ribs, these ware One Nation formaley and Speke the Same Languegs at [th]is day [38] ye Yantonose are faroshas and Rude in thare Maners Perhap Oaeing in Sum masher to thare Leading an Obsqer [obscure life] in the Planes as thay are not Convarsant with Eney other tribe. Th[e]y Sild[om] Sea thare Nighbers Thay Leade a wandring Life in that Exstensive Plane Betwen the Miseeurea & Misisippey thay dwell in Leather tents Cut Sumthing in form of a Spanis Cloke and Spread out by thirteen [poles] in the Shape of a Beel the Poles Meet at the top But the Base is fortten In Dimert [diameter] thay Go into it By a Hole Cut in the Side and a Skin Hung Befour it By way of a Dore thay Bild thare fire in the Middel and [d]ue all thare Cookerey over it at Night thay Lie down all round the Lodg with thare feat to the fire thay Have a

[38] The "band of the leaves" is the English translation of the name Wahpeton, a branch of the Dakota Indians whose habitat was on the upper St. Peter's River. See Doane Robinson in South Dakota Historical Collections, 2:23. A map may be found in Newton H. Winchell, *Aborigines of Minnesota* (St. Paul, 1911), opposite p. 73. The "band of the west" was probably the Wahpekuta, who occupied the area along the Cannon River and the Blue Earth Valley. When Le Sueur reached the mouth of the Blue Earth River, he was told that the river belonged to "the Sioux of the west." Winchell, *Aborigines*, p. 73; Edward D. Neill, "Dakota Land and Dakota Life," Minnesota Historical Collections, 1:211. The "band of the Stone House" refers to the Sisseton branch, who roamed through the region about Swan Lake and the Cottonwood River, and also on the upper St. Peter's River in the region of Lake Traverse and Big Stone Lake. In 1853 the Sissetons about Lake Traverse were still called the Chonkasketonwan, meaning "dwellers in a fort." See Neill in Minnesota Historical Collections, 1:210, and William W. Folwell, *History of Minnesota*, Vol. 1 (St. Paul, 1956), p. 183. The two northern tribes mentioned are not strictly Minnesota Indians. The Assiniboines are supposed to have broken away from the Yankton branch of the Dakotas, but they drifted northward and came to occupy the region of Lake Winnipeg and the Assiniboine and Saskatchewan rivers. Hodge, *Handbook of American Indians*, Part 1, p. 102. The Dog Rib Indians were members of an Athapascan tribe who made their home in the vicinity of Great Slave and Great Bear lakes. Hodge, *Handbook*, Part 1, p. 108; Part 2, p. 744.

Grate Number of Horseses and Dogs which Carres thare Bageag when thay Moove from Plase to Plase thay Make yous of Buffeloes Dung [*for fuel*] as thar is But leattle or no wood apon the Planes thay are [*Contin*]uely on the Watch for feare of Beaing Surprised By thare Enemise [*who are*] all Rund them thare ware Implements are Sum fire armes—Boses and arroes & Spear which thay have Continualy in th[*are hands.*] When on the March at Nite thay ceep out Parteas on the Lookou[*t.*] thay Ran down the Buffelow with thare Horseis and Kill as Much Me[*at as thay*] Please; in Order to have thare Horseis Long winded thay Slit thare Nos[*es*] up to the Grissel of thare head which Makes them Breath Verey freely [*I Have*] Sean them Run with those of Natral Norstrall and Cum in Apearant-[*ley*] Not the Least Out of Breath; these when a parson Dies among them in Wint[*er*] thay Cairrea the Boddey with them til thay Cum to Sum Spot of Wood and ther Put it up on a Scaffel till when the frost is out of the Ground thay Entare [*it.*] [39] thay Bileve in two Sperites on[*e*] Good & one Bad thay Genaley Get whare wife By Contact Betwene the Parians thay are Verey Gellas of thare women it Sumtimes Hapens that a Man will take his Nighbers Wife from him But Both are a Blige to Quit the tribe thay Belong to But it [*is*] Sildum you Can Hear of Murders Cummited among them thay have Punneshment for thefts among themSelves Thay Sumtimes Retal [retaliate?] By taking as Much Property from the Afender if thay Can find it But I Sildum Hard of thefts among themselves what Ever thay Mite Due to other When thay are Marching or Rideing Over the Planes thay Put on a Garment Like an Outside Vest with Sleves that Cums Doun to thare Elboes Made of Soft Skins Seve[*ral*] thicknesis that will turn ann arrow at a Distans and a targ[*et*] two & half feet in Diamerter of the Same Matearals & thicknes; hung Over thare Sholders that Gards thare Backs when thare is a Number of them to Gather Going in front of

---

[39] The use of aerial burial was not uncommon among the Indians of the Northwest. See Winchell, *Aborigines*, pp. 512–514.

thare Bands thay Make a warlike, apa[*rans.*] the Planes where these People wander is about four Hundred Miles Brod Eas & West three Hundred North & South thay Make all thare Close of Skins of Differant [animals.] these Parts Produse a number of Otters which Keep [*in*] Ponds and Riveleat on these Planes and Sum Bevers But the Land Anna[*mels*] are the Mane Obgect to the Natives— The Spring is now advan[*s*]ing fast the Chefes Cuming with a Number of the Native to Go [*with*] me to Mackenac to Sea & Hear what thare farther Had to Say

THE DIARY
OF JOHN MACDONELL

The Diary of John Macdonell

Introductory Note

Of the author of this diary, which represents a future Nor'wester at the beginning of a long and interesting career, little was known until recently, when his papers came into the possession of that prolific historian of Catholic Canada, the Reverend A. G. Morice.[1] According to these papers, writes Father Morice, John Macdonell was born in Scotland on November 30, 1768, the son of John Macdonell, who migrated to New York in 1773 and thence to Canada. Thus John, Jr., was twenty-five years old when he started West. The comments of the diary reveal that this was the young man's first trading trip.

The portion of the diary here printed is owned by McGill University. It carries the narrative only to Macdonell's arrival at his post on the upper waters of the Assiniboine River, but another manuscript, also in the possession of McGill University, continues the story through June 6, 1795. Both manuscripts are copies, but the later one seems to be in the author's autograph; presumably it was made in response to Roderic Mackenzie's circular letter sent to the fur traders in the spring of 1806.[2] It has been published in abridged form in Louis R. Masson's *Bourgeois de la Compagnie du Nord-Ouest*.[3] The portion of the diary printed below is here published for the first time.

[1] See Morice's article "The Macdonell Family in Canada" in the *Canadian Historical Review* for September and December, 1929.
[2] See Louis R. Masson, *Les bourgeois de la Compagnie du Nord-Ouest* (Quebec, 1889), 1:51. A copy of Roderic Mackenzie's circular letter to several wintering partners and clerks of the Northwest Company, dated April 21, 1806, is in the collections of the Minnesota Historical Society. See page 199n. for a further explanation of this letter.
[3] Vol. 1, pp. 266–295.

In 1797, according to Morice, Macdonell became a partner of the Northwest Company. For at least eight years after his arrival in the West his post remained in the general locality of his first station. By 1804 he was in the Athabasca country. In 1807 he was back on the River Qu'appelle. In 1809 he appears to have been stationed at Isle à la Crosse, and in 1812 at Lesser Slave Lake. Thus he saw, first and last, a large part of the West. His wife *à la façon du pays* was Magdeleine Poitras, a half-breed daughter of a trader on the Qu'appelle River, doubtless the same André Poitras who in 1805 was listed in the records of the company as a clerk on the Upper Red River.

Macdonell must have left the Indian country temporarily in 1812, for in October of that year he was made a captain in the corps of Canadian voyageurs which was the Northwest Company's rather spectacular response to Canada's enlistment call. He saw active service and was taken captive at the Battle of St. Regis, losing a sword with silver hilt, a spy glass, and other articles to the enemy. In 1814 he must have been living at the Long Sault on the Ottawa River, for there he entertained the Astorians of Franchère's party on their return trip from the Pacific.[4] One of their number represented him as being at that time "a cheerful, healthy, and contented old man," despite his nickname of "the Priest," by which his voyageurs distinguished him from the many other Macdonells and MacDonalds in the fur country. There at Point Fortune, near Vaudreuil and close to the scene of the famous Dollard massacre, Macdonell established himself in his "Poplar Villa," where he kept a store and directed a line of boats that plied between Point Fortune and Montreal. He also

[4] He stated on the witness stand that he was in the interior in 1814. Probably he came out in that year. See *Report of the Proceedings Connected with the Disputes between the Earl of Selkirk and the Northwest Company at the Assizes Held at York, in Upper Canada, October, 1818* (London, 1819), p. 155.

served as judge of the district of Ottawa. He seems to have preserved his former reputation of piety, for he raised a fine calvary in front of his house, where his neighbors assembled for prayer.

John "the Priest" acted also as the banker of the family, especially while in the West, and he is known to have given lavishly to churches and schools. In later years he lived in more straitened circumstances and was embittered by a burden of debt that rested heavily upon him. In spite of all he seems to have been able to care for his brother Miles, who is well known for the prominent part he took in the affairs of the Red River Valley, and to provide for his own eight children. A tombstone in the cemetery of St. André (d'Argenteuil) tells us that the old trader died at Point Fortune on April 17, 1850. On April 24, 1853, an act of posthumous marriage was performed.[5] His wife, Magdeleine, survived him for twenty years. She died in 1870 at the age of eighty-seven.

Macdonell's diary has been preserved only in the form of an early, perhaps nearly contemporary, copy. Corrections seem to indicate that the author himself read it and emended it. Later an editor, probably Louis R. Masson, made still further corrections. Hence it is not always possible to be absolutely sure of the original form. In general, the copyist's text has been followed. Only that portion of the manuscript which relates to his trip to the interior is presented in this volume. Excerpts from the remainder have already been printed; moreover, his life in the Saskatchewan country does not have so direct a bearing on the development of the Minnesota area as does the journey to the interior, especially the trip along the canoe route from Grand Portage to the Lake of the Woods. Of particular value are the references to the manner of life and the customs of the voya-

[5] This posthumous marriage was explained by Father A. G. Morice in 1933 after the original edition of this book appeared. Father Morice wrote that in 1853 after Macdonell's death a "French act of remarriage for legal ends" made it possible for Magdeleine Macdonell and her children by Macdonell to be his legal heirs. See *Minnesota History*, 15:92. T. C. B.

geurs. Macdonell evidently was much interested in this class of men, in whose company it was to be his fate to spend nearly twenty of the best years of his life.

Here, unlike the previous diary, an occasional period has been inserted where two sentences have been run together without punctuation by the diarist. Such lapses are obviously inadvertent and out of keeping with Macdonell's customary style, and hence it has seemed justifiable to make the correction. Similarly, an occasional misspelling of a word habitually spelled right has been corrected. Other misspellings have, of course, been allowed to stand. Words struck out by the diarist have been included within brackets with a *d*. ("deleted") before them.

G. L. N.

The Diary

1793. May 10th. Signed my Engagement with the North-West Company for five years to winter in the Indian Country as a clerk. The terms are £100 at the expiration, and found in necessaries.[1]

May 25th Saturday. Embarked at Lachine on board of a Birch Bark canoe, the first that I remember to have been in — my foreman's name is Joseph La Tourelle, and my steer's-man Pierre Valois, both of the parish of Berthier.[2]

---

[1] The discovery of the engagement to which Macdonell refers has furnished proof of his identity. Dr. Wayne E. Stevens has found the document in the notarial records in the archives of the district of Montreal. A transcript is now in the possession of the Minnesota Historical Society. As a clerk in the service of the Northwest Company, Macdonell held a position next in rank below the partners in the trade. Such clerks were apprenticed for a period of five or seven years at a fixed wage, with the understanding that at the end of this term of service they would be eligible for promotion to the rank of partner. They then assumed greater responsibilities in the administration of the fur posts and were entitled to a share in the business of the company. For an account describing the various ranks of *engagés* in the service see Gordon C. Davidson, *The North West Company* (University of California Publications in History, Vol. 7, Berkeley, 1918), pp. 226–231. For an enumeration of the necessaries that composed a clerk's personal outfit see Captain Thomas G. Anderson, "Personal Narrative," in Wisconsin Historical Collections, 9:139.

[2] Brigades of canoes en route to the interior embarked from a point above the rapids at Lachine and usually followed the route over the Ottawa or Grand River, as Macdonell traces it in his journal. Ascending to the forks at what is now Mattawa, the canoes left the Ottawa and proceeded up the Mattawa River and by a series of portages reached Lake Nipissing. They then descended the French River to Lake Huron and skirted the shore to Sault Sainte Marie. Here they portaged over to Lake Superior, on the northern shore of which was situated Grand Portage, the rendezvous of the fur traders. The Montreal canoes used over this route were about thirty-six feet long and six feet wide at the middle. They carried a load of some three or four tons and were paddled by eight or nine voyageurs. The foreman and the steersman were required to be particularly skillful and were paid double the wages

This brigade of Berthier men, was to be guided by Jos. Faignan, a faithful servant and favorite of Jos. Frobisher Esquire, for many years in the North west.[3] But Mr Frobisher wishing to keep Faignan for the last or June [*d*. Brigade, say] Canoes, gave the Brigade in charge to François *Huneau* of Isle Perrault, nick named by the men *Le mangeur de Bled,* who directed the brigade to go and camp at Isle Perrault that he might pass another [day] in the bosom of his family and equip himself for the voyage.[4] A Brigade of Canoes in the Grand River is generally four. The canoes when fully loaded carry about three Tuns.

May 27th Monday. At nine A. M. Crossed over to S[t] Anns where we found the Priest saying mass for one Lalonde, who had been drowned, by the mens account, one hundred and ten leagues above this place; I. E. above the Roche capitaine.[5]

of the middlemen. See Davidson, *North West Company,* pp. 216–219, for a short description of canoes used in the trade. For a descriptive account of the Canadian voyageur see Grace Lee Nute, *The Voyageur* (New York, 1931). Berthier is situated on the St. Lawrence about fifty miles below Montreal.

[3] Joseph Frobisher was a well-known trader and explorer of the Canadian Northwest during the last three decades of the eighteenth century. He built a fort on the Red River and also on the Churchill River, to which he penetrated in 1774. In 1775 he accompanied Alexander Henry on a trip up the Saskatchewan. He was later a partner of the Northwest Company and maintained an active interest in the fur trade until his retirement in 1798. Lawrence J. Burpee, *Oxford Encyclopaedia of Canadian History* (Makers of Canada Series, Vol. 12, New York, 1926), p. 224.

[4] The nickname *"Le mangeur de bled"* (wheat-eater) is an alteration of the term *mangeur de lard,* which was applied with some derision by the Northmen to the voyageurs who paddled between Montreal and Grand Portage without pushing farther into the wilderness. The English translation of the term is "pork-eater." The Montreal voyageurs did not live on a diet of hulled corn and tallow, as did the Northmen, but included pork in their rations, a luxury seldom enjoyed in the north country. Huneau was apparently still more extravagant, requiring even breadstuffs in his diet. Isle Perrault is the Ile Perrôt of today.

[5] The Church of Ste. Anne was located on the western extremity of the Island of Montreal. It was the custom of the voyageurs to stop there before embarking on an expedition inland. See the reference in Pond's narrative, page 30, above. Roche Capitaine was the name given to a series of rapids in the Ottawa River below the forks at Mattawa. The portage around the

THE DIARY OF JOHN MACDONELL 69

Tho drowned near twelve months ago his remains were only brought down by his brothers this spring on their return from the upper country in a coffin made for the purpose in order to give him Christian Sepulture, according to the Catholic Rites. At the church of St Anns the crews of the Canoes collected a voluntary donation amongst themselves to which I contributed my mite, in order to have prayers said for the prosperity of the voyage and a safe return to those engaged in it, to thier friends and families; and here we left two of the canoes to wait for Mr A. N. McLeod, who is to be my fellow traveller, and who returned to Montreal from La-Chine to take a final adieu of his fair acquaintences there.[6] The Guide & I with a Monsr Le Moine proceeded to *pointe au gravois* opposite the Indian village of *Lake of two-Mountains* where we put up for the night.[7] Next morning the guide & I went accross to the Indian

rapids went by the same name. Macdonell later mentions the passing of Lalonde's grave. See below, page 79.

[6] Archibald Norman McLeod entered the service of the Northwest Company some time before 1790 and remained an important figure in the fur trade until his retirement in 1821. His journal covering the winter of 1800–01, which he spent at Fort Alexandria, appears below, pages 125–185. He must not be confused with Normand McLeod, an earlier trader who died in 1796, or with Alexander McLeod, another trader active in the early 1800s. Macdonell met the latter at Grand Portage, returning to Montreal to regain his health. See below, page 95; also Elliott Coues, *New Light on the Early History of the Greater Northwest: The Manuscript Journals of Alexander Henry and of David Thompson, 1799–1814* (New York, 1897), 1:277n. The latter work will be cited hereafter as Coues, *New Light.*

[7] Le Moine was probably the Lemoine whom David Thompson found in charge of the Fond du Lac House, near the mouth of the St. Louis River, when he reached that post in May, 1798. See Davidson, *North West Company,* p. 94. The Lake of the Two Mountains is still so called. It is formed by a broadening of the Ottawa River for a distance of several miles above its confluence with the St. Lawrence. The Indian village remained for many years. Nicholas Garry mentions it as the Indian missionary village of the Seminary of St. Sulpice, and Bigsby also makes reference to it. See " The Diary of Nicholas Garry, Deputy-Governor of the Hudson's Bay Company from 1822–1835," Proceedings and Transactions of the Royal Society of Canada, 1900, Section 2 (Second Series, Vol. 6), p. 94, and John J. Bigsby, *The Shoe and Canoe, or, Pictures of Travel in the Canadas* (London, 1850), 1:135.

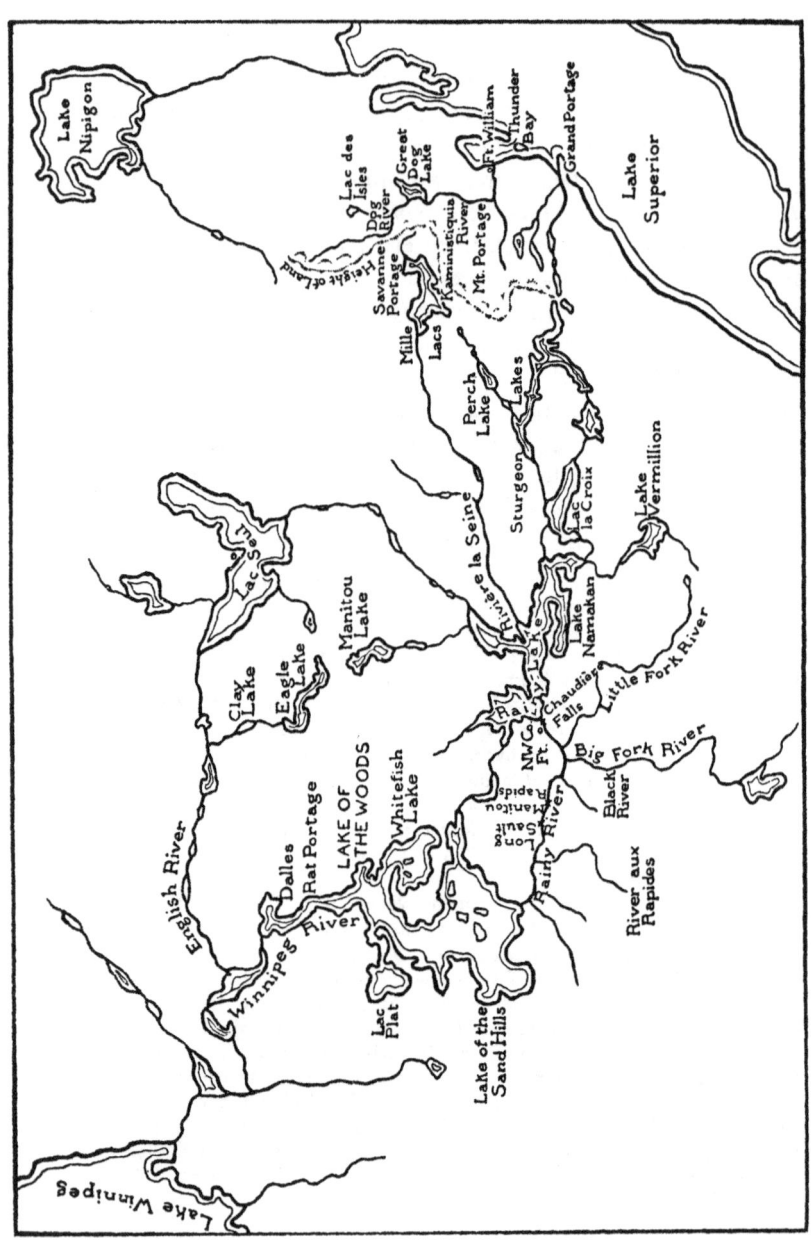

THE RAINY LAKE POST AND THE SURROUNDING AREA

THE DIARY OF JOHN MACDONELL 71

Village for a supply of bark, gum, and wattap, to mend our canoes in case of need, for all of which I gave a receipt.[8]

Mr A. N. McLoed [*sic*] and the two canoes that waited for him came up and we slept at the foot of *petites Ecors,* Carrillon Rapids, opposite to *Pointe Fortune.*[9]

May 29th. Slept at the *chute a Blondeau.*

30th. Walked up the *Long-sault* which the men call three leagues long. In it they made three portages and we slept two nights at the head of the third of these portages where I saw the first cross or grave mark. I am told it is that of a young Christian Indian who was drowned in attemping to run the Rapid in his canoe.[10]

The reason of our staying two nights at this place was to wait the arrival of our associate brigade conducted by an old guide named Denis who we find broke one of his Canoes and

[8] The gum used in repairing canoes was a resinous substance made by boiling the pitch from pine trees. It was pressed along the seams, and when it hardened it made them water-tight. Wattap was used to sew the pieces of bark together. This fiber was furnished by small roots of the spruce or hemlock tree.

[9] Petites Ecors was apparently a place where the river was confined between steep banks. It is mentioned by Belcourt as marking the boundary of Upper Canada. Georges A. Belcourt, *Mon itinéraire du Lac des Deux-Montagnes à la Rivière-Rouge* (Bulletin de la Société Historique de Saint-Boniface, Vol. 4, Montreal, 1913), p. 8. Carillon, Point Fortune, and Chute à Blondeau are all modern towns that still bear the names used more than a century ago to indicate landmarks along the river. Macdonell made Point Fortune his home in later years.

[10] Long Sault Rapids are of historic interest chiefly because they mark the spot where in 1660 Adam Dollard des Ormeaux and his little band of followers gave their lives in resisting an attack by the Iroquois Indians. The Iroquois were planning the destruction of Montreal, but upon encountering such heroic resistance, they abandoned the project. See Ralph Flenley, trans. and ed., *History of Montreal, 1640–1672, from the French of Dollier de Casson* (Toronto, 1928), pp. 253–265.

It was a custom among the voyageurs to erect a cross to mark the grave of any of their number who met his death along the trail. When passing such crosses the voyageurs always pulled off their hats, made the sign of the cross, and repeated a short prayer. Daniel W. Harmon, *Journal of Voyages and Travels in the Interior of North America* (Trail Makers of Canada Series, Toronto, 1911), pp. 6, 9.

is gone back to the village of the Lake of the two mountains, either to get another or materials to repair the broken one. The guides orders being to wait for the associate Brigade, we are likely to lose much time on the road.[11]

June 1st. We left our campment at the head of the *long sault* at 3 P. M. A League farthur we came opposite to a very beautiful mountain on the north shore of the Ottawa; The men tell me it is part of a Ridge of mountains that extends along from Temiscamagne to Tadosac perhaps to the *Labrador* Coast.[12] At [word missing] the guides who shoot the Canoes down the long sault and *Carrillon* Rapids have their huts erected. The fare to a guide is five Dollars. From the long Sault we have twenty leagues of still water to navigate. The Ottawa in this distance runs a N. E. [?] to an E. N. E. Course. After ascending fourteen leagues of smooth water we came to La parents settlement at the barrier where our guide attempted in vain to hire a man in lieu of one who had turned back from the long sault on account of a rupture with which he was afflicted.[13] The land on the south side begins to rise to some heighth. On the north the Ridge of Mountains which came to view at the head of the Long Sault is still to be seen. The water of this river is of a browner cast than that of the St Lawrence and much warmer at this time of the year.

[11] One or more guides were usually attached to each brigade of canoes. Their task was to point out the best course through the various streams and lakes, and to have general charge of the canoes and the property on board. Harmon, *Journal*, p. 2.

[12] David Thompson found that the "league" of the canoemen averaged about two miles in length. See David Thompson, *Narrative of Explorations in Western America, 1784–1812* (edited by J. B. Tyrrell, Publications of the Champlain Society, Vol. 12, Toronto, 1916), p. 172. Lake Temiscaming is a long body of water formed by the broadening of the Ottawa River. The foot of the lake is about fifty miles north of the forks at Mattawa. Important fur posts were located in the vicinity. Tadoussac is situated on the left bank of the St. Lawrence directly across the mouth of the Saguenay River from Baie Ste. Catherine.

[13] The settlement was located a few miles below the present city of Ottawa. Belcourt speaks of a small settlement which was doubtless the same one. Belcourt, *Itinéraire*, p. 10.

THE DIARY OF JOHN MACDONELL 73

Monday June 3rd. Left our campment for the first time before sun-rise. After paddling about a league & a half, the land on the South shore began to be rocky and steep from the edge of the water. Passed opposite the mouth of the Rideau River, the water of which falls perpendicular from the top of a Rock fourteen to sixteen feet high into the Ottawa.[14] The Rideau may be about twenty five yards wide. About fifty paces from this is a second channel seperated by an Island that extends to the brinck of the fall. Both these channels are of an equal size and in the form of crescents with the upper channel of the round side turned towards the stream and the concave to the Ottawa, but the upper channel of the rideau is always dry at low water. When the water is high in the Rideau it is dangerous for canoes to pass near the mouths and on that account they pass on the opposite side of the ottawa. A mile farther on we came to a large fall called le *grand des Chaudieres*.[15] The water being high we turned to our right into a long narrow cave surrounded with steep Rocks called *La Cave* which we ascended upwards of 300 Yards to its North Western extremity and there unloaded our canoes; the shore being too steep to haul up the canoes they were brought round light to the ordinary portage at low water and from there carried to the head of the falls. Mr McLeod and I went to fish, and take a view of the Rapids, but to our great surprise caught nothing. However our pains were amply paid by the view; this fall I have since found to be the most curious and picturesque in all the *grand River*. On the North shore the fall is about ten feet high but on the south side it comes down a

[14] The present city of Ottawa is situated on the Rideau or Curtain River a short distance above its junction with the Ottawa. At the time Macdonell wrote there was no settlement either on the Rideau River or on the north bank of the Ottawa where in 1800 Philemon Wright laid the foundations of the modern city of Hull. For the story of this region in early times see Alexander H. D. Ross, *Ottawa Past and Present* (Ottawa, 1927).

[15] Garry is eloquent in his description of these falls, which in English would be called Kettle Falls. "Diary," Proceedings and Transactions of the Royal Society of Canada, 1900, Section 2, p. 95. It was at this spot that Wright built his settlement.

steep Rush or Race-way between an Island and the shore and since the country is settled tis here they float down the timber. There are several small rockay Islands looking over the brink of the fall. The rock which occasions it has several curious crevises in it through which the water pours with a wild appearance.

There are ten Portages following each other of this name in the space of about five miles and some discharges between them. At the uppermost or *portages des Chiens* we slept.[16] The mosquitoes intolerable.

The Ottawa at this place seems little inferior to the St Lawrence at Cornwal in size. Above the *portage des Chiens* we entered the *Lac des Chaudiers* a piece of dead water called ten Leagues from W. to E. and not above one in width. After ascending the Lake about three leagues, we got sight of the Ridge of Mountains to the N. which we had not seen since we reached the Rideau yesterday, owing to our rout laying close under an extensive point along the North Shore of the river. Eight miles farthur we came to *pointe aux Irroquois* or *Pointe a la bataille,* so called from a party of that nation skirmishing with the Traders here in former times to way-lay them. Came to the Chats.[17] Just below this portage is a pretty farm which was formerly a place of some trade.

Leaving the Chats we took but half the cargoe on board for the space of a league during which we voyaged among a number of small Islands divided from one another by various

[16] This place is not Portage des Chiens or Dog Portage, as the author has it, but rather Portage des Chênes or Portage of the Oaks to which Garry makes reference. Garry, "Diary," Proceedings and Transactions of the Royal Society of Canada, 1900, Section 2, p. 97.

[17] Garry found the Falls of the Portage du Chat even more romantic than the Chaudière: "The Chaudière is one Fall, but here the whole Body of the River being fully two miles in Breadth runs over rocky Islands in Pinnicles and covered with Wood, and forms an innumerable number of falls (you see at once fifteen), the Water appearing angry with the Obstacles which oppose its Progress; a Battle between Rock and Water over a mile of Rocks ragged and uneven. The Portage is here very difficult and dangerous but only 270 Paces." Garry, "Diary," Proceedings and Transactions of the Royal Society of Canada, 1900, Section 2, p. 97.

rapidious channels where we had to use the lines to haul up the canoes. The canoe line is not a stout cable such as used by Boats but consists of fine Hambro lines loosely twisted upon one another and is about 60 Yards long.[18] After Gumming which is generally done before embarking on a Lake after passing a portage or *rapid* we entered the *Lac des Chats* which is [d. after] seven Leagues long and near one in breadth. At the western extremity of it we found ourselves amongst a cluster of Islands separated by Channels of different sizes and strong currants frequent; There is great plenty of Pine growing here on each side of us on the Ridges. A white rock of coarse grain is now mixed with the black one we had before Passed the night at the Fort Ducharge.[19]

June 6th. Started from *Ducharge du Fort*. Made the portage; In these channels the water is sometimes swift and narrow and the course winds for we have gone sometimes North and at others due South. It would be difficult to find the rout at all without an experienced guide for setting aside the intricacy of these turns and windings the guide must have a competant judgement to choose the proper channel for the state of the water is [word illegible] in the Ottawa and it is known to rise and fall to great extreames in the Ottawa. Lost the half of this day by rain which must be much wanted in the inhabited parts of the provinces though a perfect nuisance to us voyageurs. Next morning we steered a N. E. Course to the portage called *la Montagne* where we carried Goods & Canoe up a steep hill. After embarking proceeded E. & North. Made *D'Argy* and reached the Grand Callumet. This portage, the

[18] Hambro lines were, according to Landmann, part of the standard equipment of every canoe, but neither he nor Macdonell gives any description of them. Landmann is quoted in Davidson, *North West Company*, p. 216.

[19] Garry notes that Lac des Chats was so named because of the number of raccoons that formerly filled the adjacent woods. See his " Diary," Proceedings and Transactions of the Royal Society of Canada, 1900, Section 2, p. 97. Macdonell confuses Fort Ducharge with Décharge Dufort, which, according to Belcourt, was named after a man called Dufort, killed there in an attempt to run the rapids. Belcourt, *Itinéraire*, p. 14. The present name of the place is Portage du Fort.

longest in the Ottawa is ½ a League across. Upwards of three hundred yards from where we unloaded is a pretty steep ascent.[20] This Portage took more than twenty four hours of our time, before we cleared it, what with Gumming and mending our canoes. This is the first place I saw Fred Signorat who was since so esteemed a servant of the North West Company; He invited my fellow travellers and self to a supper of the best in his possession.[21] The voyageurs called the Grand Callumet sixty Leagues from Montreal and I think it much about opposite to *Kingston* or *Lake Ontario*. There is a quarry of Marble on the opposite side of the River to where we unloaded our canoes at the foot of the Grand Callumet Rapid & I presume the portage takes its name from the Indians making use of this stone to make their pipes or calumets of it.

8th June. [*d.* Started from the Du] We embarked on the Smooth water above the Grand Callumet with a fair wind which blew straight up the river; After proceeding a few leagues the shore on both sides of the River began to get high and rocky particularly that on the left hand which was frequently one hundred feet perpendicular from the surface of

[20] The Portage d'Argy is called by Belcourt the Portage des Dargis. It was supposed to have taken its name from two brothers who perished in an effort to run the rapids. See Belcourt, *Itinéraire*, p. 14. Associated with the Grand Calumet is the legend of Cadieux, which takes various forms as different narrators tell it. Cadieux fell into the hands of the Indians and met his death at the Calumet Portage. His friends buried him there, and he became a legendary figure to whom was attributed the composition of "Petit Rocher," one of the favorite songs of the voyageurs. For the story and the song see Nute, *Voyageur*, p. 147; Belcourt, *Itinéraire*, p. 14; and Garry, "Diary," Proceedings and Transactions of the Royal Society of Canada, 1900, Section 2, p. 99. Alexander Henry the elder explains that the portage was named for the "pierre à calumet," a kind of limestone found there, a material easily worked from which the Indians shaped their pipes. Alexander Henry, *Travels and Adventures in the Years 1760–1776* (edited by Milo M. Quaife, Chicago, 1921), p. 25 and note.

[21] Belcourt found at this place a Northwester called Severight, who was by that time a well-known trader. See his *Itinéraire*, p. 15. Some years later Franchère wrote of one Sicought stationed at Fort Coulonge. See Otto Fowle, *Sault Sainte Marie and Its Great Waterway* (New York, 1925), p. 387. Fowle probably misread Franchère's writing.

THE DIARY OF JOHN MACDONELL 77

the water, with which it formed a right-angle. In one place in particular I think it was so narrow that a stone might be cast by a good thrower from one shore to the other. This is called *les Rochers du Grand Callumet,* and here I saw for the first time, *tripe de Roche,* (rock weed) — which the men tell me is the last resource men have to subsist upon in the inhospitable regions of the dreary North, and has been Know[n] to keep men alive for months, boiled in water, after having the sand well washed off it. Six leagues [above] the Grand Callumet we came to the grand marais, on the North Shore of the River, for it has changed its course back to what it was at the entrance of the Chenaux 5 Leagues below the Grand Calumet.[22] Opposite to this marais on the south shore there is a fine sand bank 30 to 40 feet high near a mile in length which bounds prettily around this point of the Grand Marais in the form of a Crescent having the same gradual *penchant* from one end to the other, from its summit all the way to the waters edge. It is shaded on top by fine groves of Norway Pine whose stalks grow up fifty feet frequently without branches. At intervals through the pines we could see like a large clearing apparently made by fire and which the Canadians would call a Grand-Brulé. This brulé came to the water's edge about two miles below the bank above mentioned.[23]

Sunday 9th June. Left our campment at the head of the Grand marais where a branch of the *Ottawa* issues to the southward and joins the River some where near the entrance of *Lac des Chats* — making thus an Island of the *Grand Calumet* Portage. This Small channel it is said is only passable for small canoes. A league beyond the *Grand marais* we got sight of *Fort Coulonges,* a sorry hut, situated near the foot of the

[22] The French word *marais* means swamp or marsh. The phrase *grand marais* was descriptive of many places along the canoe routes of the Canadian Northwest and in early times was not used as a specific place name.

[23] The literal translation of *brulé* is "burnt." The term was commonly applied to the clearings that appeared when areas of forest were laid waste by fire.

mountains; Entered *Lac Coulonges;* these lakes are in this River what knots would be on a cord; two or three times the breadth of the River and of various lengths.[24] *Lac Coulonges* is about two leagues long and is near two miles broad. At the upper end of it is another brulé with which such another sand bank as that opposite to the grand marais but on a smaller scale. The *Allumets* are the next rapids two Decharges and a Portage. The portage is fifteen to twenty paces, over a pretty steep ascent. This portage would be worth a good deal of money in a flurishing settlement being the best mill seat I ever saw.[25] The water at the lower end of the portage is from ten to fifteen feet lower than that above it, so that a canal might be made through the rock to act on machinery. After emptying our canoes of their cargoes they were hauled round the point of which this portage is the Isthmus. A mile farthur we came to the *Lac des Allumets* about four miles wide and nine long from north to south. It is shallow and abounding in shoals, and rocky lands; around it, especially on the East, are very fine Groves of pine. We are now directly towards the chain of Northern mountains as if we meant to cut through them. Turned to the north West and entered the *Riviere creuse* still a part of the *Ottawa* under another name, which is

[24] The town of Fort Coulonge preserves the name of this trading post, which was established by the Northwest Company in 1784 and named after a French officer who spent the winter in the vicinity in 1694. Commission de Géographie de Québec, *Nomenclature des noms géographiques de la province de Québec* (Premier Rapport, Quebec, 1916), p. 28. See also page 368 of *Along Quebec Highways, Tourist Guide,* published in 1930 by the Quebec Department of Highways and Mines.

[25] The Allumettes Portage, called by Belcourt the "Portage de la Culbute des Allumettes," was short but very steep, and all the skill and strength of the voyageurs were called into play in lifting the heavy canoe to the summit. Garry reports that bedding was placed in the declivities of the rock, which served as steps upon which one end of the canoe could be rested. On the return trip down the portage the voyageurs, finding it inconvenient to load the pieces of baggage on their backs in the usual manner, passed them from hand to hand or tumbled them down the cliff (*leur font faire la culbute*). Belcourt, *Itinéraire,* p. 15; Garry, "Diary," Proceedings and Transactions of the Royal Society of Canada. 1900, Section 2, p. 99.

twelve leagues long to the Portages called Les *Joachims* and so straight withall that you can see as far as the Lake a mile broad extends, the chain of mountains running parallel close along side of us on the right hand.[26] The land on the left is covered with p[l]enty of excellent Pine.

Tuesday 11th June. We made the two *Joachims* which together, are reckoned eaqual to the Grand *Callumet*. Camped at the settlement of the *River du moine*. My bowman had the misfortune of breaking his Canoe to-day and stowing in three of her ribs. This house at the *riviere du Moine* — is the last we shall see to Sault of St Marys.[27] The *Roche Capitaine* is the next portage we came to, a rough turbulent Rapid. A League above it I saw the grave of poor lalondes the Body had been taken out of, to be buried at St Anns as before mentioned.[28] Detained half a day on account of Titiche Lafrênieres having broken the bow of his Canoe by running it against the Shore.

15th June. Left the *Grand River* at *Mattawin* in which we made eighteen portages and about as many discharges. It is said there was four days Voyage for a loaded canoe from this place to lake Temiscaming.[29]

[26] The Rivière Creuse or Deep River was the name given to the Ottawa as it flowed through a narrow valley from the lower Joachim portage to the Lac des Allumettes. See Belcourt, *Itinéraire*, p. 16, and Henry, *Travels and Adventures*, p. 27n. The Minnesota Historical Society has a photostatic reproduction of an old French map (Map B 4044 No. 15), the original of which is in the Paris Archives, library of the Service hydrographique de la Marine, which shows a Creuse River as a tributary of the Ottawa. Between the two Joachim portages was a small lake or basin scarcely fifty yards in width. When crossing this the voyageurs told one of their standing jokes about a canoeman who had been stopped there at one time because of a head wind. Garry, " Diary," Proceedings and Transactions of the Royal Society of Canada, 1900, Section 2, p. 100.

[27] Alexander Henry mentions the post at the mouth of the Rivière du Moine as being in operation in 1760. *Travels and Adventures*, p. 27.

[28] See above, page 69.

[29] "Mattawin" is one of several ways in which the name of the settlement at the forks was spelled. "Mattawan" and "Mattaouan" were also used. "Mattawa" is now the accepted form. Eugène Rouillard, *Noms géographiques de la province de Québec* (Quebec, 1906), p. 58.

Entered the little river which runs east at its entrance and is so narrow that a good gun would carry Shot from side to side, further on it is considerably wider. *Mattawin* means a fork in the *Algonquin* or Nipising Tongue. A league up the little river which we now navigate made the *portage du plain Champs,* a considerable one where we passed the night.[30] Here the brigade was separated so that only two canoes travelled together, owing to the portages being frequent and only affoarding room for two canoes to load and unload at a time.

Saturday 16th June. We are now going in a deep glen of still water called 3 leagues long, very straight and from three to four hundred paces wide, between two ridges of Rocky Mountains.

Monday 18th. We passed a cave called by the men *Porte de l'enfer;* it is a cave in the face of the Rocky mountain on the north side of the River, thirty to forty paces from the water, the entrance to it appears to be from six to eight feet high and arched; they Say this cave receives light from the top and is very spacious within; about a mile farthur on we found the *paresseu Portage,* a pretty long one: the rapid that occasions it has a perpendicular fall of about ten feet; this is the fifth portage we made since entering the little River.[31] At some of

---

[30] Macdonell's version of *Plain Champs* is not the same as that of Belcourt, who calls the place *Plain-Chant* (plain song) and traces the origin of the name to voyageurs who claimed to have heard spirits singing melodies of this sort. See Belcourt, *Itinéraire,* p. 17. The difference may be accounted for by the fact that the pronunciation of *champ* and *chant* is almost identical in French. The Little River, by which the author says the party proceeded from Mattawa to the height of land, was the Mattawa, and was known to the elder Henry by that name. The latter goes on to mention a "little river by which we descended into the lake" (Nipissing), and it is possible that Macdonell confused the two. He gives no name to the "small rivulet" mentioned on page 82. Belcourt calls this short stream the Nipissing River. Henry, *Travels and Adventures,* p. 29; Belcourt, *Itinéraire,* p. 19.

[31] In mentioning Porte de l'Enfer (Hell Gate), and the Paresseux Portage, Macdonell reverses their order. Hell Gate, so called because of the gloom of the ravine and the restless agitation of the stream near the cave, was located several hundred yards above the Paresseux Portage instead of being below it as is stated. See Belcourt, *Itinéraire,* p. 19; Bigsby, *Shoe and Canoe,*

the portages a tree would bridge the river across. Eight or nine leagues above the paresseu is *l'anse au Perches* where the setting poles are thrown away to the reserve of two per canoe which the Bowman and Steers-man keep. The ceremony of throwing away the poles our men performed with a loud huzza.[32] The next impediment our navigation met with was the portage of *Talon* occasioned by a fall nearly forty feet high which is not perpendicular but has two cascades. The portage is long and difficult, at the west [?] end [?] of it we encamped and passed the night. About three leagues beyond this portage we left the Little River and made two portages called *Les Musiques,* one of them is horrid, nothing but ups and downs among broken and rugged rocks. After passing the last of the *musiques* we proceeded about a quarter of a mile in a ditch not much wider than the canoe, which nature seems to have made through the centre of a *cedar Swamp* for the convenience of the North west Trade; then we embarked on a small lake two Leagues long which brought us to the Portage *la Tortue* being the last. Came next to *Lac la Tortue* three leagues long and one in breadth. This lake is the [d. main] source of the Little River the whole of which from *Matawin* is computed by the men to be thirty leagues to the first portage of the *vases. Lac La Tortue* is much clearer water than the little River. Leaving this lake we have three portages running called the vases.[33] The men will have the first vase to be some perches longer than the *Grand Callumet* and is the hight of land dividing the waters which fall into

1:161. See also a photostatic reproduction at the Minnesota Historical Society of Map B 4040 No. 13a in the Paris Archives, library of the Service hydrographique de la Marine.

[32] The setting poles were thrown away at the height of land since they were not necessary on the journey downstream. Apparently paddles were adequate after passing the Anse aux Perches despite the fact that the actual divide was above Lac la Tortue.

[33] The propriety of the name Portages des Vases, or Muddy Portages, was attested to by Henry the elder, who noted the term with understanding in 1760, and by Bigsby, who passed that way more than half a century later. Henry, *Travels and Adventures,* p. 30; Bigsby, *Shoe and Canoe,* 1:164.

the *Ottawa* from those which fall into *Lake Huron*.[34] After passing *le grand des Vases* we found a small rivulet which brought us to Lake nipising. It is curious to see the North West and mackinac trade carried on through a small creek that a man can in many places jump over.[35] After following this brook for half a league we came to the second Portage of the *vases,* after which the brook is joined by another about as big, which made it sufficiently deep to float a loaded Canoe, until you came to the third or last vase. At the entrance of this little River into *Lake Nipising* or *prairie des vases* we encamped four nights without even shifting the place of our tent.[36]

Monday 24th June. Left the Prairie des *vases* and crossed a large Bay of the Lake *Nipising,* which is called from 16 to 20 leagues Long but we only pass twelve of it from East to west and in that distance it does not appear to be more than from three to four leagues wide in the outmost extent from North to South. I have been informed it is so shallow that they spear fish in winter in the middle of it under the Ice not exceeding three to four fathoms: its water is of a Grayish muddy colour. About the center of this lake is point aux Croix on which is erected the crosses of eleven men who were swallowed up in it canoe, & Cargoe, some years ago.[37] Three leagues beyond

[34] The *perche,* an old French unit of distance, was eighteen feet.

[35] The Northwest and Mackinac trade during this period was a very considerable one. The total value of exports of furs from Quebec reached an annual figure well in excess of two hundred thousand pounds sterling, and the business is stated by Innis to have brought to the Northwest Company an average annual return on the capital investment of seventy-two thousand pounds during the years 1790–95. See Harold A. Innis, *The Fur Trade in Canada* (New Haven, 1930), p. 260. What proportion of the trade went over the canoe route via Lake Nipissing and the Ottawa River it is impossible to determine accurately. Boats were being introduced, and the route by way of Niagara and the Great Lakes was used to some extent. The larger part of the trade, however, was dependent upon canoe transportation. See below, page 94.

[36] Prairie des Vases is mentioned by Belcourt as a point of land situated at the entrance of the river into Lake Nipissing. *Itinéraire,* p. 20.

[37] Roderic Mackenzie in his "Reminiscences" states that one of those who lost their lives was a man by the name of Smith and that the tragedy oc-

this point we met an Indian and two little girls in a small bark Canoe to whom we gave some buiscuit in exchange for fish. Seven leagues from the Prairie des *vases* we entered among a number of Islands through which we have five leagues to navigate before reaching the Chaudiere des francais and left the Lake to continue its course farthur than our sight could extend to the West North West.[88]

At the chaudiere *des Français* we carry from the Lake nipising to a deep still water cove of the River *des Français*, which issues out of the Lake by a variety of channels to the North North West of the portage and are too rapidious to be navigable above if they are to be judged of by [the] nearest of them to the portage which is steeper than a mill race and not wider in places. After proceeding about two miles down the cove [where] we carried from *Lac Nipising* the current of the main body of the Français River comming from the N.N.E. took us broad side and carried us down merrily being the first current able to make an impression on the canoe that we have drifted with. At the Chaudiere des Français I saw the first Juniper berry growing but now they are to be met with all along the French River.

June 26th. Came down the following Rapids, Les Pins, Rapide Croche, La Fausille, Le Parisien, petit parisien. The day is a beatiful clear day and sun shine. Have seen nothing but rocks since we entered the French River producing moss and some ever-greens stinted in growth, one would think that a bird could scarcely live on these Rocks.

Fourteen leagues from *Lake Nipising* is *L'Enfant perdu* a fine encampment where according to the Story an Indian child that was bathing in sight of his parents was suddenly pulled under water and not coming up soon his friends repeatedly dived for him, but to no purpose. Some time after

curred in 1785, on Mackenzie's first venture into the fur country. Masson, *Bourgeois*, 1:8.

[88] The potholes worn in the rock along the course by water and pebbles gave to the Chaudière des Français its name. Henry, *Travels and Adventures*, p. 31; Belcourt, *Itinéraire*, p. 20. The French River flows from Lake Nipissing into Lake Huron.

they heard moaning under the ground they were encamped upon, they then began to dig with sticks and paddles and only gave up their attemps as vain when they heard the cries of the child proceeding under the high rocky ground and wood back of their encampment. It is said the Boy's cries were heard for six days during which his friends used all their endeavours to relieve him until discouraged by the above mentioned circumstance.[89] A league below *l'Enfant perdue* under the high rocky ground and wood back of their encampment is a portage called le Grand Recolet where one of the North West Companys canoes manned by brothers of the name of Majeau [upset] and lost half the cargo about fifteen days ago.[40] The few survivors and the goods that floated were picked [up] below the Rapid by the other canoes of the Brigade. These unfortunate men had made portage and loaded their canoe below it, but had neglected to put a man or two on shore with a bit of Line to stem the strong eddy which carries back to fall, from a foolish confidence in their own power, and in consequence were drawn down by the eddy under the pitch of the fall where the canoe instantly filled and sunk. Though some of the bodies were found far below this the seven crosses are erected here as a warning to others along with seven others in memory of former casualties. Two leagues below the *Grand Recollet* is *Derraud's Rapid* named after a voyageur of that name who broke his Canoe in it; this being the communication between *Lake Huron* and the *ottawa River* appears to have been much frequented by the *savages* of old, as may be judged from the various figures of animals &c. made by them on the face of the steep Rocks in many places along the banks. Some leagues below *Derreaud's*

[89] The story of the lost child was one of the narratives that formed a part of the folklore of the voyageurs. It is repeated in essentially the same form in Harmon, *Journal*, p. 8.

[40] This incident also was one that was recalled each time a brigade passed the portage, being preserved in this way for many years. Seven men lost their lives in the accident. Belcourt was told of the tragedy when he passed over the route in 1831. *Itinéraire*, p. 20.

THE DIARY OF JOHN MACDONELL   85

Rapid is the figure of a man standing over an animal that lays under him, with a sun on one side and a moon on the other side of him each surrounded by a large circle — a little farthur on, is at least sixteen figures of different animals standing promiscuously together on the face of a steep Rock. Amongst them may be seen fish, flesh, and Tortoise all of them painted with some kind of Red Paint. These figures are made by scratching the Rock weed (moss) off the Rocks with the Point of a knife or some other instrument. Two leagues from Lake *Huron* there is a figure of an ox which gives name to a fine long View of the river called *Lad* [*sic*] *du Boeuf*.

After passing a narrow Racy rapid named the Dalles we saw an Island on which as the story goes, the Irroquois in former days, say 40 or 50 Years ago tried to cut off a strong Brigade of trading canoes. But upon finding themselves discouvered by the French they abandoned their ambush with precipitation and the canoes pursued their rout. It is said this was amongst the last attempts the Irroquois made in the long wars they had with the french in Canada. I think it strange that the Irroquois should have come so far out of their own territories to wadge war; But it is known to be a fact that a strong body of them consisting of not less than 800 to 1000 men had been surprised [and] cut off by the Chippewa's on an Island in *Lake Superior* opposite to the *Gros Cap*.[41]

Thursday June 27th. After coming 25 Leagues yesterday and today, which is, the full length of the *French River,* from *Lake Nipising* to lake *Huron,* we entered the latter with a very strong head wind which compelled us to put ashore as soon as we found a suitable place to unload and haul up the

[41] The conflict between the French and their Indian allies and the Iroquois dates back to the middle of the seventeenth century. See accounts in George M. Wrong, *Rise and Fall of New France* (New York, 1928), 2:493–550, and in Kellogg, *French Régime in Wisconsin*, Chapters 11 and 12. Miss Kellogg shows that the Iroquois penetrated as far west as Wisconsin. The massacre of a band of Iroquois by the Sioux in the vicinity of Lake Superior is mentioned in Edward D. Neill, "History of the Ojibways and Their Connection with the Fur Traders," Minnesota Historical Collections, 5:402.

canoes.[42] The French River enters the Lake by a great number of branches separated by high rocky Islands. The Lake appears like an Ocean no land to be seen but that of the side we are upon and a few petty Islands belonging thereto. About the mouths of the French River are a few rocky shoals where the natives find a variety of water fowls eggs in the season; baskets full of which they brought to our tents for sale, and tried all the ways they could devise to make us give them Rum, but finding us staunch in our refusal offered to appease the wind if they could be indulged with something to drink, and, taking no more effect than the rest of their loguick, they departed much disatisfied, vowing they would conjure and cause the wind to blow with increased violence from the same quarter for eight days.[43]

The account the guide gives me here is " The entrance of the *French River* into the *Lake Huron* is nearly at an eaqual distance from *Detroit* on the S. S. E., *St Mary's Falls* on the W. N. W. and *Malkinac* on the W. S. W. which is farthur by ten leagues than either of the other two places. The Canoes to & from *Malkinac* keep the same course with those bound for *S*^{t} *Mary's,* till they reach Pointe Tessalon whence they cross amongst Islands to the *Pointe du Detour* fifteen leagues from Mackinac. The whole distance from Tessalon to Mackinac is twenty five leagues." This is certainly a mistake for

[42] It was no uncommon thing for the voyageurs to put ashore because of wind when they were traveling across broad expanses of water. The canoes they used were primarily adapted to river travel and were in danger of being broken or swamped if the waves were high. Duncan McGillivray and Harmon both tell of similar delays, and Kennicott explains the difficulties he encountered some years later. *The Journal of Duncan M'Gillivray of the North West Company, at Fort George on the Saskatchewan, 1794–1795* (edited by Arthur S. Morton, Toronto, 1929), p. 5; Harmon, *Journal,* p. 3; "Biography of Robert Kennicott," Transactions of the Chicago Academy of Sciences, 1869, Vol. 1, Part 2, p. 158.

[43] The Canadians thought of the wind as *la vieille* or "the old lady." When they wished to encourage her to give them a favorable breeze they would throw small pieces of tobacco or other insignificant articles into the water as a sacrifice, saying at the same time, *"Soufle, soufle, la vieille."* Grace Lee Nute, " The Voyageur," *Minnesota History,* 6:161.

Detroit is farthur from the entrance of the French River than either of the other places though I cannot specify the distance.[44] The following are the names of the portages from Montreal line in the order in which they occur in ascending the *Ottawa River* &c. to *Lake Huron*. Viz — 1st *Chute a Blondeau*. N° 2.3.4. *Long Soult*. N° 5.6.7. *Les Chaudieres*. N° 8 *Les Chats*. N° 9 *Portage du Fort*. N° 10 *La Montagne*. N° 11 *D'argy*. N° 12 *Le Grand Callumet*. N° 13 *Allumettes*. N° 14.15 *Les Joachins*. N° 16 *La Roche Capitaine*. N° 17. *Les deux Rivieres*. N° 18 *Le Troue*. Those of the *Little River* N° 1 Le *plain Champs*. N° 2. *Les Roses*. N° 3. *Campion*. N° 4 *La Gross Roche*. N° 5 *Le Paresseu*. N° 6 *La Prairie*. N° 7 *La Cave*. N° 8 *Talon*. N° 9 and 10 *Les Musiques*. N° 11 *La Tortue*. N° 12.13.14. *Les vases*. And the portages in the French River N° 1 *La Chaudiere des Français*. N° 2 *Parisiens*. N° 3 *Le Grand Recollet*. N° 4 *La Petite Fausille*.

        18 portages in the Ottawa
        14 " " " Little River & Vases
        4 " " " French River

In all 36 portages to the entrance of Lake Huron and there are besides these about an eaqual number of Décharges.

[44] Reference to a map of the region will show how justified Macdonell was in his objection. The distance from the mouth of the French River to Detroit is something over three hundred miles, whereas the distance to Sault Sainte Marie is more nearly two hundred miles. Point Tessalon is on the north shore of Lake Huron southeast of the Sault; Detour Point is situated on the straits between Lake Huron and Lake Michigan, opposite to Mackinac. Mackinac was one of the important distributing points for the trade of the Northwest. Situated on the boundary line between the territories of the Ottawa and the Chippewa Indians, it was in a position to encourage the trade of both, and it served as a depot to which furs were brought from the area south of Lake Superior and west and south of Lake Michigan. See Ernest A. Cruikshank, *Early Traders and Trade Routes in Ontario and the West, 1760–1783* (Toronto, 1893), p. 259. Although Sault Sainte Marie was not as valuable as Mackinac as a depot, it was nevertheless a post of some importance to the Northwest Company as a station on the route to Grand Portage. For the story of the Sault see Otto Fowle, *Sault Sainte Marie and Its Great Waterway* (New York, 1925).

In the evening of the 27th in spite of the fellows conjuring the wind abated, and according to Mr Jos: Frobishers written instructions to Mr A. N. McLeod we lightened the guide's canoe of forty five peices, which were distributed among the other canoes and shipped all M^r McLeod, Lemoine, and my effects on board of it and took a man out of each of the other canoes which made us a crew of fourteen paddles, and set out on our journey leaving the brigade to wait the arrival of Dannis our associate guide whom we had not seen since the *long Soult* but who we since learnt came to them that same evening. We are now but a single canoe making the best of our way to the Grand Portage.[45] After proceeding four leagues we put on shore for the evening.

The 28th. Being a fine sunshiny day we made good progress — next day we had a thick fog in which we were bewildered for some hours and camped at the serpents point — halfway to the Sault.

Saturday 29th. Met a number of canoes coming from Michilimackinac and passed point Tessalon. We continue coasting the North shore of the lake.

Sunday 30th. Arrived at the Sault St Mary's. The only settlements are on the South shore of the straits divideding Lake Superior from Lake Huron at the bottom of a large Rapid which makes us carry our goods a mile to their head. Mr Nolin who transacts the North West Companys business here has much the best improvements of any of those settled here.[46]

[45] The usual load for a Montreal canoe was about sixty pieces. The term was applied to the bundles, each weighing some ninety pounds, into which the cargo was packed. When crossing a portage each man carried two pieces on his back and shoulders, using a leather sling over his forehead to support one piece, while the second rested on the first. Garry, "Diary," Proceedings and Transactions of the Royal Society of Canada, 1900, Section 2, pp. 90, 96; Henry, *Travels and Adventures,* p. 16. A single canoe such as Macdonell was using would now be called a light, or express, canoe. For a note on the Grand Portage see below, page 92n.

[46] At the time Macdonell visited Sault Sainte Marie no substantial improvements had been made. A few years later the Northwest Company

From this gentleman M^r McLeod and I received every attention, and rooms in his House while we remained at the Sault.

Vast numbers of white fish are taken, here, of an excellent quality many of which are salted and sent to *Mackinac* & *Detroit* where they ought to sell well to bear the expense and repay the export, for salt sells at the Sault for 1/8 p^r lbs.

July 2nd. We left the hospitable roof of Monsr Nolin who escorted us to the western end of the portage where we pitched our tent and finished the Madeira that remained in our care with Monsr Nolin, Monsr Lemoine &c. Lemoine remains here to shift for himself — stopped at pointe au Pins where two leagues above the Sault we found Mr Nelson building a vessel for the North West Company to navigate the Lake Superior and to be called the Otter. She is to be launched shortly.[47] Left Pointe aux Pins at 4 P.M. with a fair wind which soon Brought us opposite to the Gros Cap after which we entered the great Lake Superior the Mother & mistress of the other Lakes; its water is so green and transparent that I am confidently told the bottom can be seen in 30 fms [fathoms] water.

The 4th. We were prevented from stirring by stormy weather — a cold raw day.

located on the Canadian side of the Sault and built locks by which the canoes could pass from Lake Huron to Lake Superior without a portage. A road was also constructed and a sawmill built, which furnished boards and timber for Grand Portage. See Innis, *Fur Trade in Canada*, p. 226; Fowle, *Sault Sainte Marie*, p. 235. "Mr. Nolin" was probably Augustin Nolin, who traded in the vicinity of Sault Sainte Marie and later built a home there. See Wisconsin Historical Collections, 20:155n.; Michigan Pioneer and Historical Collections, 15:113.

[47] Pointe aux Pins was a spot peculiarly suited to the building of boats, since there was an abundance of pine timber there. There were but few ships on the Great Lakes at this time. The "Athabasca" had been built at Pointe aux Pins for service on Lake Superior, but having been found inadequate for this purpose, had been floated down the falls to be used on the lower lakes with the "Beaver." The "Otter" now took the place of the "Athabasca," under the command of Captain John Bennet, who sailed her on Lake Superior for the Northwest Company for a number of years. See below, page 96; Masson, *Bourgeois*, 2:149; and Innis, *Fur Trade in Canada*, p. 226.

July 5th. Passed the Bay of Michipicotton in which the North West Company have a trading post.⁴⁸ This bay runs a long way into the Country and its shores run so parrallel that the head wind we had upon one side of it was aft-wind on the other side, for the space of ten leagues. We made by the men's Compute twenty four leagues this day. Next day we passed Tête a la loutre where it is said a collumn of Rock stands upon a lofty round mountain to the height of ten to Twelve feet perpendicular; Twelve to fifteen leagues furthur on we found the entrance of the Pic River where there is a Trading Post belonging to Mʳ Coté and associates situated within half a mile of our encampment.⁴⁹ This was the coldest night ever I felt at this time [of] the year, and in the vicinity of our encampment there are eleven Crosses in memory of that number [of] men that are buried here most of whom perished last winter by various casualties.

We keep our arms in good order ever since we parted from the canoes being told the Indians are apt to attack a single canoe. The crews of the canoes have seldom any arms of their own. At l'anse a la Bouteille met a canoe of Forsyth Richardson & Cᵒˢ, that had wintered in Nipigon alongside of the H. B. Company's Traders, who did not make a single pack,

⁴⁸ The post at Michipicoton had been found to be a profitable one for some years. It had been auctioned for 3,750 livres in 1743 and in one year produced, according to the account of Count Andriani cited by La Rochefoucauld in 1791, forty bundles of fine furs. Innis, *Fur Trade in Canada*, pp. 111, 268n.
⁴⁹ Tête à la Loutre, or Otter Head Point, took its name from the unusual shape of a large block of stone there, which was a standard landmark, commonly taken to be halfway between Kaministiquia (Fort William in later years) and Sault Sainte Marie. See William H. Keating, *Narrative of an Expedition to the Source of St. Peter's River, Lake Winnepeek, Lake of the Woods, etc.* (London, 1825), 2:184.
  The yield of the Pic River post about 1790 was thirty bundles of furs. See Innis, *Fur Trade in Canada*, p. 268n. Gabriel Cotté, son of Nicholas Cotté, was an outfitter and trader at Mackinac for a number of years, having located there as early as 1768. See Jean Baptiste Perrault, "Narrative of the Travels and Adventures of a Merchant Voyageur in the Savage Territories of Northern America Leaving Montreal the 28th of May 1783 (to 1820)," Michigan Pioneer and Historical Collections, 37:536 and note.

THE DIARY OF JOHN MACDONELL 91

for Mr Hudson their cheif, had been frozen to death in [the] winter seeking subsistance for himself and his fellow sufferers.[50] This Canoe was loaded with the same goods they took into the interior last autum. Next day we passed the *Nipigon* River which appears a large [one], saw the mamel two round mountains in the form of Sugar Loaves whose bases seemed united. After which we passed the *Bay noir,* which is so deep that the eye cannot see the land that terminates the bottom of it, though the mouth is but moderately large, passed close to the *Thunder* Mountain one of the highest land about the lake though the whole of its Northern Coast be an Iron bound one; one half of *thunder* Hill rises in about the proportion of 45 Degrees from the waters edge and is toped off by the other half of its height a perfect perpendicular. So that at a distance it resembles an extensive citadel wall, sloping from above half its height in a regular proportion to the waters edge.[51]

From the *Tosinerre* to the *Pâte,* another curious round mountain upon an Island of near the same height with the

[50] Lake Nipigon, situated due north of Lake Superior, dates back in the history of the fur trade well into the seventeenth century. Posts in this area were very productive during the French régime, but their output declined during the period of British occupation. Duncan Cameron, stationed there by the Northwest Company, suffered from competition with the Hudson's Bay Company, whose traders penetrated south into the Nipigon area from the Albany River and established a fort at Osnaburgh Lake in 1786. Cameron's report of 1804 described the country as very much impoverished. See Burpee, *Oxford Encyclopaedia,* p. 455; Innis, *Fur Trade in Canada,* pp. 157, 268n.; Masson, *Bourgeois,* 2:232, 292-300.

A pack of furs refers to the bundles into which the peltries were pressed and tied up. Packs were made up according to weight, each containing about ninety pounds of furs. It was common to mix the different kinds, though some bundles were made up of peltries of a single kind. Each pack was marked, and a bill of contents made out to show what it contained. Elliott Coues, ed., *The Expeditions of Zebulon Montgomery Pike to Headwaters of the Mississippi River, through Louisiana Territory, and in New Spain, during the Years 1805-6-7* (New York, 1895), 1:284; Harmon, *Journal,* p. 16; Anderson, "Personal Narrative," Wisconsin Historical Collections, 9:143.

[51] Major Long, passing Thunder Hill in 1823, estimated its height as eight hundred feet. Keating, *Narrative,* 2:173.

Thunder, is a traverse of about two leagues, passed which, we paddled against a strong hard wind till we reached *point au Père* where we passed the night. This point tradition says had its name from a *Père Jusuite* murdered here upon it of old by the Indians.[52] Here M^r McLeod and I shaved and shifted being the last night we shall sleep out, wind and weather permitting; this side of the grand portage. Leaving pointe au père we paddled two pipes and put to shore to give the men time to clean themselves, while we breakfasted — this done a short pipe brought us to *Pointe au Chapeaux* around which we got a sight of the long wished for Grand Portage.[53] The beach was covered with spectators to see us arrive, our canoe went well and the crew sung paddling songs in a vociferous manner.

The Grand Portage is situated in the bottom of a shallow Bay perhaps three miles deep and about one league and a half wide at its mouth from *Pointe aux Chapeaux* to *pointe a la*

[52] Macdonell apparently intended to write "Père Jesuite." Belcourt speaks of the point as being named for a Jesuit father, but states that he died of some sickness during the course of a missionary expedition. Belcourt was unable to learn the man's name. *Itinéraire,* p. 33.

[53] The "pipe" was one of the units of time commonly used by the Canadians. It was apparently a flexible unit, for there seems to be no agreement as to the length of time it covered. The editor of Belcourt's *Itinéraire* says (page 55 note) that the voyageurs would stop every half or three-quarters of an hour, rest a few minutes, and light their pipes. Davidson asserts that they stopped much more infrequently, every two hours only. See his *North West Company,* p. 218n.

Pointe aux Chapeaux is the Hat Point of today, which guards the northeastern entrance to Grand Portage Bay. Grand Portage was the general rendezvous of the Montreal fur traders until the opening years of the century when the Northwest Company moved their post northward along the shore of the lake to Fort William. Most of the pork-eaters who brought goods from Montreal went no farther, but returned to the St. Lawrence, their canoes loaded with the packs of furs that the Northmen had brought down from the interior. Although the name Grand Portage at first referred to the nine-mile trail over which all goods and furs had to be carried between the harbor and the waters of the Pigeon River, it later came to be applied to the post at the eastern end of the trail, Fort Charlotte being at the upper end of the portage. The rendezvous was an active place during the summer when the canoes from the fur country met those from Montreal. Nearly a thousand

Framboise having a small Island just opposite the fort about half way from one of these points to the other: on a low spot which rises gently from the Lake. The pickets are not above fifteen to twenty paces from the waters edge. Immediately back of the Fort is a lofty round Sugar loaf mountain the base of which comes close to the Picket on the North West Side.

The Gates are shut alyways [*sic*] after sunset and the Bourgeois and clerks Lodge in houses within the pallisades, where there are two Sentries keeping a look out all night cheifly for fear of accident by fire. A clerk a guide and four men are considered watch enough. These are Montreal engagees.

The North men while here live in tents of different sizes pitched at random, the people of each post having a camp by themselves and through their camp passes the road of the portage. They are seperated from the Montrealeans by a brook. The Portage is three leagues from one navigation to the other which caused great expense and trouble to the company. The men have Six Livers of this currency for every peice of Goods or pack of Furs they carry from one end of it to the other — the currency of the North west is double that of Canada which currency had its origine, I presume, from the mens' wages being formerly paid in peltries and it was supposed that one *liver's* worth of Furs would be worth two livers to the person that took it to Montreal to be paid. The currency existed long before the North West Company

men were there (see below, page 95), engaged in transferring goods and furs over the portage, while agents and wintering partners of the company held their annual meeting and laid out plans of action for the coming year. Macdonell's description of Grand Portage, quoted by Davidson on page 237 of his *North West Company*, is one of the best that has been preserved. The transfer of the post to Kaministiquia was effected after a move by the United States to collect customs duties made its advisable to establish headquarters on British soil. See Solon J. Buck, *Story of the Grand Portage* (Minneapolis, 1931), for further details. This pamphlet is a revised reprint of an article with the same title published in *Minnesota History Bulletin*, 5:14–27.

had a being and I believe before Canada was taken from the French.⁵⁴

All the buildings within the Fort are sixteen in number made with cedar and white spruce fir split with whip saws after being suquared [*sic*], the Roofs are couvered with shingles of Cedar and Pine, most of their posts, Doors, and windows, are painted with spanish brown. Six of these buildings are Store Houses for the company's Merchandize and Furs &c. The rest are dwelling houses shops compting house and Mess House — they have also a warf or kay for their vessel to unload and Load at.⁵⁵ The only vessel on the Lake Superior is the new [one] Mr Nelson was building when we passed at *Point aux Pins* and is to be called the *Otter*, the *Athabaska* which sailed the Lake before her is to be [*d*. called the otter] floated down the falls of St Mary, to help the Beaver to bring the needfull [supplies] from Detroit and Mackinac to the Sault, which the otter is supposed sufficient, to convey from St Mary's to the Grand Portage and in return she takes a cargo of Furs to the Sault when they are arrived from the North.⁵⁶ Part of the Company's Furs are sent Round the Lakes in Shipping, but the major part goes down the ottawa in the montreal Canoes. Every improvement about this place appertains to the North West Company. Between two and three hundred yards to the East of the N. W. Fort beyond the Pork eaters camp is the spot Messrs David and Peter Grant have selected to build upon, as yet they have done nothing to it but marking out the four corners of the ground they mean to occupy with posts stuck in the ground. They are now

⁵⁴ Grand Portage currency was reckoned by units usually designated as G. P. C. Twelve of these units were equal to a pound sterling. See Masson, *Bourgeois,* 1:61–66. The livre of Canada after the conquest was worth about seven-eighths of an English shilling. Davidson, *North West Company,* p. 202n.

⁵⁵ Macdonell's reference to the wharf at Grand Portage is one of the few that have been preserved. The dock was reconstructed in 1931, the project having been executed in connection with the celebration of the two hundredth anniversary of La Vérendrye's exploration of the harbor.

⁵⁶ See above, page 89.

off for the interior without leaving any vestage of their having been here but the four posts above mentioned.[57] It is called Sixty leagues from here to *Fond du Lac* where the *Rivier St Louis* enters Lake Superior and which is half the Lake, measuring either side from thence to the Sault St Mary.[58] Fogs are frequent on this immense Lake which renders the navigation difficult. The New Ship otter has been expected some time now and we are anxiously looking out for her; provisions have turned so scarce that near 1000 men upon the ground in the company's service have been put upon half allowance. A full allowance to a voyageur while at this Poste is a Quart of Lyed Indian Corn or maize, and one ounce of Greece. It is reckoned there is only six days allowance remaining in the Stores, and should the vessel protract her arrival beyond that period I am at a loss to think what shift the gentlemen would adopt to subsist their servants.

August the 1st. M^{rss} Robert Grant, Peter Pangman, Alex. McLeod and Wm Thorburn set out in two Large Canoes for Montreal. These Gentlemen are universally regretted; the

[57] David Grant, mentioned by John McDonald as an old experienced trader in the Northwest, is credited with the leadership of a group organized in opposition to the Northwest Company which had its headquarters in 1793–94 at Sturgeon River. See Masson, *Bourgeois*, 2:20; Innis, *Fur Trade in Canada*, p. 258. Peter Grant, clerk of the Northwest Company in 1784, had become a partner in 1791, but at the time of this narrative he was associated with David Grant. The two men apparently planned an independent post at Grand Portage in 1793, but left it unfinished to go to the interior. According to later entries in Macdonell's journal (Masson, *Bourgeois*, 1:284), Peter Grant made a temporary encampment five miles from Macdonell's fort on the Qu'appelle River. In 1794 he established a post on La Coquille or Shell River, representing one of the five different oppositions who were trading in that year in the region of the Assiniboine and Qu'appelle rivers. After these opposition activities in 1793–94, Peter Grant again joined his fortunes to the Northwest Company, serving as proprietor of the Rainy Lake post in 1799 and later taking charge of the Red River department. See Masson, *Bourgeois*, 1:66, 294, and Coues, *New Light*, 1:80n.

[58] Fond du Lac was the name given to the region around the southwestern end of Lake Superior. In the parlance of the fur trade the department of that name embraced not only the lake shore but also the territory around Leech and Sandy lakes and the upper waters of the Mississippi. See Thwaites in Wisconsin Historical Collections, 19:173n.

two former retire from the concern with handsome competancies and the two later merely to recruit their health, injured through bad fare and fatigues in the interior.[59]

Augt 2nd. Old Bazil Ireland the guide arrived with two Montrèal canoes and brings the agreeable news of the Otter lying off *Pointe au Père*. Early next morning a Boat well manned was sent to tow her up into port, and to their surprise spied her behind the point a la Framboise after passing before the fort in the Night with a North West wind. It was ten o'clock before She anchored at the wharffe having entered partly by sailing and partly by towing.

Monday 5th Agu^t. I left the lake Superior and walked over the Grand Portage to Fort Charlotte accompanied by M$^{rss.}$ Cuthbert Grant and John Bennet the sailing master of the otter.[60] The Portage is full of hills is divided by the voyageurs into sixteen *Poses* or resting places, its soil is cheifly composed of copper coloured clay the cheif vegetable produc-

---

[59] These men were all traders connected with the Northwest Company. Robert Grant, whose trading career dated back at least to 1778, had been stationed in the Red River department with William McGillivray and had traded at that time in competition with the opposition company organized by Pangman, Gregory, and McLeod, to which reference has been made (page 12 above). About 1784 Grant established Fort Espérance on the Qu'appelle River, the post at which Macdonell was to spend the winter. See Innis, *Fur Trade in Canada,* pp. 200, 236. Davidson in his *North West Company,* page 46 and note, gives the date of the founding of this post as 1787. See also Coues, *New Light,* 1:47n. Pangman, the organizer of the Montreal Company in 1784, afterwards joined the Northwest Company, and at the time of his retirement in 1793 was apparently in sufficiently good standing to be "universally regretted." See Burpee, *Oxford Encyclopaedia,* p. 479. Thorburn was a trader who had a post on the Qu'appelle River. See Innis, *Fur Trade in Canada,* p. 252, and Coues, *New Light,* 1:300n. Alexander McLeod had been in the Athabasca region for some years, wintering in 1789-90 at Fort Chipewyan. Coues, *New Light,* 1:277n.

[60] Cuthbert Grant was one of the leading traders of the Northwest Company in the decade 1780-90. He had been on the Athabasca River with Peter Pond and had established a post near the mouth of the Slave River in 1786. At the time he met Macdonell he was on his way to Fort Qu'appelle, where he was to spend the winter. Grant was associated with the opposition movement of the decade following 1790 which finally led to the organization of the X. Y. Company in 1798, and he was one of those who

tion of which is spruce, fir and other evergreens.[61] Mr Donald Ross has been so long in charge of Fort Charlotte that he has acquired the respectable name of Governor.[62] Next day I assisted my Bourgois in sending off fourteen canoes for the Red River. These N.W. Canoes are about half the size of the Montreal or Grand River Canoes and when loaded to the utmost can carry à Tun and a half. The number of men required to navigate them is four to five i.e. the near hand posts have but [?] four men. A head clerk or Bourgeouis is allowed by the concern to have an extra man in his canoe to wait upon him. There has been great abuse in these things formerly certain gentlemen who were fond of Dashing taking an unecessary number of chosen men into their canoes from motives of vanity. I set out after the fourteen Canoes above mentioned to winter in the Red River.[63] The River we navigate from Fort Charlotte falls into Lake Superior in l'Anse aux [d. Trembles] Tourtes three leagues to the East of the Grand Portage.[64] This river is both narrow Shallow and full of falls and Rapids. The first carrying place we came to was

later signed the agreement by which the two companies were consolidated. See Burpee, *Oxford Encyclopaedia*, p. 247; Davidson, *North West Company*, pp. 73, 93, 243; Coues, *New Light*, 1:80n.; and Innis, *Fur Trade in Canada*, p. 253.

[61] The term " pose " was of French origin, and was applied to the stopping places which were to be found at intervals on every long portage. A pose was not merely a resting place; it was also a temporary depot, and all the packs were brought to the first pose before any were carried to the second. This arrangement was designed as security against possible raids by the Indians. Inasmuch as the same places were used as poses by all who passed, it came to be the common thing to measure the length of a portage by the number of poses along the trail. The distance between two poses varied from six to eight hundred yards, depending upon conditions on the trail. Michigan Pioneer and Historical Collections, 37:172n. Wisconsin Historical Collections, 19:180.

[62] This statement by Macdonell is evidence that Fort Charlotte was already, in 1793, an old post. See Buck, *Story of the Grand Portage*, p. 9.

[63] At the time of Macdonell's journey the Assiniboine River was called the Upper Red River, while the present Red River was distinguished from it by the name Lower Red River.

[64] The Anse aux Tourtes is Pigeon Bay.

Perdrix caused by the Rivier falling over a Rock from the height of about fifty feet.[65] Here I was surprised to see two men shoulder the canoe mouth upwards and from end to end of the portage. Passed the night at the prairie along with M[r] John Finlay, so far on his way to fort des Prairies.[66]

Wednesday 7th Aug[t]. Passed the carribeau and slept at the Outarde from whence we had to send a canoe back to the Caribeau for seven pieces that are missing out of a brigade caused by a throng of canoes together. The Outarde Portage is longer than the Grand Callumet.[67]

[65] Portage Perdrix was known to English-speaking traders as the Partridge Portage. Coues, *New Light*, 1:8.

[66] The North canoes used on the voyages from Grand Portage to the interior were considerably smaller and lighter than the Montreal canoes used on the lower part of the route. Two men, the bowman and the steersman, were able to carry these canoes over the portages, whereas six men were usually required to carry the Montreal canoes. The larger canoes were carried bottom up. See Alexander Mackenzie, *Voyages from Montreal on the River St. Lawrence through the Continent of North America to the Frozen and Pacific Oceans* (London, 1801), pp. xlvii, xlviii.

The "prairie" or "meadow," which was the usual camping ground the first night above Grand Portage, was situated about two and a half miles above the Partridge Portage. Coues, *New Light*, 1:8 and note.

John Finlay was one of the wintering partners of the Northwest Company, trading in later years in the Athabasca region. Masson, *Bourgeois*, 1:61; 2:498.

It is difficult to determine the location of Fort des Prairies, since the name seems to have been applied to several different posts. Pond puts it above the forks of the Saskatchewan on the North Branch, whereas Bain says it was just below the junction of the two branches. See Davidson, *North West Company*, p. 37n. In tracing Thompson's route of 1808, Tyrrell says the explorer passed Fort à la Corne "on the site of the old French Fort des Prairies," some miles below the forks. Coues points out that as the trade pushed up the river, the name was applied to establishments on the upper reaches of the North Branch, such as Forts George, Vermilion, and Augustus. When two of these were operating, they were sometimes called Upper and Lower Forts des Prairies. Thompson, *Narrative*, pp. lxxxviii; Coues, *New Light*, 2:481n.

[67] The Carribeau, or Caribou, Portage was also called the Deer Portage. Literally *outarde* would be translated "bustard," but the portage was more frequently called Goose or Fowl Portage. See Coues, *New Light*, 1:9n. For Macdonell's description of Grand Calumet, which he had crossed two months before, see above, page 75.

THE DIARY OF JOHN MACDONELL 99

Messrs Robert Thomson and W^m McKay both bound for the English River came up and passed the night with us.⁶⁸

Thursday 8th. Made the Orignal and Grand des Cerises Portages and Passed another night with our agreeable friends Me^ssrs Thomson and McKay.⁶⁹

Friday 9th. Passed the petit portage neuf and Part of the Grand Portage neuf at the N.W. end of which we Passed the night with Mr Simon Fraser.⁷⁰

Saturday 10th. Passed the whole day at the Grand Portage neuf waiting our canoes that are behind.

Sunday 11th. It was noon when we left Grand Portage neuf. Passed the Martes, les Perches and Slept at the height of Land, where I was instituted a *North man* by *Batême* performed by sprinkling water in my face with a small cedar Bow dipped in a ditch of water and accepting certain conditions such as not to let any new hand pass by that road without experiencing the same ceremony which stipulates particularly never to kiss a voyageur's wife against her own free will the whole being accompanied by a dozen of Gun shots fired one after another in an Indian manner.⁷¹ The intention of

⁶⁸ The Churchill River was known as the English River, Joseph Frobisher having given it the name. Davidson, *North West Company*, p. 39.

Robert Thompson and William McKay had been located for some years on the Churchill and Nelson rivers and succeeded in offering considerable competition to the Hudson's Bay Company at York Factory, situated near the mouth of the Nelson River. Thompson was killed in a quarrel with some Indians in the winter of 1794–95. Thompson, *Narrative*, p. xxxix.

⁶⁹ Portage Orignal was called by its English equivalent, Moose Portage. Grand des Cerises was translated Great Cherry Portage. Coues, *New Light*, 1:9n.

⁷⁰ Coues says that the Portages Neufs (New Portages) were so named from the fact that the old route had originally followed a different track. The name Watab Portage was later used. Coues, *New Light*, 1:10n.

It is probable that the Simon Fraser here referred to was the man who was a partner in the Northwest Company from 1795 to 1804 rather than the younger trader of the same name who did not become a partner until 1802 and who later became famous as an explorer. See W. S. Wallace, "The Two Simon Frasers," in *Canadian Historical Review*, 13:183 (June, 1923); Burpee, *Oxford Encyclopaedia*, p. 219.

⁷¹ Some form of initiation or celebration at the expense of the passengers was customary among the voyageurs. The amount of formality varied on

this Bâtême being only to claim a glass. I complied with the custom and gave the men, between Mr Neil McKay and self a two gallon keg as my worthy Bourgeois Mr Cuthburt Grant directed me.⁷² We are now at the head of the waters that run into Lake Superior.

Monday 12th Augt. Steered off the height of land upon the waters running to the North West into Hudson's Bay. Passed the Epingl[e] Décharges. Entered *Lac de la Piere a fusile*.⁷³ A pretty Lake having beautiful well wooded mountains running parallel to it, forming its south shore, it is from two to three miles wide and barely [?] double that in length. A fine calm sunny day the water smooth as Glass. Passed l'Escalier and the cheval de Bois. Camped at the Gros des Pins.⁷⁴ Messrs Angus Shaw, and Duncan McGillivary [*sic*] came up and passed us on their way to *Fort des Prairies*.⁷⁵ Mr Shaw

different occasions, but the desired dram remained the underlying motive for whatever ceremony or other persuasion there might be. See Harmon, *Journal*, p. 2; Coues, *New Light*, 1:11; and "Robert Kennicott" in *Transactions of the Chicago Academy of Sciences*, Vol. 1, Part 2, p. 155.

⁷² There were several persons named McKay in the fur trade. Neil McKay was at this time headed for the forks of the Qu'appelle River where he wintered near Peter Grant at a point about five leagues from Fort Espérance. See Masson, *Bourgeois*, 1:284. The opposition activities of David and Peter Grant during this year have already been noted (page 94 above). Apparently David Grant was on the Sturgeon River while Peter traded on the Qu'appelle.

⁷³ Lac Pierre à Fusil is now called Gunflint Lake. Harmon called it Flinty Lake and attributed the name to the stones found along its shores. Harmon, *Journal*, p. 18.

⁷⁴ The Gros des Pins is the Portage des Gros Pins (Portage of the Big Pines), which later became simply Pine Portage. It was a carry of 640 paces over a high ridge. L'escalier (the stairway) and the Cheval de Bois (wooden horse) are mentioned by Alexander Mackenzie. The former was a portage of 55 paces around a waterfall; the latter, a longer carry of 380 paces. See Coues, *New Light*, 1:12n., and Alexander Mackenzie, *Voyages from Montreal*, p. li.

⁷⁵ Angus Shaw was a well-known trader of the Northwest Company who during the previous year had established Fort George on the north branch of the Saskatchewan River. Shaw had been active in the Nipigon region during the decade from 1780 to 1789, and from 1789 to 1791 he had been developing the trade in the vicinity of Moose Lake. See Innis, *Fur Trade in Canada*, pp. 157, 206, 237, 253, 262, and Masson, *Bourgeois*, 1:31, 61; 2:17. Duncan

being a dashing Bourgeois gave the men of my fifteen canoes a dram out of a big keg he had upon Tap.

Thursday 13th. Mr Daniel McKenzie in the light canoe with the Arabaska papers came to our fire before we left it in the morning so far on his way to montreal to recruit his injured health. Went down the little fausille, Descharge du vaseu, the cedars, and a number of shallow little Rapids called the Châts.[76] Cleared the Marabeau at 1 P. M. Made the two little Rochers of saguinage and camped at l'Anse au Sable. Next day made the little Rocher and Prairie Portages also Rocher des Couteaux and entered the Lake of that name, the clearest water in the North.[77] Passed the Rapids des cauteaux and slept at the second Portage below them where our Bourgeois came up with us and ordered each man a dram, which I served out to them.

Thursday 15th. Waited at the Carpe for the Canoes behind. Mixed nine Gallons of Indian Rum it being customary for Bourgeois to wet the whistle of every Indian they met on the

McGillivray was a *bourgeois* of the Northwest Company, a younger brother of William McGillivray and a nephew of Simon McTavish. In 1800 he made an expedition to the source of the North Saskatchewan through Howse Pass. He also took part in the effort, vain though it was, to negotiate with the Hudson's Bay Company regarding the transfer of goods and furs to and from the interior by way of the Bay instead of sending them through the Great Lakes. See McGillivray, *Journal;* also Davidson, *North West Company*, pp. 83, 85, 96; Innis, *Fur Trade in Canada*, p. 281; and Coues, *New Light*, 1:439n.

[76] Daniel McKenzie was a *bourgeois* of the Northwest Company for a number of years. In 1797 he was stationed at Fort des Prairies and the Red Deer River. Two years later he was the proprietor of the department which included Upper Fort des Prairies and the Rocky Mountains. In 1806 he was proprietor of the Athabasca department. See Coues, *New Light*, 1:216n.; Masson, *Bourgeois*, 1:62; and manuscript minutes of the Northwest Company. The "Arabaska papers" were the dispatches and letters sent by the traders in the Athabasca region to those located at posts farther south and to officials of the company at Montreal.

[77] Marabeau was also spelled Marabou or Maraboeuf. Saguinage should probably be Saganaga, although the spelling varies on different maps and in different accounts. See Coues, *New Light*, 1:12n. Lac des Couteaux is known as Knife Lake.

way. At Gros des Bois-Bleus Mr Grant bought a canoe for old Aguse, his, being the worst in the Brigade.[78] Slept at Petit des Bois bleus.

16th Augt. Passed Grand des pins at 6 A.M. Pointe de Bois at 7 A.M. Breakfasted at the Galais du Lac Croche.[79] Cleared the Rideau portage at 3 P.M. Dined at Flanon [*sic*] and Slept there.[80] Here I saw the first dog (a large Black Indian one that Augé the interpreter killed in Lac Croche) eaten. He castorated him as soon as he fell to prevent rank taste in the flesh. The hair of the animal was singed off as canadians singe their hogs and then washed clean with water. Next day we were stopped at our last nights quarters by a strong head wind till half after twelve. Killed a cub Bear on an Island in Lac la Croix and slept in sight of the *Mai*.[81]

Sunday 18th. Lac la Croix is twelve leagues long. Made the Portage of La Croix. Passed Lake Vermillion,[82] three leagues long, seperated from Lac la méccan by a shallow straight.

Monday 19th. Passed the remainder of Lake Miccan with

[78] Obviously the copyist has made an error here. This is the Portage Bois Blanc or Basswood Portage. Macdonell so lists it at the end of the journal. See below, page 117.

[79] Lac Croche is Crooked Lake, so named from the extreme irregularity of its shore line. The canoe route varied in direction through ninety degrees in crossing it. Coues, *New Light*, 1:15n.

[80] Flanon should be Flacon, referring to Bottle Portage. Macdonell spells it correctly in his list; see below, page 117.

[81] Lac la Croix or Cross Lake later became the junction where the Grand Portage canoe route and the route from Fort William came together at Pointe du Mai. See Coues, *New Light*, 1:218. The northern route, which passed from Fort William, via the Dog and Savanne rivers and Sturgeon Lake, to the Maligne River and Cross Lake, was at first very unpopular. It was used because it was an all-Canadian route that was not subject to diplomatic controversies, as was the Grand Portage route. The question of British transit rights over the latter was not definitely settled until 1842.

The *Mai* was probably a lobstick, or maypole, a favorite landmark of voyageurs. Such a pole was made by cutting away all but a few branches of a tree, usually one which stood on a headland or promontory. Nute, *Voyageur*, pp. 67, 208.

[82] On Lake Vermilion see below, page 202n.

THE DIARY OF JOHN MACDONELL 103

a brisk fair wind.[83] Made the small portages neufs, at 9 A. M. Entered Lake La Pluie at 10½.[84] A fair wind carried us over the Grand Traverse of four leagues and we camped at the petit detroit about three P. M. to wait the canoes behind. Rained hailed and thundered in loud peals accompanied by a tempestuous wind. Some of the hail stones we picked up were as big as the yolke of an egg. After the shower the weather cleared up but it blew so fresh that one of our canoes who staid behind to feast on a large white dog they had stolen was unable to come to us.

20th. Sent a light canoe and guide in search of the canoe missing. As soon as it appeared we set out intending to reach the Fort of Lake Lapluie, but a strong head wind forced us a shore five Leagues from the first detroit. Here we found the Premier, *Nectam,* with twenty young men; to whom, the Bourgeois gave a treat of Rum and Tobacco.[85]

21st. Left the place of our Degrade[86] and made five Leagues which brought us to the end of the lake which is called 18 Leagues Long — from the N. W. End of the Lake issues *Lake Lapluie river* which is supposed to be 40 Leagues

[83] Coues explains that the name of Lake Miccan, now known as Lake Namakan, is not of French origin but is rather a modification of an Indian word. The spelling of the name varied, a more acceptable form being Namaycan. It refers to a place where the natives formerly speared sturgeon. Coues, *New Light,* 1:17n.

[84] Lac la Pluie is Rainy Lake. The name is traced to Joseph la France, who maintained that the name originated in the fact that the cascade, near the discharge of the lake into the Rainy River proper, raised a mist like rain. See Coues, *New Light,* 1:18n. The Rainy Lake fort was a post of considerable importance to which the Athabasca traders came to exchange their furs for supplies and goods brought from Montreal. After the union of the Northwest Company and the Hudson's Bay Company in 1821 the Athabasca traders received their supplies from York Fort in Hudson's Bay. Garry, " Diary," Proceedings and Transactions of the Royal Society of Canada, 1900, Section 2, p. 125. The diary of a trader stationed at the Rainy Lake fort appears below, pages 195–241.

[85] For mention of the Premier, a noted chief, see below, page 212.

[86] When the Canadians were forced by adverse winds to land and wait for more favorable sailing conditions, they were said to have made a " degrade."

long emptying itself into the Lake of the woods. In sight of the fort of Lake La Pluie is the Kettle fall, causing a portage. The Fort stands on the top of a steep bank of the river. It has two wooden Bastions in front flanking the Gate.

Thursday 22nd. Left the Fort at 10 A. M. and slept below the manitou Rapid.[87] This is deemed the most beautiful River in the N. W. and is generally about ¼ mile wide.

Friday 23rd August. Slept at the Isle au sable three leagues from the mouth of the main channel of the River at the foot of the widest traverse in the lake of the woods. Next day we proceeded to the *Roche Rouge* having been detained in exchanging our old canoes for new ones we found at Isle au Sable in possession of the Indian makers.[88]

Sunday 25th Augt. Left our fires at 3 P.M. Made the little portage of Lac des Bois which is made merely to avoid a circuitous rout — at the most western part of this lake. Made Portage du Rat into the River Winipic [Winnipeg] which issues out of Lac des Bois in a number of different channels. Lake of the Woods is called thirty leagues the way the canoes come — but like the River of Lac la pluie is made much longer than it really is. The portage du Rat is said to [be] the place where the american Line by the treaty of 83 finishes having followed the Canoe track from the Grand Portage to here and from this place it is to take a due west course till it intersects the Mississippi — a thing impossible in the nature of things, for the source of the said Mississippi is said to be 300 Miles due south of the portage du Rat. Camped at Mr Frobisher's Galais about the Dalls.[89]

[87] Manitou Rapid was on the Rainy Lake River. See below, page 218.

[88] Sable Island, lying in Lake of the Woods near the mouth of the Rainy River, is mentioned by Bigsby as being five and a half miles long and made up largely of sand hillocks and granite mounds. *Shoe and Canoe*, 2:288.

[89] It is interesting to note that although the British and American foreign offices did not have satisfactory information regarding the geography of the upper waters of the Mississippi River, it was nevertheless common knowledge among the fur traders that the Treaty of 1783 was impossible of execution. Peter Pond's part in the story has already been suggested (page 13 above). The need of exact data was appreciated by the two governments, and Article

THE DIARY OF JOHN MACDONELL 105

Monday 26th. Passed the Grand Décharges, terre Jaune, petit Rocher de Chaurette, Terre-Blanche and cave Portages and Slept at the old fort of Portage de l'isle called by the natives *Wabartim*.[90] Next day passed the Portage de l'isle Below which we were informed by Indians that a party of Traders from Hudson's Bay consisting of three boats and two canoes, had for the first time descended the waters about 8 days ago — and in testimony showed us where one of them had been shot through the arm by the Indian who guides these Hudson's Bay Traders. Slept at *Chûte à Jacqueau*.[91]

4 of the Jay Treaty of 1794 provided that a joint survey of the upper Mississippi should be made. Although David Thompson, surveying for the Northwest Company, determined the location of the Northwest Angle of the Lake of the Woods and the source of the Mississippi in the years immediately preceding 1800, the official survey was delayed until after the War of 1812, and the boundary line was not precisely drawn until 1818. Even then a dispute remained unsettled regarding the details of the boundary between Lake Superior and the Lake of the Woods. According to the agreement finally reached in 1842, it was decided that the line should run along the canoe route from Grand Portage, but that transit rights should be enjoyed by both parties. Rat Portage was not, however, the northwesternmost point of the lake to which the line extended, as Macdonell here states. That point was found to be at the head of a bay to the west and south, later named Monument Bay. For the text of the treaties of 1783, 1794, 1814, 1818, and 1842, see William M. Malloy, *Treaties, Conventions, International Acts, Protocols and Agreements between the United States of America and Other Powers, 1776-1909*, Vol. 1 (Washington, 1910); see also Alexander Mackenzie, *Voyages*, p. lviii; Thompson, *Narrative*, pp. 170-180; Buck, *Story of The Grand Portage*, p. 13; James White, " Boundary Disputes and Treaties," in the Edinburgh edition of the series edited by Adam Shortt and Arthur G. Doughty, *Canada and Its Provinces*, Vol. 8 (Toronto, 1914), pp. 751-878. The Dalles are rapids just below Rat Portage, where the river, some forty yards wide, flows between perpendicular granite cliffs. A " galais " (" galet ") was a gravel bank in the voyageur's vocabulary.

[90] Macdonell's log of the route may be checked by reference to Belcourt, *Itinéraire*, p. 50; Mackenzie, *Voyages*, p. lix; and Coues, *New Light*, 1:27. The spelling of " Wabartim " is not clear in the manuscript.

[91] The post at Portage de l'Ile was situated on the Winnipeg River a short distance below the entrance of the modern English River. The trail by which the Hudson's Bay people pushed inland in 1793 from Fort Albany via the Albany River became an established route which joined the Winnipeg River route near Portage de l'Ile. See maps in Masson, *Bourgeois*, Vol. 1, and

Wednesday 28th. Mr Grant's Canoe and mine set out in pursuit of the Hudson's Bay Traders leaving the rest of the Canoes with the guide to follow as fast as they can. Made the Pointe de Bois, Petit Rocher, Rocher Brules and Chute aux Esclaves by 9 A.M.[92] Proceeded to the Barriere at noon Grand Rapid at 2 P.M. and slept at the *Grand Galais* of the *Riviere Blanche*. Having performed a journey of 25 Leagues and made 8 Portages since morning — all hands quite fatigued. This Rivier Blanche is but a part of the River Winipic under another name.

The River winipic is full of shocking rapids which occasions this frequent carrying. The Country from *Matawin* but more particularly from Lake Nipising is hardly fit for cultivation except in certain choice spots such as sault St Mary and Rivier of *Lac Lapluie*.

29th. Made three running portages of the Rivere *Blanche* and two small *Rochers* above the *Bonnêt,* passed Lac du Bonnêt two leagues in this direction with a stiff aft wind. Overtook the Hudsons Bay traders with their three boats and two canoes as the Indians had informed us in the Bonnêt, where they had slept, having done as much in two days as they had in ten; this party is headed by Mr Donald McKay late of pointe Claire and a Mr Sutherland.[93] This day we

in Thompson, *Narrative;* also the reference in Harmon, *Journal*, p. 21. Chute à Jacqueau was spelled in various ways, being anglicized by Mackenzie as Jacob's Falls. C. N. Bell, *Some Historical Names and Places of the Canadian North West* (Transactions of the Manitoba Historical and Scientific Society, no. 17, 1884–85), p. 2.

[92] Tradition has it that Slave Falls took its name from a slave of the Chippewa who escaped from his captors and procured a canoe, but either by design or accident went over the falls and was killed. Bell, *Historical Names*, p. 2.

[93] John Sutherland was a few years later to be in charge of the Hudson's Bay Company post at the Elbow of the Assiniboine River, near the site of Fort Pelly. He is mentioned frequently in McLeod's diary. See below, page 126. Little seems to be known about Donald McKay other than that he was a Hudson's Bay Company trader who sometimes went by the nickname " Mad " McKay. See below, page 107.

THE DIARY OF JOHN MACDONELL 107

made nine carrying places and passed the night at the *Grand des Eaux qui remeuent*.[94]

Friday 30th Augt. Passed the three Decharges and the last portages of the River Winipic. Upon a high round knoll between the last Rapid on the N. E. Shore of the River stood a french Fort of which there is now not a vestige remaining except the clearing. This place is now called by the men Pointe au F——e. Two leagues lower down on the opposite side of the River is the North West Company's Fort built by Mons[r] Toussaint Le Sieur a year ago. This is also called bas de la Riviere Fort, for three miles below it the Rivier Winipic discharges into the lake Winipic after a course of an hundred computed Leagues from *Lac des Bois*.[95] This fort is chiefly dependant upon fish taken in its environs for subsistance except when the provisions from the Red River are deposited here. The remains of the Biscuit we brought from the Grand Portage has been so bruised in the carrying places that we find it now most convenient to eat it with a spoon.

31st Aug[t]. D. M[c]K. alias Mackay *le malin* passed with his three Boats and two Canoes. Attended our ladings giveing the canoes 21 [ps] and the Boats, three in number, 23 [ps] each, of the largest and most clumsy [articles] such as cases of guns, Iron, knives, hats, with cassettes and sacks flour.

[94] The Portage des Eaux qui Remuent would be in English the Portage of the Troubled Waters. It is mentioned by Belcourt, *Itinéraire*, p. 52, and by Garry, " Diary," Proceedings and Transactions of the Royal Society of Canada, 1900, Section 2, p. 133.

[95] Fort Maurepas was an old post built by La Vérendrye in 1734. It was originally situated near the mouth of the Red River but was soon removed to the mouth of the Winnipeg, where it was re-established on the eastern shore. Although this fort was not maintained by the British, a post was built by the Northwest Company on the opposite bank which was variously known as the Bas de la Rivière post or Fort Alexander. In 1800 Harmon reported that the Hudson's Bay Company had located a post in the immediate neighborhood. After the merging of the two companies a single post was maintained, which was called Fort Alexander. See McGillivray, *Journal*, p. 5; Innis, *Fur Trade in Canada*, p. 237; Harmon, *Journal*, p. 46; Bell, *Historical Names*, p. 2; Coues, *New Light*, 1:35n. The voyageurs were not squeamish in giving names to topographical features, as Pointe au Foutre shows.

Sunday Sept. 1st. Left le Sieurs Fort, a head wind prevented our reaching the *Isle a la Biche* till about ten P.M.

2nd. Made a large Bay called la *Baie du Portage,* at sunset when the wind fell.[96]

Thursday 3rd. Made the Grand marais where we were stoped by the same wind that kept us back since we entered the lake. At this last campment had to shift some of the bagages, six times during the night the shore being flat and the wind violent of the Lake. The Hu[d]son's Bay Party is here with us.

Wednesday the 4th. Started after sunrise, made the traverse to the entrance of the red River Streight. The men call it six leagues, entered the long wished for Red River. It is only reckoned 18 Leagues from the mouth of the River winipic to the mouth of the Red River; that is, six from the latter to the Grand Marais, six from the Grand Marais to Fall a la Biche and six from the latter place to the entrance of River Winipic.

The Red River enters Lake Winipic by a variety of channels seperated from one another by low Islands full of Rushes and Reeds, one only of which produces a few conspicuous trees for land mark; A sand bank stretches from the shore for two miles opposite to their channels. Got provisions of fish from all the Indians we saw at the mouth of the River of which we are in great want having left the Grand Portage with only 3 Sacks corn to a canoe which were out at *bas de la* Riviere and they have had nothing since but half a sack of flour per canoe and whole one to each Boat excepting what little provisions we got from the Indians; but the Red River abounding in fish the industrious at that employ caught a

---

[96] Ile à la Biche is Elk Island. The regular canoe route from Grand Portage to the Assiniboine area followed the river system through Rainy Lake, Lake of the Woods, and Lake Winnipeg. From Fort Alexander traders paddled across the bay at the southeastern end of the lake, passed inside Elk Island, and turned due south past Portage Bay. Having crossed a large bay known as Grand Traverse, they entered the mouth of the Red River, which they ascended to the forks where the Red and the Assiniboine rivers join.

sufficient number to relieve their hunger. The Trading with the Indians prevented our proceeding farthur than Six leagues into the River this day and put up for the night at old seite of Mr Jos. Frobishers Fort, the first he ever entered [wintered?] at in the interior of the North West. This place is now over grown with brush so as [not] to be known except from the traditions of the antients. The *Rivier aux morts* is about half way between this siete and the lake — a league from the Lake you have the whole Red River together which is here a ¼ to ½ mile wide.[97]

[*d*. Tuesday] Thursday 5th September. Overtook D. McKay and his Hudson's Bay Party in the Rapid of sault a la Biche, (they having passed us while trading withe the savages in [?] the entry of the Red River) about noon. Here I broke my canoe, being the eighth stove, in so as to be hauled up in this Rapid, slept at the head of the sault a la Biche which is mashy and shallow and called by the voyageurs 3 Leagues long. The Great Plains began at the River aux morts, but the soil is so rich that grass grows nearly as tall as a man upon them, so that it is impracticable to walk and keep up with the canoes.

Friday 6th Sep^t. Arrived at the Forks after comming five leagues from the head of the sault a la Biche.[98] The Distance from here to lake Winipec is reckoned twenty leagues and

[97] The Dead (or Death) River was originally the Indian equivalent, Nipuwin or Nipuwinsipi. The melancholy name recalled the tragedy of a camp of Crees, old people and children, who were attacked and massacred by the Sioux while their warriors were taking furs to Hudson's Bay. In later years the stream went by the name of Nettley Creek. A short distance above the mouth of the river was the spot where Joseph Frobisher spent the winter of 1770–71. Coues, *New Light,* 1:41, 42, and note.

[98] The junction of the Red and the Assiniboine rivers had been the site of Fort Rouge, established about 1738 by La Vérendrye. This was the earliest white settlement in the Red River area. At the time of Macdonell's voyage, no post was maintained at the forks, but in 1806 the Northwesters built Fort Gibraltar, and from that time a post under one name or another was operated by the fur traders. Agricultural settlement began with Lord Selkirk's project of a Red River Colony in 1811 and persisted until Fort Garry, which replaced Fort Gibraltar, came to be known as Winnipeg.

from thence to *Bas de la Rivier* eighteen so that the whole distance from *Bas de la Rivier* to here is about 38 Leagues but as all these accounts are exaggerated I think a fourth may be deducted to come at the truth. At the Forks we found two lodges of Indians who have a Moose deer killed not far off, sent six men for the meat of it which they are to bring on their backs, our flour and Biscuit, are now, entirely out, and we shall have to live like Indians upon fish or flesh; as providence supplies us. At these Forks we leave the Main Red River that comes from the Scioux country to our left and enter the small branch called the *assinibouan River*.

Saturday 7th Sept. Rain-bound till Sunday late in the afternoon — so we may only be said to have shifted our camp.

[*d*. Monday] Sunday 8th Sept. At the passage we found a Buffalo Bull which the men killed; Being the first I saw, I was struck with its coarse aspect.

Monday 9th. Rained and loud peals of Thunder. Our hunters killed another Buffalo.[99] Ever since the *forks* we have walked on delightfull plains — so extensive that the view is only terminated by the horizon; the country perfectly level. The River windes so that we can keep a head of the canoes and have time enough to hunt and fish.

Tuesday 10th. Passed the place where Mr Blondishes Fort stood.[100] Slept opposite to a large morass or swamp in the plains which resounded all night with the various cries of Swans, geese, Ducks &c.

Wednesday 11th. The Strip of wood that lines the River has now got so large that we remain in the canoes as it might be trouble some to find them when required. Passed the seite

---

[99] A trading party always hired hunters, whose task it was to supply meat for the men. These men went out, often for days at a time, sending in to camp occasionally for men to come and bring in the game they had killed. In regions where it was possible, the hunters were active even while a party was en route, as here, to the post where they were to spend the winter.

[100] The trader here referred to seems to have been Maurice Blondeau, who was one of the first to penetrate the Red River district after the British conquest. See Innis, *Fur Trade in Canada*, pp. 192–196.

THE DIARY OF JOHN MACDONELL 111

of an ancient Fort *de la Reine*.[101] The spot on which it stood can scarcely be known from the place being grown up with wood. Supped upon a Bear killed by the hunters and while at supper a Snake came into the Tent and was not perceived till it got half its length across Mr Neil Mackay's plate.

12th. The Hunter requested our staying where we were till we heard him fire. An hour after his departure we heard him fire about twelve shots. Upon his return we sent for the meat of an Elk or Moose Deer, with her fawn and a Red Deer he had killed — bringing and dividing the meat most of the day.

13th. The Hunter killed a Red Deer.

Saturday 14th. Raised Bark to mend our canoes. Passed the seites of several old Forts particularly that of Monsr de St Pierre near the portage de la Prairie.[102] Slept three pipes above the last mentioned place. From the portage La praierie the French used to carry their goods and canoes three leagues across the plains to Lake Manitou-a-barac [?] which communicates with our present rout to Fort Dauphin.[103]

[101] Fort la Reine was a post established about 1738 by La Vérendrye's men as a basis of operations from which a line of posts could be organized extending north to the Saskatchewan. The exact location of the fort is uncertain, but it appears to have stood near Portage la Prairie, possibly a short distance below it. It was burned by the Crees about 1752, and Fort des Trembles replaced it as a fur post. See below, page 112; Bell, *Historical Names*, pp. 4, 5; Masson, *Bourgeois*, 1:270; and Innis, *Fur Trade in Canada*, p. 195.

[102] Jacques le Gardeur, Sieur de St. Pierre, became, during more than thirty years in Canada, one of the most noted officers in the service of New France. He gained an unusual familiarity with Indian languages and was very skillful in dealing with the natives in war, as well as in diplomacy and in trade. In 1750 he was sent west to continue the explorations of La Vérendrye, and penetrated as far as the Saskatchewan. In 1753 he was in western Pennsylvania, where he received George Washington, then messenger from Governor Dinwiddie of Virginia. He met his death in the Battle of Lake George in 1755. See a sketch of his life in Wisconsin Historical Collections, 17:165. It is suggested by some historians that the Rivière St. Pierre, later to be called the Minnesota River, may have taken its name from Jacques le Gardeur.

[103] Lake Manitou-a-banc is Lake Manitoba. The younger Henry uses the same nomenclature in his journal of 1803 and 1804. See Coues, *New Light*,

Sunday 15th. Buried John Miln's child who died last night at the seitt of the *Fort des Trembles*.[104] This fort was abandoned twelve years ago (or the year of the small Pox). The savages having attempted in a treacherous manner to take the property and murder all the whites in it, they were beat off with the loss of seven Indians killed; the whites also lost three men killed. Camped at L'Anse aux Pieres.

Monday 16th. Took the land road on foot with Mr C. Grant with all the clearks and Interpreters to lighten the canoes, the water being very low. Some time ago a courier was sent to *pine fort* for Horses to lighten the canoes. This day we met four young Indians who left the fort after hearing of the canoes by our emmissary, from them we learnt the tragical end of Mr David Monin the North West cleark whom Mr Robert Grant left in charge of Pine fort last spring. He undertook a jaunt to the Mississoury country contrary to his duty by the solicitations of Morgan, Jussomme and Cardin free men who accompanied him, for the austensible motive of providing himself with a capital horse; but on his return from there accompanied by Morgan, he fell in with a war party of Scioux, who had just cut off fifteen lodges of Assinibouans near tête a la Biche, and who instantly dispat[c]hed both.[105]

1:236. The French could easily reach the lake by way of the Rat and White Mud rivers; they then paddled north through the lake to Fort Dauphin, then situated at the northern end. The dotted line on the map on page 128 shows the usual route of the British to Lake Manitoba. In the British period, Fort Dauphin was the name given to a post built by Peter Pond on the north shore of Lake Dauphin and later removed to the Ochre River a few miles south of the lake. Ernest Voorhis, *Historic Forts and Trading Posts of the French Régime and of the English Fur Trading Companies* (Ottawa, 1930), p. 58.

[104] According to Coues, John Miln was at this time in charge of Pine Fort, one of the Northwest Company's posts on the Assiniboine. But Macdonell speaks of David Monin as having been left in charge of Pine Fort the previous spring. Possibly Miln replaced Monin when the latter was killed by the Sioux, as mentioned in the next entry. Fort des Trembles was situated on the south bank of the river about five miles above Portage la Prairie. It was abandoned about 1781 because of Indian raids. Coues, *New Light*, 1:292; 3:986; Innis, *Fur Trade in Canada*, p. 195.

[105] The upper Mississippi and Missouri valleys were a region in which there was considerable rivalry between the British traders in Canada and the

Below River du milieu, we [?] met five Horses with all the provisions that were at Pine Fort on their Backs. Disagreeable news to us who had been on Short allowance for a fortnight. Horses came to this country from the Spanish settlement, and are spread all over as far as the plains extend — the native use them in war and to [word illegible] down Buffaloes, some are very fleet. Stealing them is an endless source of quarrel

Spaniards to the south. During the period of the American Revolution the Spanish, finding themselves unable to supply the Indians with the goods they desired, gave the British permission to engage in a trade with the natives which had previously been closed to them. This was the beginning of the decline of Spanish control in the northern area, a decline to which the activities of the Canadians during the decade from 1790 to 1800 further contributed. The expedition of Monin with Morgan and Jussomme seems not to have been undertaken as a trading project of the Northwest Company. In December, 1793, an expedition of nine men was equipped by Macdonell to go to the Mandans and trade with them, but the goods supplied were charged against their personal accounts. Eight of these men returned the following spring, Macdonell entering their arrival in his diary under the date of March 13. According to Captain McKay, who mentions the incident in his journal, the Canadians were not successful in their trading efforts because of rivalry among themselves. Chrysostome Joncquard, a member of the expedition, who remained behind on the Missouri, was taken south in 1795 by Jacques d'Eglise, and gave to the Spanish at St. Louis important information regarding the activities of the Canadians. In October, 1794, Jussomme, who had escaped the fate of Morgan and his companions, led a party sent by the Northwest Company from the Mouse River post to the Mandan region. This time Jussomme established a more permanent post, where the British carried on their trade until dislodged in 1796 by John Evans, an explorer in the service of a company of Spanish merchants at St. Louis. For further detail regarding the trading efforts of the British and of the Spanish see Abraham P. Nasatir, "The Anglo-Spanish Frontier in the Illinois Country during the American Revolution, 1779–1783," *Journal of the Illinois State Historical Society*, 21:291–358; Nasatir, "Jacques d'Eglise on the Upper Missouri, 1791–95," *Mississippi Valley Historical Review*, 14:47–56; "Documents on the Spanish Exploration of the Upper Missouri," translated and edited by Nasatir, in *Mississippi Valley Historical Review*, 14:57–71; Milo M. Quaife, ed., "Extracts from Capt. McKay's Journal — and Others," Wisconsin State Historical Society Proceedings, 1915, pp. 186–210. The original manuscript of Macdonell's journal covering the period from October 11, 1793, to June 6, 1795, gives information regarding expeditions to the Mandan region which does not appear in the printed portion of the diary as published by Masson. Pertinent entries are those for December 6, 8, 10, 1793; March 13, 1794; October 6, 1794; and May 21, 1795.

amongst the savages. The Indian's horse is accustomed to provide for himself during winter; It paws away the snow to get to the Grass.

Wednesday 18th. The canoes [that] came to us at Rivier du Millieu were lightened of some peices to be forwarded on Horseback to the Pine Fort for which place Mr C Grant and Augé started on horseback, leaving me to give their ladings to the horses when they came.

Saturday 21st. Every thing having gone I set out on foot for Fort distant ten leagues and arrived at it two hours before sunset. Starvation worse at the Fort [than] along the road. The people who were out in various directions looking for Indians with provissions returned on the 26th with nine lodges of assinibouans well loaded with peices [of] meat. These people formerly a tribe of the Scioux or Naudawessi; live in Tents made of leather which they carry with them when they remove from one place to another. They make each Dog haul a trunk [?] (made of two sticks tied close together right over the dogs head, the other end of which drags upon the ground as far asunder as a pair of Cart wheels, upon which they put from 50 to 100 lbs weight according to the dog's strength) both summer and winter.[106]

Saturday 28th. Sent off the canoes and goods for the upper posts. It begins to freeze hard at night. Indeed it is remarked that the frost invariably [begins] here about the 25 September.

Monday 30th. Left the Pine Fort on foot having a few horses to carry our provisions and bedding for we are not to sleep with the canoes any more. There are two sorts of Juniper in the plains, one of which grows in tufts while the other runs on the ground like a vine. The berries of each are so alike that I would find no difference; the leaf of the latter is verry like Red Cedar. These berries are not yet quite ripe.

Tuesday 1st Octb. Mr C. Grant placed Augé in opposition

---

[106] This crude form of drag was called the *travois* and was used rather commonly by the plains Indians. See Hodge, *Handbook of American Indians*, Part 1, p. 802.

THE DIARY OF JOHN MACDONELL   115

to Mr Ranald Cameron whom Mr Peter Grant settled at a new place two miles above the mouth of the River La Sourie; a small river from the S. W. that empties itself into the Assinibouan River.¹⁰⁷

Thursday 3rd Oc^t. After walking till 3 P. M. I mounted a high round hill from the summit of which I spyed three Buffaloes on a hill at some distance. Having got two men to accompany me we killed one of the three, a thigh of which I carried to our campment to make Steaks.

Friday 4th. We killed five large Bulls.

Saturday 5th. Overtook Mr Peter Grant and his canoes above the River au *bois de flêche*. The River continues so crooked all this time that in two hours we can travel as much as the canoes can do from sunrise to sunset. Our remaining time is agreeably spent in hunting Buffaloes many of which we kill, or in fishing, the River abounding in fish.

Monday 7th. Incredible numbers of Buffaloes to be seen in all directions.

Friday [*sic*] 8th Oct. Arrived at the Fort of the River qui *appèlle* where I am to winter. This place is built upon the banks of the small river qui appèlle, four leagues over land from where it falls into the Assinibouan River. I am informed it was established by Mr Rob. Grant in the year 1787.¹⁰⁸

The Red or rather Assinibouan River is the part most abounding in all the north west, the following animals are natives of it, viz — Buffaloes, Moose Deers, Orignals, Elks,

---

¹⁰⁷ Ranald Cameron was later to be active in the trade of the Nipigon region. He was a clerk there in 1797, and was reported as being there with Duncan Cameron in 1799. Masson, *Bourgeois*, 1:64; Coues, *New Light*, 1:189. He is mentioned by Faries, below, page 225. For the activities of David and Peter Grant in opposition to the Northwest Company see above, page 95n. The Souris (Mouse) River is a considerable stream in North Dakota.

¹⁰⁸ Masson speaks of a legend which grew up around the name of the Qu'appelle River. The stream was supposed to have been haunted by a spirit whose voice wailed in the night, causing the natives to call it *la rivière qui appelle*. Masson, *Bourgeois*, 2:274n. In regard to the founding of the fort see above, page 96n.

Red Deer, Cabeniers [?] of various kinds, Grizzly, Black, Brown, and yellow [sic] Bears, carcajoux, Badjers, Raccoons not plenty, skunks, large ground squirrels of two kinds, Fishers, Minks, Martins, Lynx, Wolves, Foxes, Kitts, the common Red wood squirrel, and the striped Swiss — moles and mice in great abundance, Eagles, Vultures (*oiseau Puant*) Crows and Rooks, a variety of Hawks, and Owls. The water fowls are Pelicans, swans of two kinds, Gray or Bustard Geese of two kinds, stock Ducks (*canard de France*), several kinds of Teals and Divers or Poule d'eau; with beavers, Otters, and Musk Rats, weazels and two kinds hare; i.e.; the common wood and the *lievre de Prairie* twice his size. Pheasants are very plenty about as big as house hens, something like the Grouse or Moor fowl at home.[109] The River is stocked with the following fish viz — Sturgeons which ascends it to spawn in the spring of the year, Breams, suckers or carpes, Pike, Doré, Cat fish or *Barbue*, Mullets, *Mâe Achigan* called by the Men Mâle Achigan and Nacaishe. The men call these latter Lacaiche, and they abound in some places to that degree that I caught a score of them with a hook while the canoes stopped to smoke their pipes.[110] The wild plumb, and Grape, the pair, choak and sand cherries, Summer berry and the Rasp-

---

[109] Professor Innis suggests that *kitts* may have reference to the small prairie fox, commonly known as the kit fox. The carcajoux is the *Meles labrodorica,* or the American badger. The *lièvre des prairies* is the prairie hare. See Monseigneur Taché, *Esquisse sur le Nord-Ouest de l'Amérique* (Montreal, 1869), p. 112. The *poule d'eau* is the water hen or grebe. Four varieties are listed by Taché, who makes a distinction between these and his classification of divers. The *canard de France* is the mallard, a species of large duck found in abundance in the Canadian Northwest. Taché, *Sketch of the North-West of America,* translated by Captain D. R. Cameron (Montreal, 1870), pp. 197, 201.

[110] The malashegané is mentioned by Taché as having the peculiar power of producing a noise like a distant beating of a drum deep in the water. It is a good fish for eating. The doré is another name for the American sandre, also a palatable species. Suckers or carps were used for food, though without enthusiasm, especially when the diet was restricted in variety. The catfish, or barbue, takes its name from its beard appendages (barbes) and its broad, square head. The meat of the fish is rich and well-flavored. Taché, *Sketch of the North-West,* pp. 207–210.

THE DIARY OF JOHN MACDONELL 117

berry are also natives of this country. Names of the Portages from Lake Superior to Red River — 1st Grand Portage 3 Leagues Long, 2nd Perdrix, 3rd Grosse Roche, 4th Carribou, 5th L'Outarde ½ league long, 6th L'Orignal, 7th Grand des Cerises, 8th and 9th the two vases, 10th Petit Portage Noeuf, 11th Grand Portage noeuf ½ league long, 12th La Marte, 13th Les Perches, 14th Heighth of Land, 15th l'Escalier, 16th Le Cheval de Bois, 17th Gros des Pins, 18th Petit Rocher de Saguinaga, 19th Petit Rocher de la Prairie, 20th La Prairie, 21st 22nd 23rd The 3 Rochers des Couteaux, 24th La Carpe, 25th Gros des Bois Blancs, 26th Petit des Bois Blancs, 27th Grand des Pins, 28th La Pointe de Bois, 29th Petit Rocher du Lac Croche, 30th Le Rideau, 31st Le flacon, 32nd 33rd 34th Les 3 Portages La croix, 35 & 36, Les deux petits Portages Neuf, 37th La Chaudiere in view of Fort L. L. P.

The Portages from Lac La Pluie to Lake Winipic are, 1st Portage in Lake of the woods, 2nd Portage du Rat, 3rd La terre Jaune, 4th Petit Rocher de Charette, 5th La Terre Blanche, 6th Portage de l'Isle, 7th Chûte a Jaco, 8th Pointe de Bois, 9th Petit Roché, 10th Roché Brulé, 11th Chûte des Esclaves, 12th La Barriere, 13th 14th, 15th, 16th, 17th, 18th The six Portages of the Riviere Blanche, 19th & 20th The 2 Petit Rochers du Bonnêt, 21st Le Bonnet about a mile Long, 22nd Galais du Bonnêt, 23rd La Terre Blanche, 24th 25th 26th Les trois eaux qui Remuent.

From Lachine to Lake Superior	36 Por^g
From Lake Superior to Lac la Pluie	36 "
From Lake la Pluie to Lake Winipic	26 "
Total Portages from Montreal to Lake Winipic	98 "

I add for your information all the portages from York House H. B. to Lake winipic and consequently to the Red River settlement p^r Ja^s Halero who knows the Road well having been twenty years voyaging in the Hudson's Bay Service.

Hill River

1st	The Rock	10 yds long		
2nd	White mud	50 " "		
3rd	Little Rock	30 " "		
4th	Burnt wood	60 yds long		
5th	Upper Burnt wood	60 " "		
6th	Swamp in yᵉ hill	120 " "		
7th	Little Rocky Portage	50 " "		
8th	Mossy	350 " "	or ¼ mile	
9th	Little Rock	100 "		
10th	Mr Thomson's Porᵗ	50 "		
11th	Upper "	50 "		
12th	D—l's Creek	20 "		
13th	Grownwater's Island	15 "		

now pass swampy Lake
and then Jack River

14th	Handᵍ place Jack Ri.	130 yds		
15th	Long Portage	400 "	¼ mile	
16th	Swampy "	400 "	¼ "	
17th	Little Rock	12 "		
18th	Uppermost Jack River	70 "		

then pass Knee Lake

Trout River

19th	Trout fall	50 yds Long		
20th	Middle Portage	60 " "		
21st	Upper "	60 " "		
22nd	Crooked Chute above	20 "		
23rd	Back Creek	200 "		

Then holy Lake Oxford house

Jack River

24th	Wapanapans	40 "		
25th	Middle Portage	20 "		
26th	Upper Spout	25 "		
27th	Hill Portage	800 "	½ mile	
28th	White Fall	1200 "	¾ "	

29th	Painted Stone	40	"
30th	Stony Beaver Dam	40	"
31st	Little " " "	20	"
32nd	Sea River	25	"
	Jack River — Riviere au Brochêt		
	Plea Gru & Lake Winipic		

My informent says this is utmost number of portages to be carried over at the lowest he ever saw the water.

THE DIARY
OF ARCHIBALD N. McLEOD

The Diary of A. N. McLeod

Introductory Note

McLeod alone of the diarists of this volume was a *bourgeois,* that is, a partner of the company. As already pointed out, Pond was an independent trader, whereas Macdonell, Faries, and Connor were clerks of varying experience and authority; McLeod was a *bourgeois* in full command of a large and important department. His diary gives quite as detailed a picture of fort life as does that of Faries. The scenes he describes are representative of life at the prairie forts and those at the edge of the prairies; he records even more fully than does Faries the traders' relations with the Indians: the Assiniboine, Cree, Fall, and Blood and to some extent the Chippewa, Sioux, and more distant plains Indians. The diary entries also reveal clearly the lines of communication with the large neighboring forts of the Northwest Company, and suggests the keen competition of the Northwesters with the traders of the Hudson's Bay and the X. Y. Company.

Archibald Norman McLeod was active in the service of the Northwest Company as early as 1796, and he was made a partner in the firm some time before 1799. He joined the Northwest Company and was influential in the management of its affairs until his retirement in 1821. McLeod's duties as a *bourgeois* carried him to a number of different posts. At the time he began the diary he had been for three years at Fort Alexandria. In 1799 he was proprietor of the Fort Dauphin department, and during the following year he was in charge of the Swan River department, supervising the trading activities in the country between Lake Winnipeg and the Red and Assiniboine rivers. In 1802 he removed to the Athabasca department, where he remained until 1809. He was transferred to New Caledonia (British Columbia) for a few years, but returned to the Athabasca department in 1815 and was instrumental in breaking up Fort Wedderburn, a post of the Hudson's Bay Company near Fort Chipewyan. In 1816 he was at Fort William and led a party from that post against the Hudson's Bay Company establishment at Fort Douglas, the center of Selkirk's Red River Settlement. With the surrender of Fort Douglas after the skirmish of Seven Oaks, he was placed in command of the post, but his services there were of short duration, for the fort was recaptured within a year by a Hudson's Bay Company party under D'Orsonnens.

McLeod adjusted his business interests to the changing organization of the Northwest Company, and in 1808 became a partner in the new company, McTavish, McGillivrays, and Company, successor to McTavish, Frobisher, and Company. For this later period he has been called second in importance to William McGillivray at Fort William. He apparently took no part, however, in the negotiations with the Hudson's Bay Company, and retired from active trading when the consolidation of the two companies was arranged in 1821.[1]

The diary is here printed through the courtesy of McGill University. In editing the manuscript, an occasional period was inserted where McLeod had left a space in the manuscript between independent statements but had omitted punctuation. No capital letters were supplied, however. The letter *d.*, signifying "deleted," has been used to indicate words struck out by the diarist.

C. M. G.

[1] See Lawrence J. Burpee, *Oxford Encyclopaedia of Canadian History* (Makers of Canada Series, Vol. 12, New York, 1926), p. 395; Gordon C. Davidson, *The North West Company* (University of California Publications in History, Vol. 7, Berkeley, 1918), pp. 13–15, 157, 189; Elliott Coues, *New Light on the Early History of the Greater Northwest: The Manuscript Journals of Alexander Henry and of David Thompson, 1799–1814* (New York, 1897), 1:277n.; Chester Martin, *Lord Selkirk's Work in Canada* (Oxford Historical and Literary Studies, Vol. 7, Oxford, 1916), p. 77.

The Diary

Alexandria November 1800 [1]

Kept by Norman McLeod

That the Occurrences, &. events, of which this is destined to be the testimonial, may prove prosperous, &. pleasant, in the same degree that the uneasy writer is agitated, by anxious, and fervent wishes; is the Sincere prayer of one, who by no means regards, himself, as acting for or persuing his own private interest, but is spurred, and actuated by reflecting, that

[1] Fort Alexandria, the post at which McLeod spent the winter of 1800–01, was situated on the upper waters of the Assiniboine River, some nine miles above the post of the Hudson's Bay Company at the Elbow. The location was well suited to the needs of the superintendent of the department. The Assiniboine River was the common line of travel to the posts on the Qu'appelle and Red rivers, while an easy march brought a trader to the Swan River, near the mouth of which stood the Swan River fort, a hundred miles east of Fort Alexandria. Harmon reports that Fort Dauphin could be reached in four days by horseback, although it took considerably longer by canoe. The buildings at Fort Alexandria were well constructed and were plastered on the inside and the outside and smeared with a white earth which served as a sort of whitewash. Across the river stretched a broad expanse of prairie, while behind the fort, groves of poplar, birch, and pine lent a pleasing variation to the landscape. A brief description of the post is given in Daniel W. Harmon, *Journal of Voyages and Travels in the Interior of North America* (Trail Makers of Canada Series, Toronto, 1911), pp. 31–33, 39. Harmon entered the country for the first time in 1800, and reached Fort Alexandria in the fall of the year. His journal may be used to gain a knowledge of events immediately preceding the opening of McLeod's diary. The principal geographical features of the region, and landmarks such as the Spunk or Touchwood Hills, Nut Hill, and Beaver Hill are shown on the map given on page 128. The habitats of the Indians are also shown, the information being taken from the map in Alexander Mackenzie, *Voyages from Montreal to the River St. Lawrence through the Continent of North America to the Frozen and Pacific Oceans* (London, 1801), and from the frontispiece map in Davidson, *North West Company*. Harmon reports that the Cree Indians stayed for the most part in the woody part of the country, hunting moose, elk, and beaver, while the Assiniboine hunters remained on the prairies and hunted buffalo and wolves. *Journal*, p. 34.

he is entrusted with, not only the property but confidence, of others.

On his arrival here last Fall, the writer of these lines entertained the most sanguine, &. lively hopes, of converting the property he brought into the Swan River to good account, by the following separation of it; He intended to leave a few pieces for the Expenditure of Swan River House, as there are 2 Indians only there, with La Verdure (the Guide) to take care of the property &c. Perigné with 15 Ps [pieces] goods, Liquor, &c, was settled for the Montaigne des Oiseaux with 6 Indians, &. as Mr Sutherland for the H. Bay's C° winters at the *Recoude* it was projected to send Mr Harmon with some person there, to have a little ammunition &. rum in case any of our debtors should go to see the *English* or rather the Hudson's Bay C^{os} Servants there;[2] In the month of December he intended sending people with a few pieces goods &c to settle at the Nut Lake, & he himself to move from Alexandria there, if, &. whenever necessary; but the last of these plans viz. the purposed establishment at the Nut lake was knocked in the head, as was the plan for sending people to the Elbow, by the arrival of Mr Harrison from River a la Biche with a letter from M^r McGillis wherein he mentions if he has not sent him one half of the goods &. Liquor originally brought to Swan River, (for his demands amount to that) &. a number of men, the opposition (or the X Y) will make as many packs

[2] Louis Perigné had been in charge of the Swan River fort, but in the middle of October he had been sent to establish a new post at Montagne des Oiseaux (Bird Mountain), about fifty miles up the Swan River. See Harmon, *Journal*, pp. 30, 56, 57. John Sutherland is probably the man whom Macdonell met on the Winnipeg River in 1793. See above, page 106. Daniel Williams Harmon was a young man of twenty-two who had just entered the employ of the Northwest Company. He remained in the Northwest until 1819, being stationed for four years at Swan River and later at Cumberland House under Peter Fidler. He also traded at McLeod Lake and Stuart's Lake in New Caledonia. He is known chiefly through the journal referred to here, which he kept while in the West.

McLeod follows a common custom in calling the traders of the Hudson's Bay Company "English"; those of the Northwest Company, on the other hand, were regarded as Canadian or French.

as he will, &. as every other consideration must give way to that it of course superseded the idea of makeing so many establishments.³

By the visit made to Fort Dauphin between the 12th &. 27th of October, by the Schemer of the above mentioned Plans, he found that a demand for a quantity of Goods &. Liquor would be made on him for the four Posts established there. In fact the apparent scarcity of goods, liquor &c. throughout the whole of the Department fills his mind with the greatest anxiety and most severe apprehensions for the consequences. But Lays his trust in God to help &. prosper his honest endeavors, &. crown with Success his unremitting, exertions for the performance of his Duty.

At the same time that he relies on the candour of such

³ Edward Harrison was a trader who clerked for the Northwest Company for several years in the Fort Dauphin and Red River departments. The younger Henry speaks of him in terms somewhat derogatory. See Coues, *New Light*, 1:203, 237, 238, and Vol. 3, the index volume. Although several persons named McGillis figure in the accounts of the period, there is no doubt that the man to whom McLeod refers was Hugh McGillis, one of the leading partners of the Northwest Company, who was wintering at the company's post on the Red Deer River (Rivière à la Biche). He visited McLeod later in the fall (see below, page 143), and wintered at Fort Alexandria himself from 1802 to 1804. See Coues, *New Light*, 1:215n.

The decision to restrict the number of posts was made because of the limited amount of goods on hand. Macdonell reports that the usual practice of the Northwest Company was to meet competition by establishing new posts, thus making it impossible for their rivals to meet them everywhere at once. See Louis R. Masson, *Les bourgeois de la Compagnie du Nord-Ouest* (Quebec, 1889), 1:274. The X. Y. Company, or New Northwest Company, had been organized in 1798 as a coalition of several firms that had been trading in competition with the Northwest Company. During its first years it achieved no great success, but with the return of Sir Alexander Mackenzie to Canada in 1802 it gained new vitality, and a bitter rivalry set in between the two companies which ended only with the death of Simon McTavish in July, 1804. A policy of conciliation was then adopted, and overtures to Mackenzie and his friends led to the consolidation of the two firms in the fall of the same year. According to the agreement of 1804 the X. Y. Company was to get twenty-five per cent of the profits of the trade. See Davidson, *North West Company*, pp. 72–80; Harold A. Innis, *The Fur Trade in Canada* (New Haven, 1930), pp. 253, 259, 271; Masson, *Bourgeois*, 2:482–499.

FORT ALEXANDRIA AND NEIGHBORING POSTS

Gentlemen as read the following sheets, not to censure &. condemn the proceedings or the principles on which these proceedings were not only adopted but carried into effect, by private murmurings &. indirect insinuations, but call the writer to an open &. public account for any thing that may (to them) appear to require such; as surely they have the right so it shall be his province to provide they shall have the means by laying this before them;

It may be necessary to premise, that this journall should have been commenced on his first arrival here (8th Septr 1800) but as he was necessitated to go about from one post to another untill the 15th of November he thought it best to begin from that date, although he took minutes of all his previous transactions, which are at the service of any gentleman that may have a wish of perusing them.

Saturday 15th November 1800. A Cloudy, but mild day. Sent La Rose with Roy's step-son to the Thunder's tent, to try to prevail with his wife, (the Grey mare being the *better* horse) to send her fine [?] furs here. I sent 3 feet of Tobacco, for an encouragement to them so to do.[4]

Sunday 16th. Still Cloudy, — rather colder than usual, Col-

[4] McLeod may have been seeking to trade with the same "Old Thunder" whom Alexander Henry mentions as having a camp on La Plante's River. See Coues, *New Light*, 2:587, 593. The tobacco which the traders used so extensively in bartering with the Indians was put up in two different forms. Sometimes it was made up into carrots of one or two pounds each and packed in ninety-pound bales. Each carrot was a solid bundle of tobacco leaves laid together lengthwise and compressed, then wrapped in a cloth covering and tightly bound with cord. Such a bundle was from twelve to eighteen inches long, and tapered almost to a point at each end. See Innis, *Fur Trade in Canada*, p. 213; *American Historical Review*, 19:305n. Frequently, also, the tobacco was braided and twisted and measured in terms of length rather than of weight. Thus the three feet of tobacco refers to the length of the twisted strand. A fathom of tobacco in this form weighed about three-fourths of a pound. Davidson, *North West Company*, p. 223n.; Wisconsin Historical Collections, 19:216n.

Roy, La Rose, and others with Canadian names were the voyageurs, interpreters, guides, and other servants. Baptiste Roy and Baptiste Larose are listed as being at Lower Fort des Prairies in 1799. François Roy was in the Fort Dauphin department in 1805. Masson, *Bourgeois*, 1:63, 404.

lin came back, he brought, home 24 Catts, &. 37 Beavers, he tells me the *Vent* du *Nord,* Bear, & *Mauvais Mâl,* are in the Nut hill working the Beaver, But unfortuneately he adds they intend soon leaving that, &. steering to the plains to look for their Beloved Buffaloes.[5] Frisé came from our hunters with ¾ of an Elk, the only meat we had from them for these twelve days past, &. they are not at all ashamed to send me word if I do not send them rum they'll not hunt for the Fort, &. such is my present situation that I will be necessitated to comply with their very unreasonable, tho' common request.

Monday 17th. Cloudy, but very cold, in fact it's the only cold day we have as yet had this Fall, La Rose came from the *Tonnerres,* but brought no skins, they it seems told him, they would soon come to the Fort &. wished to be the bearers of them, themselves, they are starving, — having nothing to subsist on but Rabbits, of which Indeed there are vast numbers this year, about here. Ettiene Ducharm is unwell I gave him an emetic this afternoon. Roy is very unwell to day with a Swell'd face &. head

Teusday 18th. Cold, Clear, &. Calm. I Sent, Dauphiné, & L'Heureux with two Horses for some articles I stand in need of from Swan River. I sent Mr Perigné 2 Looking glasses, &. 30^{lb} of grease. Cadian returned to him with my men. I sent Frisé to guide La Boune (*Maron*) or Jacques (for I dont know which of these is his real name) to the Hunters as he is sent to remain his turn with them. I gave a Doze of Physic to E. Ducharm, this morning; — La Comble, &. Cadottes horses, which, when I was at Fort Dauphin, (five weeks ago) were supposed to have been stolen by, the Stone Indians, came off themselves to the Fort, in very good case. The Frêne, Tabo, Bertrand, &. 4 others (young men) arrived here very late in the evening, the first paid his Debt, the next, gave 40 Ratts en *present,* &. Told me he expected at least a large Keg, & a

[5] Collin is probably Joseph Collin, an interpreter for the Northwest Company who is listed in 1804 as stationed at Fort Alexandria and Fort Dauphin. Coues, *New Light,* 3:936; Harmon, *Journal,* p. 95; Masson, *Bourgeois,* 1:404.

little stronger than I generally made it.⁶ The Frênes wife (being Drunk) fell on a Knife she had in a smoaking bag at her girdle, &. by which she was Stabed an inch and a half Deep close under the Ribs, — she remained senseless for a long time. Roy has his face &. head amazingly swelled, & has a pretty strong fever. I gave him a little flour to make a little soup with, as he cannot open his mouth to eat any meat

Wednessday 19th November *1800*. A Cold day, the Indians are all Sober, but do not go off today. Frisé came back from the Hunters who say they cannot follow the Animals they wound, the ground being so hard frozen they have no marks of where they tread. a young Indian kill'd a Swan in the River close by the House, the poor Bird had at least Six pound of ice sticking to one of its wings, — it kept in the Rapids, as the only part not covered with ice, & no doubt would soon have perished with the Cold tho' not very poor.⁷

Thursday 20th. A Cold, Stormy morning, Snowed from nine oClock A. M. untill 2 oClock P. M. in which Short space of time there fell between four and five inches Snow. The Indians did not Stir owing to the Badness of the weather. The Frêne's wife is greatly better, tho' still unable to walk. This snow is come very opportunely for us, as our hunters

⁶ The fur traders always found it necessary to furnish the Indians and native hunters with goods on credit, trusting them to bring furs in payment during or after the season's hunt. Mention is made later in this diary of the way in which the Indians often obtained credits from one trading agent only to take their peltries to another agent and receive credit a second time. Losses of this sort were made up by charging the Indians very high prices for the goods sold to them. As the natives became increasingly dependent upon the goods and ammunition supplied by the traders, they became more and more subject to control by the whites, control based upon financial obligations which were the more exacting because of the Indian's habitual lack of providence and thrift. Thus a vicious system was generated, which, though it kept the red man alive, left him little more than the bare necessities of life. See Wayne E. Stevens, *Northwest Fur Trade, 1763–1800* (Urbana, 1928), p. 145; Innis, *Fur Trade in Canada*, pp. 153, 178, 246–248; William W. Folwell, *History of Minnesota*, Vol. 1 (St. Paul, 1921), pp. 167–168. *En present* may be translated *for the present*. Muskrats were usually spoken of as rats.

⁷ Swans, now rarely seen, formerly were not uncommon in the Northwest.

could not Kill, &. that all our piece meat is almost entirely out, &. I should be very Sorry to be obligded to make use of the little pounded meat we have at present.[8]

Friday 21st. A fine Clear day, all the Indians went off excepting the Frêne. Jacque, alias Maron, came from the Hunters to acquaint us they have kill'd 4 Red Deer; I Sold the Grey Colt to La Rose for 100^{lb} G. P. C. [Grand Portage Currency].

Saturday 22^d. Mild weather, the Frêne went off this morning, — his wife being able to walk. I sent 4 men for the four red Deer that are at our Hunters lodges, to whom I sent some Amunition &. to the *Petit Corbau* a Strip'd Blanket. I deliver'd the Blanket to La Rose with directions to deliver it, but he gave it to carry to N. Ducharm, who on his arrival at the lodges put the Blanket in the Branches &. there forgot it, &. to crown the Matter in their great hurry to get back to night they did not load their horses, well by which means a part of the meat remained. La Rose being the only one I saw, got a Severe reprehension for his carelessness, in respect of the Blanket & their leaving a part of the Meat, I told him I should charge the Blanket to his A/C untill I learned whither it is lost or not. he means to return to morrow, to learn the fate of the Blanket, &. fetch the remainder of the Meat.

Sunday 23^d. A Cold, windy day, La Rose went for the Meat that remained at the Hunter's of whom one (Petit Corbau) came to the house &. told us he had kill'd a Doe red

[8] Piece meat refers to the meat that was cooked and eaten within a comparatively short time, instead of being pounded and dried. The pounded meat, which the traders obtained from the Indians and impregnated with melted tallow, was called pemmican. Thus treated and sewed up in buffalo hides, it would keep for a long time without spoiling, and a supply of it was kept in reserve to be consumed only in case of necessity. Fort Alexandria was important for the pemmican made up there and distributed to other posts of the Northwest. Mention is made later in the journal of the pounded meat and bladders of grease that were brought to the fort and traded by the Indians. The food requirements of a fur post were great; Harmon reports that a crew of seventy men consumed about four hundred and fifty pounds in a day. *Journal*, p. 103.

Deer; he brought the Six Beaver for the Blanket, I sent yesterday, but what his most material business at the *Fort* was to get Liquor. I gave for him &. the 2 others three Gall. mix'd, &. told him they should have no more untill they kill'd ten Animals &. that then [I] would give them 2 Gall. for nothing, &. so during the winter for every ten Animals they kill they are to have 2 Gall. M.[ixed?] Rum. I sent Vallé for the other beast, that he kill'd. Indeed we stand in need of victuals for within this week we have an addition of two strangers, — two of the men's women being brought to bed the one of a Boy, the other a Girl, — and still there is a third ready to tumble to pieces.

Monday 24th November *1800.* A Fine, Mild, day, Vallé, &. La Rose, brought home the Meat from the Hunters, they tell me they have kill'd another Red Deer. Roy is pretty well recovered, as is Ducharm, &. Carron.

Teusday 25th. A very mild day, the most of the Snow melted today. I sent E. Ducharm for the Red Deer that the hunters kill'd Sunday, La Rose &. H. Ducharm I sent to look for Birch to make chairs, Vallé went to get wood for a Sledge, Roy took a Doze of Physic, I scolded Girardin, for some stupid observations of his, to Mr Harmon &. Collin, he is making me a pair of Deer skin trowsers, old Parant, is busy making a Slay to haul the fire wood home with, Danis is making a Couple of window Shuttters

Wednessday 26th. A fine day, I took Collin &. an other man with me &. went to the Indian Elbow (Recoude) expecting to find some Indians there of whom I have heard for a long time past, not a single word, or at least learn from Sutherland whether he has seen any of them.

I Slept at Mr Sutherland's &. had the *Honor* of playing *Cribbage* with Jeanny, (his wife).[9] he poor Devil complains

[9] Harmon found "Jeanny's" company very pleasant. He says of her in his *Journal* (page 39): "He [Sutherland] has a woman of this country, for a wife, who, I was pleased to find, could speak the English language, tolerably well. I understand, also, that she can both read and write it, which she learned to do at Hudson's Bay, where the Company have a school. She

bitterly of Mʳ Goodwin's usage of him, in sending him no *Goodys,* but what he had he made me very wellcome to, I am pretty well convinced he has seen none of the Indians I was uneasy about.¹⁰ There is very little Snow remaining in the plains, for it has thaw'd a good deal these two days.

Thursday 27ᵗʰ. Still fine weather we set off home after breakfast &. found everything in Statu Quo.

Friday 28ᵗʰ. The Mildness of the weather makes me fear very much that provisions will be equally scarce and Dear as last year

I sent off La Rose, Carron, &. Roy's Step Son, to the *Tonnerre's* tent for his Skins a *Second* time, with a Message if they did not give them their furs that I should go myself, &. that I would take them, I sent not even a bit of Tobacco. Three Stone Indians arrived, of whom the Red Mooss is the principall, they seem to have very little of any thing, I gave them a few pints of Liquor, &. they traded a few more.¹¹ Old La Voye (Free man) came to the Fort, he has not seen a Human Phisiognomy since Le Mire went for 100 Skins of his in September last by my orders, since which time he has kill'd 40 more but did not bring them with him. L'Heureux,¹² &. Dauphiné, & with them Bellile came here from the Montaigne des Oisaux. Dauphine broke a new Gun he was bringing up from the Lower Fort,¹³ which I have charged to his account. Bellile

speaks, likewise, the Cree and Sauteux [Chippewa] languages. She appears to possess natural good sense, and is far from being deficient in acquired knowledge."

¹⁰ Robert Goodwin was a factor of the Hudson's Bay Company post at Fort Albany. Coues, *New Light,* 3:956; Masson, *Bourgeois,* 2:272–273.

¹¹ A judicious use was made of liquor to encourage the Indians who came to the posts to trade their furs on favorable terms. During the years when the competition between the Northwest Company and the X. Y. Company was at its height, the amount of liquor used in the trade increased greatly. Innis, *Fur Trade in Canada,* p. 271; Davidson, *North West Company,* pp. 91, 224–225.

¹² François L'Heureux appears on the list of 1804 as a voyageur at Fort Dauphin.

¹³ The lower fort was the post near the mouth of the Swan River. Masson, *Bourgeois,* 1:404; Harmon, *Journal,* p. 30.

told me about the keg of H. Wines they made free with when they remained behind, he owns that he &. B^te La France Drank it, I mean to charge it to the account of La France as he was the foreman of the Canoe, Fran^s Roy is unwell I gave him a Doze of physic to take tomorrow morning.[14]

Saturday 29th. The Stone Indians traded half a Doz^n Buffaloe robes &. a few kitts &. went off, Carron came back from the Tonnerre's with a message from him &. the *Pass au Travers that I needed* not be anxious about their skins, for they intended bringing them, themselves as soon as they had any thing worth while comming to the House with. La Rose &. Piquaquit remained.[15] The Hunter's little Boy came home to inform us that they have kill'd Seven Red Deer, this has been every bit as fine a Day as yesterday, tho' Cloudy.

Sunday 30th November *1800*. Quite Mild, but Cloudy fell a few grains Snow, indeed it looked all day as if it would rain. Being St Andrew's day, the men presented me with a Cross, &. I in return presented them with a quart of H. Wines. I have made it a rule ever since I have been at this place (3 years) [16] to give no drams on any occation, by that means I always have reconciled it to myself, &. circumstances, to let them have a little debauch the latter end of Novr or beginning of Decr. it formerly was customary to give them a little liquor on putting up a flag staff. &. after they had finished either the Fort or Houses, neither of which times I give them anything; In short I gave them a quart H.W. in the morning in drams, &. 2 quarts in the evening mix'd with water &. sugar, as they danced, till three oClock in the morning to Frisés singing, but in course of the day a parcel of them bought each a pint of rum which kept their heads pretty warm

---

[14] H. Wines stands for high wines, a liquor composed largely of alcohol which was given to the Indians in more or less diluted form. See Wisconsin Historical Collections, 19:399n.

[15] Piquaquoite appears on Masson's list of 1805 as stationed in the Fort Dauphin department. Masson, *Bourgeois,* 1:404.

[16] McLeod's reference to his three years' residence at Fort Alexandria seems to show that the post was built in 1797.

all day, &. occationed a few Battles among themselves.[17] One of *Cut Lip's* widows came here, today. She goes to the plains in search of her *relations;* Collin was out along with one of the men all day looking for Birch to make Slays, but found none fit for that purpose.

Monday 1st December *1800*. A Mild day, Cloudy, and really strange weather, for daily it drops a few grains of either Snow or hail, but neither, so as to cover the earth, sufficiently for sledges to run, or mark the footsteps of animals, enough for the Hunters. Roy's step son, came from the Tonnerre's, he Says La Rose will come home tomorrow, but does not know whether he'll bring what they went for.

I sent Mr Harmon for meat with the men, the man who remained at the Hunter's is come back this evening, (Jacque).

Teusday 2d. A very mild, Cloudy, day. The men came home with the meat, The Hunter's boys came, with them to trade Six Beaver Sk[in]s. La rose came from the Tonnerre's but could not get the Skins from them, they send me word not to be apprehensive of their going to the H. Bay people at the Elbow.

Wednessday 3d. Rather colder than usual, but still Cloudy. I sent Carron to remain at the Hunter's for a fortnight, &. set off for home (Montaigne des Oiseaux), I sent Perigné a saddle by him, old La Voye untied his skins that Le Mire brought here in October. he had in all 93 Beavers, &. 7 Otters, of which he paid Credit, &. traded 43, consequently there still remains 64 [?]. I agreed to lend him a horse to go for the forty he left, behind him when he set off, to come to the Fort, he wishes to remain at the Fort to pass the winter, which I am obliged to accord to for fear of disobliding him. Fell a very few grains of snow.

Thursday 4th December *1800*. Still Cloudy, and mild, it every day threatens to Snow but imediately the clouds disperse &. remains clear for an hour &. gets overcast again.

Two men arriv'd from Jacquo Finlay's with a letter for me

[17] The St. Andrew's Day incident is found also in Harmon, *Journal*, p. 36.

&. an Inventory of what goods remained there in the Fall & what he has still remaining, the plan he &. I concerted last fall was partly frustrated in the execution by the death of the Principall Indian there viz. the *Medale* who was suffocated by the quantity of Rum he drank, & which prevented the Indians from going to winter to where they at first intended, &. from making anything of a Fall hunt. Jacquo asks for no less a matter than 3 Kegs H. W. &. Several other articles.[18]

Friday 5th. A Fine mild, but Cloudy day, Cleared up late.

Saturday 6th. Again cloudy and Mild, fell a very few grains of Snow, I sent off, Frisé & Vallé to the River Qui Appelle, by them I wrote Messrs M[c]Donell [*sic*], Chaboillez, M[c]Kay, Monro, Falcon and Malhiote.[19] I sent principally for the small knives &. fire steeles M[r] M[c]Donell promised me last fall,

---

[18] Jacquo Finlay was a half-brother of James Finlay. He had charge of Fort des Prairies in 1796, and is supposed to have been with David Thompson on the Saskatchewan in 1800. Thompson came down from the Rocky Mountain House to the mouth of the Saskatchewan in the spring of the year, and it is possible that Finlay was with him, and that he left Thompson and took a post for the Northwest Company during the summer. In later years Finlay was active in the exploration of the Rocky Mountain region. Coues, *New Light*, 3:947; David Thompson, *Narrative of Explorations in Western America* (edited by J. B. Tyrrell, Publications of the Champlain Society, Vol. 12, Toronto, 1916), p. lxxix.

[19] All these persons were clerks or partners of the Northwest Company. Macdonell is the *bourgeois* whose diary of 1793 is partially reproduced in this volume. He was in charge of the Upper Red River department in 1799. Charles Chaboillez, a veteran Northwester, was proprietor of the Lower Red River department. See Masson, *Bourgeois*, 1:63, 64. In the fall of 1804 Harmon visited his post at Montagne à la Bosse (see the map on page 128) to get goods needed for a winter at Fort Alexandria. See Harmon, *Journal*, p. 100. Chaboillez was at Portage la Prairie in 1800. See below, page 141. For a brief sketch of his career see Adrien Gabriel Morice, *Dictionnaire historique des Canadiens et des Métis français de l'Ouest* (Quebec, 1912), pp. 61–66. There were several McKays in the fur trade, but it is probable that George McKay, listed as a clerk in the Upper Red River department, was the man to whom McLeod wrote. See below, page 170; also Masson, *Bourgeois*, 1:63. Masson's list also includes William Munro and Pierre Falcon among the traders located in the Upper Red River district. François Malhiot, later transferred to Lac au Flambeau, south of Lake Superior, had been sent to the Red River region in 1796 and was probably still there in 1800. His name seems to have been corrupted into "Mallette" in Masson's list. See Masson, *Bourgeois*, 1:63; Morice, *Dictionnaire historique*, p. 194; and Coues, *New Light*, 3:982.

&. to know how the Xy. *Miscreants* are settled. Old La Voye went off this morning (for the 40 Beaver skins he left behind him) with a horse I lend him.

Sunday 7th. The weather seems bent, on continuing both mild and Cloudy, always clearing up once in the 24 hours, tho' but for a Short time, every day it has all the appearance of snowing, but it dissappoints us continually, I really begin to fear we shall starve this winter, at any rate we'll be obligded to make use of the little dry provisions the Indians may bring to the Fort, & G—d alone knows whether we'll be able to scrape together what will make a little Pimican to bring us all to the Point au *Foutre*.[20]

Monday 8th. This indeed looks something like a winters day it blows, snows, &. is with all very Cold, L'Enfant Prodigue came to the Fort with 2 wolves & a Mooss Skin the first he traded Tobacco for, &. Rum for the later.

Teusday 9th. A Cold, serene day, L'Enfant Prodigue went off in the morning, Mr John Sutherland (alias Sugar Royall) came here to pay me a visit accompanied by two of his men, &. I made him very drunk, of all the stupid Puppies I ever sett eyes on he is the most nonsencicall &. dull

Wednessday 10th (December *1800*. Still very cold, clear weather. Mr *Sugar Royall* did not think proper to leave me &. I was tormented with his Super Stupid conversation all day

Thursday 11th. I sent off Mr Harmon &. eight men loaded ([*d.* at] their Sledges) with 60 Beaver each, I likewise dispatched Jacco Finlay's men &. wrote him to send if possible two men here in the Month of Jan^y &. to send me whatever goods &c he can Spare. Mr Sutherland went off, after breakfast I sent B^{te} Roy, & Jacque to the Hunters to try to make them separate as they kill nothing at All hardly. I gave Roy ¾ of a f^m [fathom] Tobacco to cut to them, It's very mild weather, this day

---

[20] It is possible that McLeod was using "Point au Foutre" to stand for Fort Alexander, at the mouth of the Winnipeg River. See Macdonell's reference to "Pointe au F——e," above, page 107.

Friday 12th. A very mild day, Roy &. Jacque came back they brought ½ Red Deer, the hunter's boy came with three beaver skins to buy a small kettle, but I have got none of the size he wants

Saturday 13th. A beautifull day, Jacque, &. the hunters boy went off, I sent the Hunters, each some powder &. Shott, Thaws a great deal

Sunday 14th. Still a finer day than yesterday. The Sun really heated very much, &. it even thawed when the Sun did not shine. early in the morning Demarrais broy^r in law (Crapaud) came to the Fort with three young Stone Indians, they are come from the Upper part of the Lakes of the River Qui Appelle, the three Stone Indians were sent by the Old men of their Camp to tell the H. B people at the Elbow to go with goods liquor &c. to trade with them, they had a paper which Sutherland gave them last Autumn, &. which I got from them to look at [*d*. which I tore &. threw into the fire], &. I prevailed on them not to go to the Elbow. Jacque came, from the Hunter's with an old Stragling Cow they kill'd yesterday which is quite *Meagre,* by the Stone Indian's account the Buffaloes are a great way off as yet &. if it does not come Cold weather we are likely to be as ill off as other forts in the Red River were last year, all the Country round this having been hunted by a great number of Indians all last winter &. Summer has driven the Deer far off in every direction. Consequently we can have but Small hopes of Bonne Chase if the Buffaloe does not approach.[21]

It does not freeze in the tent out of doors tonight, But the Sky is quite clear &. the firmament covered with an inumerable quantity of bright Stars.

Monday 15th December *1800*. It was one of the finest mornings I ever saw, the Sun Shone forth in all its brightness, &. the weather was so very mild, that if it had not been for the

[21] Alexander Henry the younger says that the winter of 1799–1800 was exceptionally mild, with the result that there was a great scarcity of food as well as of peltries in the region of the Assiniboine. Coues, *New Light,* 1:2–4.

little Snow that covers the ground one on going out of doors would have been apt to imagine he had lain asleep for five months &. at last awakened in the cheerfull month of May, but like all other Sublunary things it soon changed, for about noon it began to blow a [*d.* mere] hurrycane, the Sky got overcast &. every thing appeared gloomy that a few hours ago, (nay a few minutes) appeared gay, & gilded with the animating Rays of the Great Parent of Day! Such is the instability of earthly enjoyments!

Jacque went off again to the Hunters, Demarrais brother in law with the three Stone Indians went off. I gave each a bit of Tobacco, &. sent a foot of Tobacco by the Cree to Tabot's son in Law. I gave a writing to the Stone Indian in place of the one I tore to pieces, & with which he appears highly satisfied.

Teusday 16th. A very mild day, &. quite thick fog; Old La Voye came back with his 40 Beaver Skins.

Wednessday 17th. It rained last night, there is a hard crust of Ice on every thing out of Doors, it is still foggy, &. Dark but very mild, the *Vent du Nord* &. an Iroquois came here, from near the spunk Hills, two Iroquois fell in with the Crees in the Nutt hill &. they continue with them for some time. it's one of them that's come here today, they tell us the Bulls are little more than a days' march from here, they (the Crees) mean to make a pound three days march off from here. about Twenty six tents of them are gathered together there.[22] I gave the Vent du Nord as much rum as he could drink, as I am very apprehensive he &. the rest of the band mean to go to

[22] The Indians of the plains caught whole herds of buffalo by making a pound or inclosure and enticing the animals into it, where they could be slaughtered easily. For a description by Alexander Henry see Coues, *New Light*, 2:518–520. See below, page 151, for mention of another pound, evidently more distant from the fort. Palliser's General Map of Routes shows a Buffalo Pound Hill and a creek of the same name far up on the Qu'appelle River. See *Papers Relative to the Exploration by Captain Palliser of that Portion of British North America Which Lies between the Northern Branch of the River Saskatchewan and the Frontier of the United States; and between the Red River and the Rocky Mountains* (London, 1859).

Lower Fort des Prairies, they hearing such tempting accounts of low goods, &. liquor are lavished on the Indians that go there both by Our people &. the *Petit Poté* as well as the Hudson's Bay C^{os} Servants.[23] Our Hunter's boy came home to inform us of their having kill'd 2 Red Deer &. a Bear. Frise &. Vallé arrived from the River Qui Appelle they brought me letters from Messrs McDonell &. Malhiot, as likewise one from Mr Bann who winters for the HB. C.o at River à la Coquill, requesting me to lend him some Books, I mean the last mentioned Gentleman.[24] M^r McDonell informs me, that Mr Ferguson has sent to him for goods, &. that he Supply'd him with a Couple p^{cs} St[rou]ds. &. a few Blkts. &. Capots, he Mentions that the X. Y. are working away at their usual trade of throwing away a great many goods &. that they have lost a Man by Poison, some time ago.[25]

Wednesday 17th December *1800.* Cont^d M^r McDonell writes me that Mr Chaboillez was to have left home (Portage la Prairie) to come all the way here on a visit the 10th Ins^t &. that the Iroquois that went to the Lakes of the River Qui Appelle finding no great quantity of Beaver there Intended to come to River à la Biche, (he means Our Iroquois) M^r M^{c}D. complains of the Scarcity of Goods &c. & asks me to let him have amunition &. Tobacco, the Buffaloe are far from them as yet. after dark, 3 Men & an Indian to Guide them arrived

[23] *Petite potée* is French Canadian for a collection of persons or things of small value. See *Glossaire du parler français au Canada* (published by the Société au Parler Français au Canada, Quebec, 1930). The term was applied to the X. Y. Company, frequently becoming simply " potties." Simon McTavish scornfully called his opponents " The Little Company." Davidson, *North West Company*, p. 77.

[24] The Rivière la Coquille, or Shell River, is a small stream that flows into the Assiniboine from the east some distance above its junction with the Qu'appelle River.

[25] In Masson's list of the clerks of the Northwest Company in 1799 an Alexander Farguson is mentioned as being in the Fort Dauphin department. See Masson, *Bourgeois*, 1:62. Strouds, a kind of cloth fabric, was one of the principal articles imported by the traders and was exchanged in the interior for furs. A *capot* was a kind of greatcoat with a hood that was used by nearly all traders and voyageurs.

142   FIVE FUR TRADERS OF THE NORTHWEST

here from Lower Fort des Prairies. they brought me letters from Messrs King, Montour, &. one from Messrs D. McGillivray &. John MacDonald dated 15th October from Fort Augustus,[26] in which they mention the XY. having gone by the Pembina River to Athabasca Six Canoes 70 Pieces; they mention that five of their men left them early in the Fall &. came to us; — Their letter is directed to the Proprietors of the N.West Company.[27] Mr King's letter informs me, of the destruction of Goods he is oblidged to, by his opponents, of the XY. he writes me Messrs Howes &. Longmoore are his neighbours for the H. Bay — C°. &. that they are on Good terms. The Bearers of these letters were sent for Tobacco &. Salt.

Mr King's letter contains a piece of information that distresses me very much; — He Says that some weeks ago his Hunters saw the Crapaud (La France's murderer) returning from some of the Forts of Upper Fort Des Prairies with 3

[26] For data on the location of Fort des Prairies and Fort Augustus see above, page 98n. The persons from whom letters were received were clerks or *bourgeois* of the Northwest Company. James King appears on Masson's list for 1799 as stationed in the Rocky Mountain department. See his *Bourgeois*, 1:63. In 1804–05 Nicholas Montour was at Fort des Prairies. See Harmon, *Journal*, p. 46; *Bourgeois*, 1:397. D. McGillivray is probably Duncan McGillivray, who had been trading and exploring in the region of the North Saskatchewan for about three years. From November 17 to December 3, 1800, he was with David Thompson on his Bow River tour. His letter to McLeod was evidently sent a month or so before his departure. See Coues, *New Light*, 1:439n. For further discussion of McGillivray's movements in 1800 and thereafter see *The Journal of Duncan M'Gillivray of the North West Company, at Fort George on the Saskatchewan, 1794–1795* (edited by Arthur S. Morton, Toronto, 1929), pages 8–16 of the Appendix. John MacDonald, proprietor at Fort Augustus, was at this time coming to be one of the leaders in the western fur trade. He was later to be proprietor in the English River department (1804) and the Red River department (1807). In 1813 he sailed for the mouth of the Columbia River, where he took possession of Astoria for the Northwest Company, renaming it Fort George. Returning overland to Fort William the following year, he took part in the Pemmican War between the Northwest Company and the Hudson's Bay Company. He retired from the fur trade in 1816. Burpee, *Oxford Encyclopaedia*, p. 379.

[27] The Pembina River here mentioned is not the river of that name that flows into the Red River, but a stream flowing north into Elk River and Lake Athabasca. See the map in Alexander Mackenzie, *Voyages from Montreal*.

stone Indians, & that they had fifteen Horses, & all saddled with saddles made by our people. among the Saddles were one with Iron Stirrups, they moreover had 2 fine white shirts, a fine Cloth Coat, &. 2 womens hoods garnished with Ribbons &. a Lodge, Mr King adds that he is very apprehensive they have kill'd some of our Gentlemen who might have been removing from one Fort to another, &. what augments his suspisions &. mine is that whenever, those Indians arrived all the Stone Indians withdrew into the Heart of the Plains, far removed from any Fort. I shall be extremely uneasy till I hear from above; God Almighty grant that my fears may be groundless, in the same degree that they are sincere; Mr King writes me the Universall Story, — Short of Goods!!! Rained a Good deal this evening.

Thursday 18th December *1800*. Foggy &. raining or rather snowing all day, the Vent du Nord traded 4 Catts, &. 1 Beaver skin he tells me he has 20 Beaver Skins at his Lodge, which he means to go to Fort des Prairies with if I dont' treat him well. I gave him a pair of Coulours, &. a 2 Gall. Keg of mix'd Rum with several other articles, for nothing, in hopes of being able to entice the whole of the Band that are along with him to come here.[28] I sent Dannis &. the Blacksmith (young one) for the meat to the Hunter's. The Iroquois went not off, today (did not go off), he being unwell, we can understand very little of what he says, — but he Makes us signes he & his 7 friends have 400 Plues

Friday 19th. A very mild, but Cloudy day, Mr Harmon &. the people arrived with the Goods &c. from below, M^r McGillis, La Comble, Cadotte Foosier, &. 2 of M^r McGillis' men arriv'd from Red D[eer] river. Dannis &. the Blacksmith came back with 2 Red Deer &. they tell us there are eight More kill'd by the Hunters. Young Le Fevre came up from Swan River [29]

---

[28] "A pair of coulours" refers to British flags, which the Indians considered very acceptable presents. The Northwest Company used the term "plus" as a unit of value, the equivalent of one good beaver skin.

[29] An Indian named the Blacksmith is mentioned in Faries' diary, below, page 233.

Saturday 20th. As Mild &. Cloudy a Day as ever, indeed the weather's keeping so very constantly Cloudy, is a thing not remembered by the oldest residenters in this Country, every day it looks as if it was going to Snow, but it clears off for about half an hour &. gets overcast again. I sent off the Fort des Prairies men for the P^{cs} to Swan River, I sent off N. Ducharm with 2 Men to go &. find &. kill a few (Buffaloe) Bulls, I sent B^{te} Roy, Dannis, Jack Old Chauvin, old La Voyé &. young Le Fevre for the meat at the Hunter

Sunday 21st. A very fine day the people came home with the meat the woods are cover'd with rhime, & the weather keeps constantly cloudy.[30] M^r McGillis tells me he is very sure he will want both H. Wines &. Goods, particularly Cloth &. Blankets, &. *God* knows I am by no means in a situation to furnish him much, I spoke to B^{te} Roy about going along with M^r McGillis for a Month & half to try what service he can render, or if he can at all be of any use. I sent Collin &. Seven men off *en Derouine* to where the Vent du Nord came from, with the value of 3 large Kegs in Rum, &. for 60 skins in Goods &c.[31]

Monday 22d. Still Cloudy &. Mild, but Rhimy; four Men arrived from the Posts of Fort Dauphin, who are sent for H. Wines &. Goods, I had a letter from Mr Fergason who visited all the four Posts but I'm sorry to observe, they have by no means kept to my directions to them, they have been trading with upwards of 40 of the Red River Indians, but indeed I can hardly blame them [32]

[30] Rime used in this connection refers to the hoarfrost that collected on the trees at night.

[31] Traders were said to *courir en dérouine* when, instead of waiting at their established posts for the Indians to come in and trade their furs, they went out to the Indian hunting camps to get the peltries.

[32] The trading area was divided up into a number of sections or departments, and the traders were expected to trade with the Indians within their own department. See Innis, *Fur Trade in Canada*, p. 246. In this instance the traders in the Swan River department were trading with Red River Indians. Apparently the Indians had taken credits (i. e., received goods on

Monday 22^d December 1800 — Continued. But I certainly think it very hard that the River la Cocquille people cannot keep their own Indians from going to trade with our people, who are so near a little *Poté* opposition &. short of Goods at the same time. Moreover that its' a trifle expence, for all those Indians have Credits from M^r McDonell's people, who were at considerable expences with them last fall, & its' rather hard that they should be allow'd to trade what little they may have a second time. By the accounts from Fort Dauphin Cardin, does nothing, &. is very quiete, but I am really apprehensive from their want of Goods &c. (our people I mean) he may get a few Packs in the Spring, they may have just now at Fort Dauphin &. all it's dependencies 25 or 20 Good Packs. The old Pass au Travers came to the Fort, with 20 Cass'd Catts &. 8 Beavers.[33]

Teusday 23^d. Fine mild weather, but cloudy, & the trees &. everything so covered with Rhyme, that all nature seems powdered, & not an air of wind to shake it off, sent off B^{te} Roy &. Decarré for River la Biche

Wednessday 24th. Snow'd a few inches deep of very light Snow last night, very mild weather, today, M^r McGillis intended going off but Lambert could not find their Horses, I sent off the Fort Dauphin men to Swan River for a keg H. Wines each, it's enormous the expense I am at in provisions for so many *strangers*. M^r McGillis takes from here 4 large Capots, 3 New Guns, 10 Pr Tranches [?], 1 Buffaloe robe 4 Casstettes à Calûmet, 1 Pr Large Steelyards, &. a Fort Flag.

credit) from Macdonell on the Assiniboine, but were taking their furs to the Swan River traders and receiving new credit from them instead of settling their previous debts.

[33] Lynx were usually called cats in the fur trade. Two principal methods were used in skinning them. Sometimes the skins were cut down the hind legs on either side of the tail and then pulled off over the animal's head and front feet, leaving the fur inside. Peltries so treated were called "cased" skins. "Open" skins were cut down the center of the belly and spread out flat. Harold A. Innis, *Fur Trade of Canada* (University of Toronto Studies in History and Economics, Toronto, 1927), p. 102.

Mʳ Perigné & La France arriv'd from the Montaigne des Oiseaux.³⁴

Thursday 25ᵗʰ. Being Christmass I gave the men a dram, Mʳ McGillis went off, &. Lambert with him, four men came from the River Qui Appelle, who brought me a letter from Mʳ McDonell in which he asks me for Powder & tells me to send him Tobacco &. Salt, I having none of those articles here I told his men they must go to Swan River, to which to get them to consent I had a great deal of trouble, &. they insisted on returning as they came from here, three off them at last consented to go but said they had neither Shoes nor Tobacco, I gave each 2 pʳˢ of Shoes &. a foot & half, Tobacco to 3 of them, They are a troublesome sett.

Friday 26ᵗʰ. Still Mild &. Cloudy. Two of the Red River Men sett off for Swan River, the third that was to have gone pays one of the others to fetch up his piece. My two Hunters came to the House, they tell me the Cows (Buffaloe) are not far off from where they are, I was oblidged to give them Liquor enough to get Drunk, theres the meat of a Red Deer at their lodge that the[y] kill'd yesterday

Saturday 27ᵗʰ December *1800*. Cloudy, &. Mild as usual, Mʳ Perigné sett off for home Via Recoude, I gave a roll of Spencer's Twist Tobacco &. 14 Quarts Powder, 10 Wampum Shells with Mʳ McDonell's cheese to his two men that did not go to Swan River, & sent them off, I mean to keep the Roll of Tobacco they are gone for below, &. 14 Quarts out of the keg of Powder to replace what I have sent him (Mʳ McD.) from here. My Hunters went off early, I had to give them each a two Gall. keg of Mix'd Rum, the two Ducharms arived with 2 Good Sledges load of Buffaloe (Cow) meat, they were many miles beyond where the Buffaloe now are, the old Pass au

---

³⁴ McLeod's *tranche* was probably a species of chisel. The "casstette" (*casse-tête*) was a club or tomahawk that was used as a weapon. Steelyards were rough balance scales, consisting of a fulcrum and a horizontal beam. The object to be weighed was hung from one end of the bar and was balanced by weights placed upon a pan that was suspended from the other end of the bar.

Travers went off with his lodge to look for Buffaloe as he says he cant hunt enough to live on in the woods

Sunday 28th. Still Mild &. Rhimy, Two of M^r McDonell's men came here they brought me a letter from him, &. inclosed was his Gen^{ll} Letter to the Proprietors of the N. W. C° West of Red River; he tells them in that letter that he has siez'd on the 4 Rolls Tobacco that were in Mr Duncan McGillivray's Canoe; for which he sends these two men; The men inform me they slept at Sutherlands at the Elbow, where they saw three Stone Indians, who were sent for the *English* to go out to their Camp to trade with them, &. that Mr Sutherland intended sending with them, but by another road so that I might have no knowledge of his Sending, although he promis'd me when he was here not to Send out without acquainting me; Altho' it was four oClock in the afternoon I determined to go down &: endeavour to prevent his Sending, by some means or other, I got there about half past six P. M. he was rather astonished to see me, &. was so confused that in place of laying my furr Cap (which on my entrance he rather snapp'd than took out of my hand) by, or hang it up any where, he put it on his head, & taking my tippit put it in his pocket, in fact he could hardly ask me how I did, in about three quarters of an hour he recollected himself a little, &. I told him my errand. he gave me a promise before we went to bed not to Send out during the winter without acquainting me, he was perfectly sober

Monday 29th. A little colder than usual after breakfast I sett off for home, in company with one of Sutherland's men that I asked him to Send up for a little Buffaloe meat for a rarity, I got home in the afternoon &. found the Fort des Prairies &. the Fort Dauphin men had arived early this morning from Swan River together tho' the later left this 4 days after the former, I arranged the Goods &c. that I intend sending to Fort Dauphin, & wrote a long letter of Directions to Ferguson, I likewise hired Thos for 4 years &. La Plante for two. Broached & emptyed a keg H. W. it contained only 17 qts.

Teusday 30th. Very Cold &. Clear weather, I gave a little Buffaloe Meat to Mr Sutherland's man with a Gallⁿ of Peas for his Master & he went off. Collin came back, he brought 19 wolves &. 14 Beavers, 7 Catts. & 5 foxes, 39 bladders Grease, & a little dryed and Green Meat. I [MS illegible] five of the Men today.

Wednessday 31st December *1800*. A real cold day but clear &. Calm

Thursday 1st January *1801*. Still Colder than yesterday, Hoole &. La Couture arrived from Swan River, &. Le Mire with them, the later brought me a keg H. Wines, the two former brought but two pieces the 3d they left at Mr Perignés, I gave all the people in the Fort a dram which took, three qts. Rum, (reduced) to effect, after that I gave them fourteen Quarts among them, there were, people from Fort des Prairies, Red River, Swan River, Free Men, &. Iroquois, in all 38 Men including my own men I likewise gave them ½ Foot Tobacco each man, they danced & sang all day &. night, but had no quarrels, one of ye G. P. kegs of H. W. contained only 20 Qts.

Friday 2d. Cold, &. Blowy, nobody went off Today; early this morning one of the old women, who are in a Small Lodge at the Fort gate was found frozen to Death, Somebody had given her a little Liquor &. it's supposed she laid down to Sleep, but the very intense cold siezed her &. carried her to her long home, the people put her body on a scaffold as the ground is so hard frozen as not to admit of digging a hole to put her in; — Severals of the Men wanted to buy rum, but I refused them all; — 2 *fills* [*fils*] of the *Cheffress* (her sons) came to the Fort late. thay are come from the Beaver Mountain where there are some of my debtors; — they only brought a Bear Skin &. 4 wolves with 1 Beaver Skin, &. 20 Pieces of dry'd meat.

Staurday 3d. Not so cold as yesterday, Amelin &. Georege (R. River Men) went off for Swan River; I sent off 2 men to remain at the Hunters, &. three for meat, this morning, Ettiene

Ducharm's youngest Boy was found dead, he had no previous sickness apparently. It is much milder than in the morning, towards sun sett.

Sunday 4th. A very fine mild day I sent off the Fort des Prairies men, &. with them Cadotte &. Vallé to bring back the winter Express,[35] I sent to Fort des Prairies 1 Roll Spencers Twist Tobacco a Bale Carrot Tob° &. a keg of salt for Mr Duncan McGillivray the two Red River men Hoole &. La Couture went off, likewise the Two Ducharms who I have sent out to hunt for the Fort as the Buffaloe are not above a Days march off, I sent two men along with them to haul the meat to their lodge as fast as they kill. I sent Collin with 2 Men along with the Fills de la Chefferess to try &. get our Debts from Petit Bled &. Petit Sonant.[36] I only sent half a keg mixed Liquor by him, &. three foot Tobacco. The 2 Iroquois went off this morning I sold them one Dress'd Skin, (2 Ignaus).

La Voye &. La Freniere went off to Hunt the Buffaloe, in Short 28 Grown people went off different ways, exclusive of Indians. The three men that went for meat returned with 2 Cows that the Hunters kill'd, who say that the Buffaloe are very numberous not a great distance off

Monday 5th January 1801. A Stormy day, Cold &. Snowing, I sent Plante and four men off for meat. Continued to Snow &. drift all day.

Teusday 6th. Not so cold as yesterday. Snow'd since yesterday about four Inches deep, but this is a fine clear day, the people came home with upwards of three Cows, I got the Chimney in the Hall mended by the old Blacksmith, and old Chauvin.

---

[35] The Northwest traders organized their winter expresses or couriers with great care, and the resulting system of communication was one of the picturesque features of the life of the wilderness. There was a reciprocal exchange of dispatches each winter among all the posts between Grand Portage and the Athabasca region. See Innis, *Fur Trade in Canada*, p. 249; Harmon, *Journal*, p. 41; Davidson, *North West Company*, pp. 301–305.

[36] Petit Sonant was one of a tribe of Indians called Sonnants. McLeod's spelling of the word varies.

Wednessday 7th. A cold serene day, the people went off for Meat &. I sent Girardin with my dogs, along with them, Blew very hard in the evening from the South East &. very cold, Old Chauvin & the old Blacksmith were hauling wood home all day for the fire.

Thursday 8th. Rather milder than yesterday, a Band of Crees &. Assiniboins (8 men) came from the Montaigne du Tondre [Foudre], the *Batard Anglois* the principall man, they seem to have a good deal of Grease,[37] 2 Iroquois, of those that came into the Red River with Mr McDonell came along with them, they have been at their Camp this long time past, as well as the Iroquois who are for the XY having found no Beaver, they are now come here to ask my advice what to do, Collin came back with very little else than fresh meat. the men who were for meat came home, they tell me the Hunters see very few Buffaloe now, the most of them having passed, downward

Friday 9th. All the Indians traded, their Grease &. few Skins. I sent five Sledges to the Hunters &. told them to tell the Hunters to go after the Buffaloe, This day is very mild & *Rhimy*.

Saturday 10th. A very fine day, All the Indians went off except the *Boeuf Blanc* &. the Iroquois the later traded a few kitts &. wolves for Rum to carry with them to Buy horses as they mean to come back imediately, with all their Baggage, &. go to River à la Biche, where I have advised them to go. I bought a Horse to day, from the *Boeuf blanc* which I think a great deal too dear but as I never wish an action of mine, concealed I here mark what I paid for him, as I purchased him for the C° a large keg, 2/3d of a fm. H. B. Stds. a Carrot

---

[37] Montagne de Foudre (Thunder Mountain) lies in the curve of the Swan River, northeast of Sutherland's post at the Elbow of the Assiniboine. See the map on page 128. In a rough census of the Assiniboine Indians, Alexander Henry lists forty tents of Stone or Rocky Assiniboines who lived about the Skunk Wood (Touchwood) Hills or Montagne de Foudre. The Touchwood Hills were sometimes called the Punk Hills or Spunk Hills. Coues, *New Light*, 2:523.

of Tobacco, & a piece of gartering, a price that I have not exceeded for any two horses, since I have been in this Department, he is a strong, able beast I mean him for my own riding as the one I have rode these three years (my own private property) is quite worn out, &. for Aught I know is dead at Swan River, having sent him there when I came back from Fort Dauphin. In the evening three young men came here from a pound that's five day's march off, they say they are come for people to go &. trade with them

Sunday 11th January *1801*. A very fine Mild day, one of the young men that came here last evening went down to the Elbow for some of the men from there to go out with them with Rum &c. the Boeuf blanc set off. blew very fresh towards evening

Monday 12th. Sent all the people for meat, Mr Harmon having a curiosity to see the Buffaloe went with them, indeed I wished him to go &. see how the Men act there, being apprehensive they destroy a great deal in feeding their Dogs. The Boeuf blanc came back &. brought me every thing I had given him for his horse he being almost inconsolate for having Sold him, not wishing to give him up the Horse I gave him a little Horse I had &. kept the Gartering, Cloth, &. Tobacco in lieu of the Horse I gave him, by which means the Horse does not cost the C° by ten Beavers value what I originally gave him, two of Mr Sutherland's men came here on their way out to the Indians they brought me a letter &. a Book from their Master, in the first he gives me a pressing invitation to go to see him. the Iroquois belonging to the XY came here late in the evening & along with them two of ours, they say they are to go for their effects to the River Qui Appelle & that afterwards they intend going to Fort Des Prairies, I told our's that I did not like their remaining with the others, so they intend setting off from this ahunting.

Teusday 13th. The XY Iroquois went off to the River qui Appelle. I wrote a very few lines to Mr McDonell informing him of *his* Iroquois being here & telling him I wished he could come up & settle with them himself, as I have neither their A/C or engagements, Pierre &. the other went off for their families &. Baggage, the English went off with the young Indians, but an Indian who came here in the evening (Shagotimoh) tells us the Indians to whose tents they are gone have got no skins, the Fort des Prairies people having lately been there en Derouine, the people came home with the meat, Frisé &. Roy came back having staid their turn at the hunters. I sold my fine Gun to one of our Iroquois he having none for two hundred livres with which I am to be Credited & debited to Tahoatianta &. Āghiscrēgo, especially the first

Wednessday 14th. A very fine Mild day, Shagotimoh gave me nine pieces of meat &. a badger Skin for which I gave him a very little keg of Rum, he went off as did the people for meat. the Red River Men came back from Swan River (Hamelin & George)

Thursday 15th January *1801*. The eight Sledges came home with four Cows. this is a very mild day snowed a little in the morning. Dannis finished a sort of Cariole he has made for me, Mr Harmon returned with the people, he saw a great many buffaloes he says [38]

Friday 16th. I sett off with the men that went for meat, to see what was going on there (at the hunters) &. to speak to the Hunters to encourage them, we got there soon after midday, the Indians were out hunting but kill'd nothing they say the Buffaloe are going farther off owing to the extremely mild weather. I brought each of the hunters a little Rum with which they got drunk; the distance from the Fort to go there may be about 18 miles, but the roads are very fine &. level. Amlin went off home.

Saturday 17th. We got back to the Fort about half past two oClock P.M. with 4 &. half Cows. I took L' Heureux

[38] A cariole was a kind of dog sled that was used to a considerable extent in the Northwest. It was made of oak or birch boards planed smooth and turned up at the front, and was fitted with parchment sides and a comfortable back. See Egerton R. Young, *By Canoe and Dog-Train among the Cree and Salteaux Indians* (Toronto, 1890), p. 95.

THE DIARY OF ARCHIBALD N. McLEOD 153

home with me as they do not furnish, even the three others to haul. it snowed most part of the day which made the roads heavy

Sunday 18th. A fine day, being Sunday I let the men rest themselves, La Frenier came from the Ducharms lodge who have kill'd he says 21 Cows, they are near the white Mud river,[39] I am *bothered* (*plagued*) with a parcel of invalides here at the Fort who cannot go even for meat, vizt — Boiselle, La Comble, Chauvin, &. now Plante is unwell, the two Iroquois are here still they are busy making snow shoes &. sledges.

Monday 19th. I sent off six sledges to the Ducharms, &. two to our Indian Hunters, La Frenier is looking for wood to make sledges &. snow shoes; blew a hard gale from the Southward but not cold, gave medicines to Plante &. Boiselle, who are attacked with the same disorder tho in different stages

Teusday 20th. A very fine day, the people that I sent to Ducharms returned well loaded with meat, The two Iroquois went off to go to the Ducharms, La Comble &. Boiselle are both very unwell.

Wednessday 21st. Quite Mild; I sent off the people for meat to the Ducharms; La France &. Cadieu came here from the Montaigne des Oiseaux they brought me a Roll of Tobacco &. a keg of H. Wines. I engaged La France for two years &. Cadieu for three, the ordinary wages of the Post, but I promised each a Gun &. Horse, One of them (Cadieu) being free at the Grand Portage.[40]

Thursday 22^d. It's a quite warm day, thaws a great deal, round the Fort, the people came home with meat & La France & Frisé went with 4 Sledges to Ducharms, as Mr Perigné

---

[39] Two streams in the vicinity of Fort Alexandria were named White Mud River. One of them has its source in the uplands west of Lake Manitoba and empties into the southern end of the lake; the other flows close by the site of the fort and empties from the northwest into the Assiniboine a short distance below the Elbow. See the map on page 128.

[40] This stipulation in Cadieu's engagement meant that his term of service would end at Grand Portage.

told La France & Cadiau to take two Sledges load down with them, Toisier came from our Indians Hunters with a Cow, the two Iroquois that were here New years day came to the Fort, they have very little dryed meat & nothing else, they found Mr Montour's Mare that he lost last fall on his way to Fort des Prairies

Thursday 22^d January 1801 Continued. Petit Bled & Petit Sonnan came here they are come for people to go for meat to their Lodge, a good days March off, the Buffaloe are going farther off very fast owing to the extraordinary mildness of the weather, people go days journeys without mittens, so very fine is the weather, I took a ride on horse back today of upwards of an hour without gloves &. felt not the least cold. Cadieu is getting himself *tatooed* by La Frenier, as has already Boiselle.

Friday 23^d. I sent the people off for the remainder of the meat that is at the Ducharms as they are to pitch off after the Buffaloe. La France &. Frisé cam'back before day as La France wishes to get *tatooed,* This has been a very fine mild day as usual

Saturday 24th. The Petit Bled went off. the Sonnant waits to go along with the Men tomorrow, the people came back with the last of the meat from the Ducharms, the two Iroquois came back with them as they are to go with the two Ignaus to Red Deers River.

Sunday 25th. Still warm weather, I sent eight sledges off with the Sonnant, John Luke &. Jibault arrived from Jacco Finlay's with ½ Rolls S. T. [Spencer's Twist] Tobacco & a few other articles. I am sorry to learn he does very little there. he has now had two hundred &. thirteen Skins that is traded Beaver Plus. La France &. Cadiau went off with a Cow I sent Mr Perigné. La Frnier went off for the River Qui Appelle I wrote M^r M^{c}D. by him, I took a ride in my Cariole &. Dogs today.

Monday 26th. Fine weather, got cloudy in the afternoon. The 4 Iroquois went off for River la Biche. I wrote M^r McGillis

Teusday 27th. Cloudy but mild weather, Collin &. the men came back the[y] brought 40 Bladders grease a little pounded meat & the rest of their loads were made up with Bosses &. Depouilles.[41] I sent Girardin for Meat, he went off before day &. came back at night, the Hunters have pitched off after the Buffaloe but they see very few, & must go far off after them

Wednessday 28th. Fine weather, the people went for meat, one of the old Pass au Travers Sons came here he tells us they have the load of 3 Sledges at their lodge of meat &. Grease, he brought us a few bladders grease &. a very little pounded Meat, I gave him a little Rum to drink. Frisé came home with a Cow &. a half on his two Sledges.

Thursday 29th. Still as mild as usual, the Indian went off &. with him I sent Collin &. 3 Sledges, the people came home with the Meat. The Buffaloe are going away very fast which makes me apprehensive that we must towards Spring have recourse to the little pounded meat &. Grease that we have, & for which I should be extremely sorry

Friday 30th January 1801. Collin came back with 3 Good Sledges loaded of very good fat meat, the people went off for meat, Roy &. 3 men arrived from Red Deers River. they brought me letters from M^r McGillis wherein he asks for Goods, Rum, &. Guns, I am informed the Beaver is getting very scarce there, Roy behaved no better than usual while there, nor ever will I am affraid, Collin brought home the accounts of the Small Pox being among the Blood Indians, &c. this was told him by an Indian he saw from the Punk hills Who had been (as we imagine) at Upper Fort des Prairies to steel horses. The *Miroire* &. a young Stone Indian

[41] A *bosse* was the hump of a buffalo; *dépouilles* were portions of a fat substance taken from the buffalo and used as a substitute for bread. The two *dépouilles* extended along the backbone of the animal from the shoulder to the last rib, lying next to the skin. They were stripped from the carcass, dipped in hot grease, and hung up in the lodge to dry and smoke before they were ready to be eaten. See E. Douglas Branch, *The Hunting of the Buffalo* (New York, 1929), p. 49.

came here late in the evening, they are come from the East end of the Punk Hills, where there are 30 tents of them, &. he is come to ask me to send out people to trade with them.

Saturday 31st. A fine day, the people came home with Meat, the Dutchman, &. Gibault went off, I wrote Jacco &. sent him a number of small articles which he wrote me for, rather colder than usual.

Sunday 1st February 1801. I sent off Mr Harmon &. Collin with eight Sledges &. Rum &. goods to the amount of 240 Sk[in]s. along with the Miroire. Snowed a little, &. got colder weather blew very high, Ettienne Ducharm came here in the evening to inform me there are six tents of Crees where they are who have got a great many Sledges load of provisions & a good many skins. the Buffaloe are by no means numerous where they are owing to the mildness of the weather they (the Buffaloe) retreat back to the plains

Monday 2^d. Sent off, Roy, Girardin, Dannis, &. Plante with 120 sks. value of Goods, Rum, &c. to trade with the Indians that are along with the Ducharms, the three Riveire à la Biche men went off, I sent M^r McGillis a keg of High wines &. near two bales Goods, with three Guns; It realy is a terrible bad day, Snowing, Blowing, &. of consequence drifting, &. Cold; the people that went off cannot be gone far owing to the extreme badness of the Day

Teusday 3^d. A Clear day, but colder than usual, Etienne went off, I gave him amunition &. Tobacco for the time he is to be absent

Wednessday 4th. This is still a worse day than the Day before yesterday, Snowing, Blowing, Drifting &. Cold nearly a foot of snow has fallen between these two Days.

Thursday 5th. A serene Cold day, I am seriously &. grivously alarmed at Cadottes long absence

Friday 6th. A very boisterous day, Cold, Snowy, Blowing &. Drifting furiously, Roy, Girardin, Plante, &. Dannis came back with four sledges loads of Dryed meat &. grease, the Rieure [*sic*] &. Tonnerre came to the fort, I gave them a few

Pints of Rum to drink. I traded 3 Beavers & a Bear Skin with the former, the roads are excessively bad owing the great fall of Snow lately.

Saturday 7th February *1801*. Cold day. Snowed a little in the morning, I sent Dannis, Girardin, &. Jack for meat to the Indian Hunters, Roy is getting wood for Snow Shoe frames, Le Fevre &. Petite Jean came here from Perignés they brought me a keg of Salt, &. a Bag of Balls, on Sledges drawn by Horses. they are sent by Mr Perigné for some Buffaloe meat.

About twelve oClock at night Cadote &. Vallé arrived, & with them Mr Montour; the[y] brought the Genl Express, along with them, for which Cadotte &. Vallé remained 15 days; it not being arrived

Sunday 8th. A Cold, & Cloudy day, Girardin &. Dannis with Jack came back with the meat, reading letters all day

Monday 9th. Still Cold &. Snowing a little, began to write my dispatches pr [per] the Express, La Verdure and Jacque came here [*d.* from Swan] River with 2 Pieces

Teusday 10th. Cold &. Clear, Jollifour, La Pointe &. La Plante arrived from Fort Dauphin they brought me a letter from Mr Ferguson wherein he tells me that Cardin has built a Fort at Turtle River, but is doing very little either there or at Fort Dauphin, he writes me likewise that Mitchel has with drawn Chenettes fort as the few Indians that were there are doing nothing,[42] La Comble is amazingly sick he neither eats, or sleeps. Pierre's band of Iroquois left this today for the River Qui Appelle where they are gone for their effects as they mean to go by land to Lower Fort Des Prairies. Gervais came here &. brought me a letter from Mr McDonell wherein he tells me, he is out of H. Wines, the XY Iroquois arrived from River Qui Appelle, &. one of the X.Y. Men along with them, they mean to sett off for Fort des Prairies imediately

[42] The Turtle River is a small stream which flows from the south into Dauphin Lake. Mitchel was probably Michel Allary, a clerk in the same department as McLeod. Masson, *Bourgeois*, 1:62.

Wednessday 11th. Cold, &. Cloudy, Mr Harmon &. Collin arrived with 8 good Sledges load of Pounded Meat and Grease. The XY. Iroquois sett off. I hired Jollifour today for 2 Years

Thursday 12th. I sent off Cadotte, &. Frise for River la Cocquile with the Express, I wrote the following gentlemen Agents NW. Co. Messrs McGillivray, Shaw, McLeod, Welles H. McKenzie, Keneth McKenzie, Peter Grant, W. McKay C. Chaboillez, John McDonell, &. Mr Malhiot.[43]

This is a fine Mild day. Sent all the men for Meat.

Friday 13th. Jollifour, &. the 2 other went off, I sent about a bale of Goods to Fort Dauphin, & wrote Mr Ferguson a long letter & told him that people ought absolutely to be sent to oppose Cardin at Turtle River, I sent Gervais, off express with a letter for M^r McDonell, in hopes of overtaking the Genl Express

Saturday 14th Feby. 1801. A Cloudy day, not Cold. La Comble is still very unwell he cannot even sit upright in his bed.

Sunday 15th. A very fine day, thaws in the Fort, the Tete Blanche &. Petit Boeuf, came here for people to go to trade to their tents.

Monday 16th. Snowing, &. Blowing, I sent Collin &. two men off with the Indians to trade, what they have with Li-

[43] According to Masson's list of 1799 the location of these men, who were proprietors, was as follows: Angus Shaw, Upper English River; Peter Grant, Rainy Lake; W. McKay, Lake Winnipeg; Chaboillez, Lower Red River; Macdonell, Upper Red River. On Malhiot and McGillivray see above, page 137n. and page 142n., respectively. Coues lists a "Mr. Welles" who was an accountant for the Northwest Company at Grand Portage in 1797 and who was with David Thompson later in the Rat River country. See his *New Light*, 3:1024. The Kenneth McKenzie here mentioned should be distinguished from the trader of the same name who made himself famous in later years by his exploits with the American Fur Company on the upper Missouri. See Hiram M. Chittenden, *American Fur Trade of the Far West* (New York, 1902), 1:384–387. H. Mackenzie was probably Henry Mackenzie, later a member of the firm of McTavish, McGillivrays, and Company, and one of the most persistent opponents of the scheme of coalition with the Hudson's Bay Company. See Davidson, *North West Company*, pp. 161, 175, 179, 187–190, 199.

quor Etcetera. I went the the [*sic*] Elbow to see whither I could make a bargain with Mr Sutherland for a few Blkts. &. some Rum, He received us very well, at least as well as poverty &. Ignorance could.

Teusday 17th. Blowing, &. of Course drifting, I passed the day with Mr Sutherland, reading &. Sometimes playing at Cards. He says he'll let me have a few Blkts. & a Gun but he can spare no Rum, he having but barely sufficient for HIMSELF, this is a pretty cold day.

Wednessday 18th. I got home in the afternoon, &. found five young Indians from the Vent du Nord's pound who are come for Tobacco for the Great Men that are there. It is a very sharp Cold day &. blowing hard, Danis killed a Bull quite close to the House in the morning.

Thursday 19th. Collin &. the two men came back, &. with them Carron &. La Rose, with old La Voye, &. Falcon's Fatherinlaw with two other Indians, I gave them a few pints mixed rum (the Indians) &. they traded a few more, Cadotte &. Frisé came back they tell me Mr Malhiot is the next thing to starving, I had a letter from Mr Bann.

Friday 20th. The people went off for meat &. others came home with meat, I sent five &. a half F^{ms} Tobacco by the young men to the Great ones at the Pound, one of them stole a Ceinture of Cadottes, which he missed not untill they had been off near two hours,[44] he took his Gun &. Snow Shoes with an intention of persuing them all day but he overtook them before noon, &. threatened to shoot one of them if he did not tell him which of them had stolen the Belt, they restored the Sash &. proceeded quitely on their journey. The Indians traded a little pounded Meat and Grease for Sundries articles. This is an astonishing Cold day, a Good many of the men have frozen faces & noses. I spoke to the Indians to come to work the Beaver, but they have not yet determined on their plan of opperations for the Spring.

[44] Voyageurs always wore gay sashes, called *ceintures fléchées*.

Saturday 21ˢᵗ February *1801*. Not so Cold as yesterday, the Indians went off, the Iroquois arrived from River Qui Appelle they brought me a letter from Mʳ McDonell, the people came home with meat & they tell me the Hunters have killed the number I asigned them, of Buffaloe.

Sunday 22ᵈ. The People are off for meat, this day is mild

Monday 23ᵈ. The four Iroquois that came from the river Qui Appelle are gone off to join the others, Le Fevre &. Petit Jean left this today on their return to the Montaigne d' Oiseau having been fifteen days absent from here to kill two Cows which the[y] fetch along with them.

Teusday 24ᵗʰ. Very mild, fine, weather. Pierre the Mohawk's brother in law came from their Lodge for a Gun they left here to be mended.

Wednessday 25ᵗʰ. I sent off Mʳ Montour along with the Iroquois, that he may take the opportunity of going back in company with them as it's absolutely impossible for me to send any men along with him. I sent a Roll S. T. Tob for Mʳ McDonald & wrote King to Send off up above with it & if he could spare another from his own place, that I should replace it by one from here if he Sent for it. I wrote Messʳˢ McDonald, McGillivray, &. Stewart.[45]

The people brought home the last of the meat at our Indian Hunters, Fine mild weather, We made 32 bags Pimican

Thursday 26ᵗʰ. Mild, &. very fine weather, our Hunters with old Pass au Traverse, his Son, &. Petit Bled, &. Petit Sonnant came to the Fort, all the Men are gone for meat to the Ducharm's; the Indians traded a few bladders grease &. pieces of meat all night, they had a few quarrels among themselves, but nobody was hurt. Collin has been busy these few days Past, preparing wood for Grease kegs. Old Parrant &. Old Chauvin are Cutting &. hauling ice for the Ice house

---

[45] Mr. Stewart was probably Alexander Stewart, a clerk of the Northwest Company located in the upper Saskatchewan district. He is better known for his activities some years later, in 1813, when he made an expedition with Alexander Henry overland to Astoria. Masson, *Bourgeois*, 1:63; Coues, *New Light*, 2:781–782.

Friday 27th. A mild &. Cloudy day; the Indians still drink. The Men came home with the Meat, & E. Ducharm along with them. The Pivard came from the *Vent du Nord's* Pound, & as he soon got drunk we know not as yet why he is come.

Saturday 28th. Blows very fresh but very mild. Pass au Travers his son, Petit Bled, & Sonnant went away, &. I Paid my hunters which as I all along dreaded has made a great deminution of the *strength* of our shop; The People are off for meat, I sent my dogs & sledge for meat.

Sunday 1st March 1801. A Charming day, the Indians went off all except L'*Homme qui se pose* &. Pivard. The people came home with the meat, *Collish* Ducharm came home *armes et baggage*

Monday 2^d. Fine weather, I sent B^{te} Roy, &. Girardin for the last loads of meat remaining at the Ducharms, Old Parrant is hauling ice &. water for the Ice House, the men making horse sledges to go down to the lower Fort, in the evening, the old Bras court, Young Premier, &. Mitchel's Step Son, (three Sauteaux) came here from the *Montaigne du Poveupiek*, with the value of 20 Plues in Beaver, &. Catts. L'*Homme Qui se pose* & Pivard went off [46]

Teusday 3^d. A very boisterous day, Blows prodigiously, Some of the men at work making horse sledges, others melting or Boiling back (Buffaloe) fat to put in the Pimican, all the women at work sewing Bags to put the Pimican into. Roy, Girardin, &. E. Ducharm came home with the last of the meat, &. brought home the Lodge &. now we have finished hauling meat, for this Season, we have now about eighty five Buffaloe Cows in the Meat house. Collin very busy making kegs to put Grease into, old Parrant, making nails for the Sledges, &. Plante hanging up the meat &. tongues he put in salt ten days ago, to day; The Indians (Sauteaux) tell me they mean to sett off Tomorrow

---

[46] Probably the reference here is to Porcupine (Porcépic) Mountain, situated between the Swan and Red Deer rivers.

Wednessday 4th. I got the last Pounded meat we got made into Pimican, vizt 30 bags of 90^{lb} so that we have now 62 Bags of that Species of provisions &. of the above weight. I likewise got nine kegs filled with Grease, or Tallow rather each keg nett 70^{lb} the men finished their Horse Sledges. in the evening two of Mr Perignés men came here for loads to carry to Swan River, Old Bras Court, &. Young Premier sett off; I gave them two Gall. mixed rum to drink at their Lodges. I likewise gave them a few Beaver's Credits. I weighed the few furrs I have here, in order to send down a Pack with each man that goes down to Swan River, the men &. women danced till twelve oClock at night.

Thursday 5th. A Beautifull day, thaws prodigiously, all the men that have horses to lead down to Swan River sett off vizt twelve men &.[*d.* twelve] 13 horses &. 13 Dogs Sledges, with 2 P^{cs} each &. each horse Sledges four pieces. I sent off old Chauvin to take care of my horses, as I told the men to leave them below vizt 5 in number.

Friday 6th. As fine a day as yesterday, I sent off 4 Men (Six dog Sledges) 15 Pieces, along with Mr Harmon, to the Lower Fort. Le Mire came back about noon to tell me that the men a head being to heavily loaded had left four bags Pimican, not far from here which I sent Girardin for with my Dogs so that there is now off with this *convoy* 58 Bags Pimican, 17 Packs, 14 kegs Grease (89 Pieces). The *Petit Bled's* son came here in the evening with a few wolves &. a little Grease. I sent Cadotte to kill some Bulls to get Canoes made with the skins

Saturday 7th March 1801. As fine a day as the two preceding. all the Ice &. Snow is entirely melted in the Fort. Old Parant has filled the Ice house, he finished this evening. Collin busy preparing Staves & hoops to make large kegs to put Grease into

Sunday 8th. A very charming day. the snow melts very fast

Monday 9th. Petit Bled went off, I sent Roy, &. *Pickaguet* along with him for a Lodge &. some Grease he has. *Michel's* step son went with them for a horse he got from the Petit Bled. I sent Girardin to the Elbow (with a letter to Mr Sutherland) for some of the articles he barters with me for wolves. Old Parant hauled wood, &. Collin worked at the Grease kegs. The wind shifted to the N. W. when the weather got colder in the afternoon.

Teusday 10th. Cold, & Blowing a fresh gale from the Westward, in the afternoon the Corn fin's son came to the House, who tells us the Day child &. two Stone Indians are not far off, on their way to the Indian Elbow. Roy &. *Picquaquet* came back with the Lodge & ten bladders of grease &. for 4 Skins of Pounded meat, Michel's step son came back with his horse, Collin was making large keg all day.

Wednessday 11th. Rather colder than yesterday. I sent Dannis &. Girardin off early in the morning to meet the Jour d' Enfant that in case he intended really to go to Sutherlands they should get what he owes here from him, but he &. they with two Stone Indians arrived in the afternoon, he made a present of 40 Skins for which I clothed him &. gave him half a keg. they traded liquor all night; They are come a great distance having Slept Six nights from their Lodges.

Thursday 12th. A Very fine day, the Indians still drunk. the Jour d'Enfant, took it into his head that we did not give him Rum strong enough. he put on his shoes &c. & wanted to sett off for the Elbow with the remainder of his furs; but on my telling him to give three Plus &. that I should let him have strong Rum he complied &. I give him a Pint of high wines &. water mixed half and half, that is half a pint of each, with which he was highly satissfied, &. I heard no more of the English. three men arrived from Fort Dauphin whome Mitchel sent for Grease, they brought me a letter from Mitchel wrote by Mr Ferguson, &. one from F. himself containing the old story of a scarcity of High Wines. Some of the men that were at Swan River are come back with two of Mr Perignés men

Friday 13th March 1801. A charming day, the Indians sett off, we saw a Swan to, day passing over the Fort from East to west. Dannis, B^te Roy, &. old Parant are preparing timber for the ice house. the snow unfortunately for us melts very fast, I am very apprehensive the people cannot make an other Trip to Swan River, which would be a bad job for us.

Saturday 14th. As fine a day as yesterday, I sent off the Fort Dauphin men long before day light. I sent by them a keg of H. W. and a little Strouds and Gartering &c, I wrote a very long letter to Michel &. one to Mr Ferguson, I hired Bois verd for four years. I advanced him for 60 livres in Goods as an encouragement to him. Mr Sutherland from the Elbow, with 2 of his men came here. I fancy he is come to get the wolves I intend bartering with him. he brought a Gun he intends to sell for wolves. I made him drink the best part of two qts. of wine which sett his head a reelling & he surely talked the compleatest jargon of Stupidity &. nonsence, that ever ignorance, &. meanness dictated. Mr Harmon &. Ettiene Ducharm arrived late at night from Swan River, who tell me the snow is absolutely quite gone the other side of Mr Perignés Fort.

Sunday 15th. A beautifull day, the rest of my people came here today from Swan River, some with broken sledges others with lame Dogs &. some with no dogs at all, having left them *en* chemin, it certainly is the finest day I ever experienced in this Country, at this Season, the little Birds sing, Eagles, &. Swans fly about &. even Butterflies, &. Musquitoes are already to be seen.

Monday 16th. Rather colder than yesterday or the four preceding days, La France &. Cachin went off home (to Perignés) they took a Taureau each on their sledges; [47] Mr Sutherland & his men sett off home. I let him have 80 wolves, if wolves they can be called, for they are pretty nearly as void

---

[47] Buffalo hides cut and made up into sacks to be filled with pemmican were called *taureaux*. McLeod uses the term here to mean a sack filled with pemmican. Such a sack contained about ninety pounds of meat and grease. See above, page 162.

of hair as he is of Sence, or Sentiment, let that be as it will he took them, & seemed glad to have them, I made him a present of my leather Cap &. a Pewter spoon.

Ten Crees arrived here in the afternoon they have very little of anything, they are our two hunters, Falcon's father-inlaw Old Pass au Traverse &. son with Petit Sonnant &c. I gave them each a pint of Liquor &. told them if they wished to drink more they should trade it, they did so all night

Teusday 17th March 1801. Cold, northerly wind, Dannis, Fra^s Roy, &. old Parrant sent off their wives as they are going to Swan River to make sugar the two former for themselves &. the later for me with whom I sent Petit Jean to help him.[48] I got 30 kegs filled with Grease, today, the Indians traded a few dress'd Buffaloe skins &. a little, very little, Pounded meat, for Ammunition &. Tobacco

Wednessday 18th. Fine weather, the Indians went off, I came to a determination of making the men attempt to make a Batteau, to send down by the Red river, as the Snow is so totally gone off I see it to be merely impossible to get all the effects here transported to Swan River. I have no person here that ever wrought at a boat, but I fancy among us we may be able to make some sort of thing to float at least, but as the River is so full of Shoals &. rapids from here to the Indian Elbow I ordered the men to carry all the kegs of grease down to Mr Sutherlands with Sledges &. I went down with them to get Mr Sutherland to Store them to which he chearfully consented. we passed the night there. I sent off Old Parrant to make sugar at Swan River. Dannis &. Fran^s Roy went off likewise.

Thursday 19th. The men &. I came back from the Elbow

---

[48] Sugar maples were rare as far north as the Swan River, but Monseigneur Taché speaks of a variety of maple peculiar to the country (*Negunda fruxinisolium*), from the sap of which sugar similar to that of sugar maple could be made. See his *Sketch of the North-West of America*, translated by Captain D. R. Cameron (Montreal, 1870), p. 24. Henry also mentions a bastard maple (*Negunda aceroides*) which grew on the Saskatchewan and furnished tolerably good syrup. Coues, *New Light*, 2:492.

in the forenoon, I found the people employed getting timber ready for the Batteau, &. Cadotte returned from his Bull hunting with nine Bull hides with which I mean to make Canoes. it is an unlucky thing for us the snow's melting so very precipitately. I got ten Iron hoops from Mr Sutherland which is very opportune, as I am at a loss for old Iron sufficient for the nails necessary for the Batteau.

Friday 20th. This is the finest day we have had this year. the snow deminishes very fast. I sent some of the men with loads to the Elbow. I have now sent 31 kegs grease &. 1 Bag Pimican down there, I sent Collin down there this morning with Hamickonitt's Debt account, as he has been Mr Sutherland's Hunter, & is about to be paid, to endeavor to get him to acknowledge his debt as in that case Mr Sutherland promised me to pay 30 skins value of the 71 that he still owes me. The people are very busy preparing Timbers &. planks for the Boat as is the Black smith Nails, he made two hundred, (with nine hoops) of 3½ In.

Saturday 21st March 1801. A very fine day, Collin, and the other men came back from the Elbow, Mr Sutherland wrote me he should pay me the thirty skin's value on his hunter's account

Sunday 22^d. Raining all day, the Old La Corn fine came here early in the morning, he brought a few pounds of dryed meat which he traded for Rum, but as he has been all winter at Riviere à la Cocquill I presume he still owes Mr Malhiot. I therefore gave him nothing to encourage him to return here. he is with the Barbue &. Six more tents two days march off. they have nothing at all according to his account; The rain has sunk the snow very much, the Hills and eminences are quite bare now. The Corn fine tells me the Buffaloe (Cows) are within two hours walk of the Fort.

Monday 23^d. I Sent off Cadotte, &. Frorsier, along with La Frenier, and old La Voye, for La Frenier's few Skins that he killed last fall. The men at the Fort are busy sawing &. preparing wood for the Boat. Demarrais is sick. Mr Sutherland sent up two of his men who arrived here before ten oClock A. M. he sent one up a mare &. a very fine Colt as the payment of the thirty skins he became responsible to pay for the Hunter, his men returned home directly. I sent him 40 wolves 20 Badgers, 2 Callico Shirts &. a white shirt with a Pack of Cards all which I barter with him for Cloth, Blankets, &. Guns, the wolves are none of the best, but the Badgers are still worse, yet he takes the 20 for ten Skins, whereas I should not be at the trouble of picking of[f] the dunghill, it rained incessantly from noon till sun sett.

Teusday 24th. The Corn fine went off, I did not even give him a bit of Tob^{co} or a shott of Amunition: The people are some at work at the Batteau wood, others at the Ice house, &. Demarrais still sick. the Snow thawed greatly this forenoon, but in the afternoon there fell six Inches at least in the short space of four hours.

Wednesday 25th. A very charming day, a great part of what snow fell yesterday melted. The people are busy at the Ice House. A young Cree came here in the evening (Falcon's brother in law) for medecines for his father he having been bit (in the leg) by a Dog, they are two days March off; The time approaches now that we must watch our horses as otherwise the Stone Indians will steal them in consequence of which I keep mine in the Fort day & night. Demarrais is very unwell, as is my Servant (Plante).

Thursday 26th March 1801. Not very warm, notwithstanding, a great part of the late Snow melted, Falcon's brother in law went off with a few Simples for his father's leg,[49] one of his brothers who passed the winter at Mr Perignés fort came here late in the evening, he brought us neither Furs, Provisions, or news; The People were busied putting up the Ice

[49] The clerks of the wintering posts were usually versed in the rudimentary principles of medicine as they were understood in that day. Bleeding was often used, and each post had its supply of simple medicines with which ordinary ailments could be cured and the misfortunes of common accident repaired.

House, the two men finished sawing the Battau wood as did the blackSmith the nails; rained a little this evening.

Friday 27th. A little snow fell early this morning, the men put up the Ice House, the others of them are working at the Batteau wood, Cut lip's widow came here late in the evening from Mr Perignés. She tells that the Ice is mostly all gone in Swan River: Joseph Fallardeau a Free Man came here from Riviere qui Appelle, he brought me a letter from M^r McDonell dated the 16th Ins^t wherein he tells me he expects I shall send him a bag of balls p[e]^r Fallardeau who intends making a Skin Canoe to drift down with the Ice in hopes of being able to kill a few Beaver, by the way, Demarrais &, Plante very little better

Saturday 28th. Cold, clear day, the people at their wonted occupations. Two Indians came here all the way from the spunk Hills with 6 Buffaloe Robes, only, one a Cree the other an Assinibouan. they slept 2 nights on the road. Falcon's brother in law went off to See his Father, to whom I sent a little healing plaister for his bit leg.

Sunday 29th. Cold, &. snowing. The Indians traded their robes for Tobacco, Bellile arrived from Mr Perignés ahorse back on old Le Fevre's Horse. Cleared up in the evening but continues still cold. Cadotte came home &. Frosier with 53 Plus & La Freniers.

Monday 30th. The Indians went away. I sent a bit of Tob^{co} For the Crapaud by the Batard Anglois to invite him to come to the House he has not been oppenly at any of our Forts since he killed B^{te} La France four years ago at Fort des Prairies, he may perhaps be led by a fatall security to come to see me which I very earnestly wish, he has been with that band of Indians most part of the winter. Snowed constanly from ten oClock A.M. untill the evening when it ceased &. the weather became much colder. I spoke to B^{te} Roy the Sauteau interpreter to pass the summer at some of the Posts of this department, for as he is free during the summer season he certainly when on the road gives all information in his power to the XY faction in return for a glass of Shrub or a drink of Grog, he consented to what I proposed

Teusday 31st. A very cold day snowing a little. Carron, Demarrais &. my Servant Plante are very unwell I gave the first a Vomite &. the later a doze of physic. Dauphiné mended the Fort gates today

Wednessday 1st April 1801. Mr Harmon went off this morning for the lower Fort there to remain untill the embarkation, Jauque went with him as he is to bring up the men's horses; the Tonnerre came here with a few pieces meat &. a few pounds of grease, soon after him arrived Oubitchigey who came for Cut Lip's widow. he brought nothing, this has been a very cold day, the people working at the Boat &. Ice House, &. Vallé riding home firewood

Thursday 2^d. Cold windy day, the Tonnerre went off, as did Bellile who left LeFevre's horse here. Two men came here from River à la Biche a horse back. they brought me a letter from M^r McGillis wherein he tells me contrary to all his former assertions that he shall [have] Blkts. &. strouds remaining on hand, but says he is in want of Rum &. silverworks with Wampum, the people finished the Ice house, but we cannot as yet get earth to cover or plaester it the ground being so hard froze

Friday 3^d. Verry cold. A band of Stone Indians came here. they seem to have a few, very few Robes, or wolves, they did not trade a sufficiency of liquor to intoxicate themselves. there is none among them that can either speak or understand the Cree tongue, so that we are necessitated to deal with them by signes, as there is no person here who understands their language, there are six men &. 12 women

Saturday 4th. Cold windy day, the Stone Indians traded but went not off, the Black Smith is working for M^r McGillis getting Guns mended &. axes made. Plante is still very unwell. I this evening gave a small cake (of flour) to two of the Stone Indians (one each) but they did not know what it was &. all our endeavours to prevail on them to eat them proved fruitless. they smelled &. tasted it but spit it imediately, &. they not understanding us we could not explain what it was but they put them up very carefully to carry to their tents where they may meet with some that may inform them what it is, it's very remarkable that in all directions there is no snow two leagues from the Fort &. all within that space is entirely covered.

Sunday 5th April 1801, Easter Sunday. A Cold, tho clear day the Stone Indians went off, we kept all the horses in the Fort all day except two poor lean horses, being apprehensive they should take it into their heads to prefer riding home to walking. Two men came here late in the evening from Shell River, with letters from Messrs Chaboillez, McDonell, &. George McKay who all &. severally complain of scarcity of Liquor, goods, &c. Mr McDonell in particular tells me he has only one Keg mixed Rum, in his house &. only half a roll Tobacco

Monday 6th April 1801. Cold &. blowing hard, the people are some cutting fire wood others hauling, some for Gum &. others working at the Batteau. Several of the people are ill with severe Colds. One of the Shell river men having brought his Violin with him the people danced all night.

Teusday 7th. Not so cold as usual. Blew fresh, a good deal of the snow thawed today, Lambert &. Beaulieu went off, I wrote Messrs McGillis, Harrison, &. Nolin by them.[50] I sent 15 steel Traps, Two horses &. a Colt, a short gun, with some other articles to River à la Biche. Cadotte killed a Swan today

Wednessday 8th. Far from being a warm day, Most of the People are ill with bad colds, the Batteau was finished today. Jacques &. &. [*sic*] the two Le Fevres arrived from the Lower Fort with the men's horses &. my black Horse. La Verdure sent up both his Horses for his boy &. some dryed meat as they catch no fish, they have already eat half a Bag Pimican, Mr Harmon writes me he found every thing in good order below.

[50] François Nolin was listed in 1799 as a clerk in the Fort Dauphin department. Masson, *Bourgeois*, 1:62.

the snow about here I believe is determined to remain with us, whilst all the Country round us has not a single spot remaining. Some of the men &. women danced this evening.

Thursday 9th. Thaws a great deal, the Red River men went away. I wrote Messrs McDonell &. Chaboillez, I sent the former 13½ Qts. High Wines altho' I have not much more remaining, rained in the evening. I saw some Geese today for the first time this season Swans are very numerous about the place, the Colds still rage in the Fort.

Friday 10th. A fine day, nothing either material, or new, reserve two of the men having fought a battle (L'orient, &. N. Ducharm) on account of the later's having played an inocent trick with the former, who had the worst of the Battle.

Saturday 11th. A very fine day, Old, &. Young Le Fevre went off, the former took a piece weight of salt Meat, &. a bag Pimican with his horse. the later took 360^{lb} of dryed meat with La Verdures Horses for themselves to eat at the lower Fort to prevent their eating any more of the Pimitigan [*sic*]. Young Le Fevre took La Verdure's little Boy down with him, the people covered &. plaistered the ice House. there is a great deal of water on the Ice in the river.

I gave Fallardeau (the free man) two Parchement Skins to make a Canoe with to drive down the Red River. I had Lemire getting ready wood to get two made for myself, to lighten the Batteau. I likewise sent 3 skins by old Le Fevre to Mr Perigné to get a Canoe Made to go down the Swan River. Collin is very ill with the tooth ache

Sunday 12th April 1801. A Beautifully fine day, very little snow remaining. Being the Lord's day the people were not at work.

Monday 13th. As charming a day as yesterday, Carron &. La Rose caulking the boat. Frisé made two kegs of Gum today.

The Jour d'Enfant, &. old [?] wife came here with a few bladders grease &. a little piece &. pounded meat. I gave him a qt. mixed rum, which was all he drunk, as he wishes to trade powder &. Ball with his Grease &c.

Teusday 14th. Raining &. Blowing fresh, so that the people could not go on with their work. A large band of Crees &. a few Stone Indians came here, vizt Frêne, Sauteau, North Wind, South Wind, Tabo, Jacco, &c. &c. in short the people of 60 Lodges. They got drunk, &. we had a few disputes with one or two but all ended well, a number of Indians from Fort des Prairies were along with them who say, Mr King told them to come on these lands, by M^r McDonald's orders as otherwise they should run the risk of being cut off by a large war party of Fall Indians who are on the look out for the Crees; the same Indians tell me that Mr Belleau was oblidged to abandon his Fort, &. that M^r McDonell was in a manner besieged by them &. expressed to Mr King in his letter to him great apprehension of his being pillaged &. perhaps murthered by the Fall Indians;[51] The Poor Old Chef des Canards was brought here on a sledge he being sick for this long time past, he is quite emaciated. Boisterous cold night, I watched all night

Wednessday 15th. All the Indians still drunk, we had a quarrel with the North wind owing to his having endeavoured to Stab one of my men. Mauvais mâle sett off with his things to the Elbow, as he generally trades with the eng-

---

[51] Pierre Belleau was in charge of the lower Fort des Prairies, which was situated on the Saskatchewan, probably near the forks northwest of Fort Alexandria, although Morice locates it near the present city of Edmonton. See Morice, *Dictionnaire historique*, p. 23, and page 98n. above.

The Fall or Rapid Indians were so named from the fact that they lived near the falls or rapids of the south branch of the Saskatchewan River. They lived for some years between the two branches of that river but later moved south and occupied the region between the south branch and the Missouri. The hostility of these Indians toward the whites in 1800–01 was aroused by the favored treatment that the traders had given the Cree and Assiniboine tribes. Harmon tells in his *Journal* of the strengthening of Fort Alexandria during the summer of 1801. Apparently the fear of attack dated back several months to early spring, and McLeod took pains to see that the defenses of the fort were put in good order before he left. See Harmon, *Journal*, p. 51; Coues, *New Light*, 2:530; and pages 178 and 183 below.

lish. Payet, &. La Plante came here from Fort Dauphin, they brought me a letter from Mitchel &. Ferguson. the[y] sent the bearers with 2 horses for stds. &. Blkts. they inform me that Cardain has not more than 40 Beavers at Fort Dauphin &. only 80 at Turtle River including the Nipisang's hunt. I put a stop to the drinking match about twelve oClock A. M. a Raw boisterous day, raining &. snowing by intervals. The Day child went off.

Thursday 16th. A Cold, ugly day, the Indians began to trade in the Shop, it's surprising the quantity of Tobacco they trade. The river is quite free from ice here &. the water seems to be high.

Friday 17th. Raining &. blowing. Most off the Indians went off. La Couture arrived here from the River Qui Appelle. M^r McDonell sent him for Tob^{co} of which article he writes me he has not Six pounds in his house. the Mauvais Mâle came back with all his skins from the Elbow, as Sutherland told him he had neither Tobacco or Rum altho' he found himself quite drunk. he traded all his furs here. Two of the Bras Courts young sons came here early in the morning, one of them has lately come from River à la Biche. he brought me a letter from M^r McGillis, but no news. I sent La Comble &. Roy off a horse back imediately along with the boys to go for the old man's skins &. those of the young Premier. I sent them 2½ qts high wines

Saturday 18th April 1801. Still raining or rather drizling all day. all the Indians went off, I gave a few C^{rs}[?] to some of those I know best.^{52} I lent a Gun to the Petite Roche, as he tells me he does not go to war. I purchased 4 Lodges from this last band; I put up about a bale of Stds. &. blkts. for Fort Dauphin with 30^{lb} shott &. wrote Ferguson &. Mitchel.

Sunday 19th. A fine day, Payet, &. La Plante sett off as did La Couture by whom I wrote M^r McDonell &. sent him 60^{lb}

---

^{52} The manuscript is difficult to decipher, but it seems clear from the context that McLeod "gave a few credits" to the Indians whom he knew best.

Tobacco. I sent Demarrais to the Montaigne des Oiseaux for La France &. Cadieu as they have horses to help to bring down some of the effects at this place to the Elbow. Fallardau, went off with his small skin Canoe, Cut finger came here from the Elbow, he has nothing whatever to trade, he says he means to return to Swan River, we made 30 bags Pimican

Monday 20th. A fine day, the people busy getting the skin Canoes &. Batteau ready, a small band of Crees &. Stone Indians came here, Cut finger went off to the Elbow for his Lodge & family

Teusday 21st. The Little band of Indians traded what Robes, wolves &. provisions they brought, we made what few Packs we have here, up today vizt 30, in the evening 2 Stone Indians &. a Cree came here for Tobacco, as a very large band of both Crees &. Stone Indians are to be here tomorrow, they slept here. The Poor old Indian (Chef des Canards) is exceedingly ill today

Wednessday 22d. The band of Indians arrived, I gave them all half a pint each to drink on arrival, vizt 39 men, they afterwards traded some, the[y] dan[c]ed &. Sung a considerable time, the Old Bras Court & family came here likewise, but I did not suffer them to drink with the others. I was forced to buy a horse from one of the Crees for 16 half pints of liquor mixed at 4 qts. to the large. Demarrais, La France, &. Candieu came from the Montaigne des Oiseau, they tell me that Bellile is gone with my letter to Mr Harmon to the Lower Fort. this is a very warm day. the men finished gumming the boat and Canoes, &. are ready to be off tomorrow

Thursday 23^d. A very fine day I sent off, the boat &. the two skin Canoes, the former loaded with 36 Pieces &. the 2 later 12 P^{cs} each, 4 men in the boat &. 2 in each of the Canoes. All the Indians danced &. Traded today & the greater part of them went off. Cut finger came from the Elbow with his lodge &c. The Jour d'Enfant &. his Lodge arrived here, in the evening.

Friday 24th. A Cold Boisterous day, all the Crees &. Stone

Indians went off, &. I gave the Jeune Premier &. Bras Court what little rum I kept for them. the former I Clothed altho' he only made a present of ten skins as M^r McGillis promised it to him last fall, we got about 50 Robes this trip &. 300 bladders of Grease. the Old Chef de Canard's son remained with his father.

Saturday 25th Ap^l *1801*. A Cloudy, raw day I went down with all the horses &. men with 14 Bags pimican, at the same time to carry the grease &c. that I lodged at Mr Sutherland's to the old houses at the Elbow to embark in the boat and Canoes, on arrival at the Elbow Mr Sutherland informed me the boat &c. passed yesterday morning, I sent a part of the pieces across but remained at Mr Sutherlands all night myself.

Sunday 26th. I got the pieces over early, &. went over to give them their loadings after breakfast. I put 14 kegs grease &. 5 Traureux into Cadottes Canoe, &. 19 kegs Grease &. 2 Traureaux into Dauphine's Canoe, in the Batteau I put 30 Packs, 34 Bags Pimican, 6 Bags salt meat 1 Cassette, besides pounded meat &. grease, &. dryed piece meat to bring the three men to the P^t au Foutre.[53] Dauphiné, Forsier, &. Jacques are to return from River Qui Appelle, as I have a Good Canoe there wherein they are to embark 30 pieces of the load of the two skin Canoes, &. the remaining ten in the boat. I bought ten of the bags of Pimican that I sent off from Mr Sutherland each 90^{lb} weight at 8 (bad) wolves a piece, after I sent off the men from the Elbow I returned to Mr Sutherland's &. thence home; It began to snow soon after I got home, I found, the Poor old Chef des Canards very low, the Seauteaux still here, as well as the Day child; Old Chauvin, Bellile, &. Le Fevre arrived with the Horses from Swan River, I had a few lines from Mr Harmon but nothing new, this is a very boisterous cold night, ten oClock at night.

Monday 27th. Cold, &. Snowing, the Chef des Canard died about 12 oClock today. I was in the Lodge when he expired,

---

[53] A *cassette* was a kind of box or basket, fitted out to be carried on the back. See *Glossaire du parler français au Canada*, p. 178.

he departed without a struggle or groan, he was quite exhausted, by his disorder which was a Dropsy. I spoke to the Jour d'Enfant, to induce him to remain here abouts all Summer which he promises to do.

Blows amazingly hard for these many days past, freezes hard tonight

Teusday 28th. This has been a most stormy, boisterous, day. none of the Snow melted, owing to the extreme coldness of the weather. We got the Corps interred, according to their rites. I clothed it with a chiefs cloathing, vizt coat, shirt, Hatt, &. Trowsers.

Wednessday 29th. A better day than any we have had for this week past tho' not warm; The Old deceased Cheff des Canard's wife &. Daughters came here. I gave them the ten qts. of mixed rum I kept for them, they lamented, & bellowed, all night. Mr Sutherland sent up one of his men for 60 wolves I traded with him for blankets cloth &c.

Thursday 30th. A very fine day, I lent a horse to the Orkney man to carry home his wolves. Sent La Comble &. B^{te} Roy for some pounded meat the Bras Court &. young Premier left behind them &. which I paid them for; I got 6 Packs of robes, Dressed skins, kitts &c. &c. made up today, dryed the pounded meat in the Sun, & made the women smoak &. dry the piece meat which was getting mouldy. one of the Sons in law of the Chef des Canards arrived from the plains with an adopted son of the old man's (a Slave) [54]

Friday 1st May 1801. A very fine day, Mr Sutherland sent up my horse by one of his men, &. 4 empty kegs with Iron hoops, La Comble &. B^{te} Roy came back with the pounded meat. I sent off Frisé, La France, Bellile, Le Fevre, &. 4 of my horses loaded with the 6 Packs, a keg marrow fat &. a bag of salted &. dryed tongues, &. Bosses; I wrote Mr Harmon to

---

[54] "A Slave" might mean either that the old man had adopted one of the captives whom he had made a slave or that he had taken a Slave Indian as an adopted son. For a note as to the tribes included in the latter designation see Coues, *New Light*, 2:523.

send up Fra^s [François] Roy &. an other man with the horses that remained below; The Indians are eating our provisions very fast, two old women with a number of children came here from the Frain's camp, &. the Cut finger and the Petit Crapaud came from an other large Camp two days march off. the Cut finger had been alone on a visit there, those that are arrived report that the vestiges of numerous bands of Fall Indians have been seen in different places, who are in search of the Crees &. Stone Indians, in hopes of meeting with detached parties of them to cut them off. I sent some men to keep the Horses on the north side of the River as the Grass is all ate up on this side. Mr Sutherland's man returned home again.

Saturday 2^d. A Rainy boisterous day, it rained incessantly all night, one of the HB. C$^{o'}$^{s} Men came here all the way from Shell river in order to get bled, as he is plagued with pains in his arms &c. which he insists is owing to a superabundance of blood. I had a few lines from Mr Sutherland by, him; he tells me he met my people one Wednessday half way between the Old Fort at the Elbow, &. River Tremblante Fort, they had then passed the worst part of the road;[55] late in the evening Jacco the Cree Bastard, came here with his wives, children, &. baggage. he says he himself has seen the vestiges of some Fall Indians not two days journey from here which, partly is the reason of his comming to the Fort so soon; he intends he says to pass the Summer here about

This night the House was filled with women & children who were affraid to sleep in their lodges, on account of the rumours abroad about the Fall Indians.

Sunday 3^d. Snowing, &. blowing, all the forenoon cleared up &. fine weather in the afternoon. I bled the HBay man today &. gave him some camphorated spirits of wine to rub his arms with, I lent him a horse to carry him home as he is very unwell. The women came in to the Fort again to night.

---

[55] The River Tremblante flowed into the Assiniboine from the east at a point several miles below Mr. Sutherland's post.

Monday 4th. I went down to the Elbow to settle finally about the Wolves I sold Sutherland, this is a fine day, I slept at the Elbow, I exchanged a fine Gun of the C$^{o's}$ for a H. B. Gun with a Bayonette

Teusday 5th. Came home in the afternoon, found Plante very ill in bed, the yellow Forehead (a cree) came here, he says his family are near here, he means to pass the summer about the Fort, snow &. sleet by turns all day. La Frenier came here late at night (The free man)

Wednessday 6th May 1801. A Cold Serene day, the people busy at the Bastions &. squaring timber for a block house. I mean to leave the Fort in a good state of defence, in case the Fall Indians should visit it. The Deceased Chef des Canard's son & son in law went off to join the war party, the Yellow forehead, &. Roche de bout with their families came to camp here, they are all in great dread of the Fall Indians; La Frenier tells me he &. old La Voye have only killed 25 Beaver since they left here, he is come now for some of the mens horses for the summer; in fact his conduct during the winter &. spring convinces me he is a trifler.

Thursday 7th. Not so cold as usual, I sent Demarrais to the Elbow for some empty Kegs, &. Iron hoops, with other old Iron works that Mr Sutherland agreed to leave there for me, he came back in the evening; he says Mr Sutherland only left there early this morning; I got 32 Bags of Pimican made today, which compleats the number 125 made here &. ten I bought, or rather bartered with Mr Sutherland. Some more old women came to the Fort today. I prevailed on Jacco, Cut Finger, Roche de Boute, Jour d'Enfant, &. Yellow Forehead, to sett off to look for Beaver, they are to go off tomorrow; If a fine day.

Friday 8th. A Raw morning began to rain &. blow about ten oClock which continued all day. Forsier, Dauphiné, &. Jacques, whom I sent down with the Batteau &. Skin Canoes came back, they came up with the River à la Cocquill men, the night of the 6th Inst. half way between River Qui Appelle

&. shell river they having left the later place the same day, one of the red river Boats took Dauphine's &. Forsier's Canoe load, which ennabled them to return, &. the rest proceeded on yesterday, as they did on their return. The Indians did not go off, owing to the bad weather. I gave the Chef de Canard's widow to the Am^t of 28 Plus, &. took the Slave Woman, whom next Fall I shall sell for a good price to one of the men. She was wife to the Deceased old man.

Saturday 9th. Raining, &. sleet all day, &. blowing very hard all the Houses in the Fort leaked considerably. The Indians could not go off, five of the Hudson's bay people's dogs came here this evening. The men preparing to be off Monday for S. River

Sunday 10th. Still raining, &. Cold the water is remarkably high, &. all the low ground hereabout is entirely deludged.

Monday 11th. Still very bad weather, the water rising very fast, snowed today. I weighed the grease that remains, vizt 2900^{lb} or 37 kegs. the people could not go off today owing to the badness of the day. Nabess, Perignés Hunter came here today he left his Lodge the other side of the river

Teusday 12th May 1801. A Cold, cloudy, day, Snowed &. rained a little all day, the Day Child pitched off, towards the source of the Swan River the other Indians are doing nothing at all nor can they be prevailed on to leave the Fort; The Men made a raft to cross the River as the water is extremely high, and far from decreasing it still increases.

Wednessday 13th. A fine day, I sent off all the people, &. Horses loaded with Pimican, grease, &. my baggage &c. I am astonished &. uneasy at Roy, or somebody's not making their appearance from Swan River with the Horses from there according to my orders. I at long last prevailed on the few Indians at the Fort to cross the River &. follow the Day-Child; The Petit Mâl accompanied by Roy's step-son left this for the plains with an intention of buying or stealing horses from the Stone Indians, the former sent his wife along with the Indians who are gone towards the Source of the Swan River; In the evening it rained &. got cold weather.

Thursday 14th. A windy, cloudy, &. in the afternoon, a rainy day — Jacco returned here early this morning early, for a Gun he having burst his own yesterday firing at Red Deer, he reports the water is so excessively high that all the plains &. in particular those bordering on Lakes and rivers are overflowed, which is far from being favorable for the beaver hunt, the water has risen 3 feet perpendicular since yesterday; Petit Mâl &. Picquaquit came back, in the evening, the Rivers are so high they could not cross them, independent of which they were affraid of meeting with a Party of Fall Indians who, it is reported are hovering about

Friday 15th. A fine day, although it rained a little in the evening. The stuttering man came here, *bag* &. *baggage* from, Mr Perignés. the Day-Child's son came from the plains, to follow the other Indians and his father, he informs us that before he left the Montaigne du Tondre, the Crapaud had returned with thirty Horses he stole at the Fort des Prairies Forts. The Stutterer tells me that my people were till this morning at the little River three leagues only from here where they made a raft to cross. I took the inventory of all the effects here as I despair of the comming of the people from below.

Saturday 16th. Raining untill half Past ten, about Eleven oClock I left Alexandria accompanied, by Collin &. my slave boy Jack all three on horse back, we took the Elbow road supposing it the best. we made a raft on the little River, which we crossed, we slept on the banks of the Swan River, supperless. I killed a Pole-cat this evening, previous to leaving the Fort, I traded twelve Beavers from the *Beggué* &. sent him &. the Day child's son to follow the others who crossed the River. I left La Comble Bte Roy, Girardin &. Jacque (*Maron*) to take care of the fort.

Sunday 17th May 1801. We sett off as soon as it was light to follow the people who could not cross at the usual crossing place of the S. River the water being so extremely high that all the points were entirely under water, &. never did I see such heavy roads, as we passed through. our light horses had great difficulty to draw their legs out of the Mire, it rained, thundered, &. lightened at a terrible rate untill noon when we came up with the men at the entrance of the large Plain, soon after we got up with the people the weather cleared up &. we sett off all in a band, but we soon were stopt by a River that runs from the South Mountain, which is very rapid &. at present very deep, we made a Raft, &. by the help of lines on either side we crossed our loads, an hour before Sun-sett we pitched for the night at the Eastern extremity of the Plains

Monday 18th. A very boisterous morning, we passed, through hills &. bogs incessantly for three leagues before we got to M[r] Perigne's which we reached before noon, when the weather got very fine; we crossed our effects with a small wooden Canoe, we took three additional Horses at M[r] Perignes with what good &. Furs remained there. I immediately dispatched Bellile on my arrival with a few lines for M[r] Harmon, requesting him to send a large Canoe to meet us from Swan River, but my Messenger did not go far having met three men who with three others M[r] Harmon sent off with a large Canoe the 15[th] Ins[t] to proceed as far up the river as possible to meet me, but by the Hieght of the water &. badness of the Canoe they could get no higher up than the place called the Drap rouge. after crossing over the Swan River we were under the necessity to make a brid[g]e over an other small but deep River, it is really incredible the quantity of water in every brook, creek, &. even in the road. We put up at the Prairie de Travers to night where we found excellent grazing for our Horses.

Teusday 19[th]. Fine weather. We got to the Canoes, (Le Fevre having made one of Parchement) a couple of hours before Sun set, &. it was full time as most of the Horses were very much fatigued.

Our men caught a great many Carps in the rapids of which we ate a hearty supper, the men tell me the Houses at Swan

River had two feet water on their floors, when the water rose, &. that they had not a Dry bit of ground, within three or four leagues of the Fort all round the overflowing of the River having laid all underwater.

Wednessday 20th. I embarked in the Bark or Large Canoe well loaded &. the people drove the Horses, for the[y] could not ride, I left three men with the Skin Canoe to wait for Mr Perigné as he is comming down with a wooden one. we crossed the people at the two different crossing places, &. got to the Fort late in the evening, where the River still overflows the banks, &. there is water on the House flour as yet; I found neither the Canoes begun, nor the press in order as I had directed, for which I did not blame Mr Harmon, he being not fully acquainted with the requisites for both.

Thursday 21st May 1801. A finer day than usual, I got the people to work at the Canoes, sent some to fish likewise, the evening brought us rain &. high wind the constant act [sic] from which it blows is the North

Friday 22d. Cold &. blowing hard, the people could not do much to the Canoes, sent people to fish, tho' the water is so high that they have very little success, rained again this evening not A fair day from one end to the other have we. Mr Perigné &. the people I left to wait for him arrived, I arranged the furs in the room to air as they are very damp, Mr Harmon is employed marking coverings

Saturday 23d. A fine morning, La Verdure began the second new Canoe, altho' we have but poor bark for both, we take very few fish, Dannis finished mending the two other Canoes. Rained most part of this night, the wind always northerly.

Sunday 24th. Cold, windy, weather, I settled with Boiselle to remain here for the Summer at his own request he being unwell. the people worked but very little at the Canoes owing to the invariable coldness of the weather, Mr Harmon writing his letters

Monday 25th. A very fine day, I made up the furs into

Packs, vizt 50 here &. 30 sent via red River = 80. I got Collin, to head, hoop, &. secure fourteen kegs of Grease, I purchased Mr Perignée's Furs

Teusday 26th. I sent off Dannis, with two Canoes loaded with 26 Pieces to make a trip to the Isle à la M[or]de, as we should not be able to carry off everything here at once, the men who remained here Worked at the Canoes, as much as the weather would permit. Thunder, &. Lightening, with prodigious down pours of Hail, & rain, all night, the wind in the old point.

Wednessday 27th. I sent off, Mr Harmon, Collin, Old Parant, &. Fran^s Roy for Allexandria to pass the Summer there, the motive that induces me to leave so many people in land at that Port, is the apprehensions entertained of a Visit from the Fall Indians, & at any event I do not see the necessity of burthening Canoes out and in with either Clerks or Interpreters, &. I presume provisions can be as cheaply provided for them at Alexandria as any where else; I sent people to fish but they had no Success. Rained all this day, &. night the people could do nothing to the Canoes, the wind still North.

Thursday 28th. Cold, raining, &. very disagreeable day, I got one of the New Canoes taken in to the House & a large fire made to render the Bark pliable in order to be sewed.

Friday 29th. Raining in the morning, the Barré, came here today he brought me about 30 Beavers, for which I gave him a Callicoe shirt &. my great coat, &. about 8 Pints mixed Rum. Rained in the evening, with thunder & lightening

Saturday 30th May 1801. Cold morning about ten oClock the Canoes that I sent to the Island arrived &. four of the R. L. [Rivière à la] Biche men along with them, they brought me a letter from M^r McGillis who informs me he has made 60 Packs independent of the Iroquois' Packs which may am^t to 23. his letter was dated the 24th Ins^t &. then he had not left his fort, the men tell me that La Bonne deserted at the Middle River to return to the Fort, he was very sick &. had almost shott off one of his fingers. came on to rain very heavyly from noon untill midnight without intermission so that the people could not finish the Canoes

Sunday 31st. Cleared up about 7 oClock A. M. & I sent off the Canoes about one oClock P. M., I took the Inventory of the effects remaining at S. River & gave Perigné orders to build a Store &. dwelling room on the most raised spot he could find about the Fort. I sent Boiselle &. Petit Jean off in a small Canoe to go to the Island in case I should have any thing to send back from there; Jabouran (the young Foutrau) arrived from Lac La course soon after the Canoes went off. the Beggue &. the cut finger are both there &. I fancy will return to Swan River.[56]

I left the Fort about half past three P. M. & I overtook the Canoes at the head of the Middle river where we encamped.

I Left 3 Bags Pimican to Perigné &. 2 kegs grease.

Monday 1st June 1801. I got to the Isle à la Morde at 8 oClock A. M. where I found Messrs McGillis Harrison, Nolin & all the River La Biche Men &. two Iroquois that hired themselves to go &. come to &. from G. P. [Grand Portage]. Mr L'Etang &. a Couple of his Clerks with only his own Canoe I found here likewise, — the scarcity of men oblidged Mr McGillis to determine along with myself that we should go out in the same Canoe &. as his Canoe is the best we take it but retain the men of mine. We settled the Canoes &. their loadings they are only 3 men to a Canoe from this to Fort Dauphin, & severall Middle men are oblidged to steer I gave charge of the Brigade to Harrison to whom I gave sugar & Provisions for his Voyage out. Mr McGillis had some wine remaining with which I made Old L'Etang very Drunk, finding we should be heavily loaded & lumbered I lent L'Etang 6 Bags Pimican to be returned at Bas de la Riviere, I had two motives to induce me to be so uncommonly accommodating,

[56] Foutreau was another name for the *vison* or mink of the Northwest. Lac la Course may perhaps be Bank Lake, which lay on the route to Athabasca between Portage de Traite and Buffalo Lake. See the map in Thompson, *Narrative*.

THE DIARY OF ARCHIBALD N. McLEOD 185

first the debarassing my own Canoes of so many pieces, next that those six pieces with what he has in his Canoe already will load it so much that, he cannot go on faster than my loaded Canoes, M^r McGillis has eighty nine Packs in all here including the Iroquois Packs

Teusday 2^d June 1801. I sent Boiselle &. Petit Jean off as soon as day light appeared, I sent back a keg of H. Wines, one half of which I sent Perigné word to keep. I likewise sent back the small keg of powder I brought from Alexandria. I wrote Mr Harmon p^r Boiselle, M^r McGillis &. I embarked together & we got against a strong head wind to the entrance of the Bark Island channels it rained all this night, with Thunder &. lightening.

Wednessday 3^d. Raining &. blowing all day, we could not stir

Thursday 4th. We left our encampment early & got in the evening to the entrance of the Middle River of Fort Dauphin where Mr Ferguson Left a Note at Pointe à la Biche (,where by the by I ordered the Canoes to meet me,) to inform me he was, but we found nobody here, we made a large fire & fired off some Guns in case they might be gone to the Point au Lille on the opposite side of the Lake, somebody answered our Guns, but I was in hopes all night of seeing any of my people that might be there across.[57] My foreman is very unwell to night we gave a Qte of Syrup to the men to eat with the Pimican

[57] Pointe à la Biche is Red Deer Point in Lake Winnipegosis.

THE DIARY
OF HUGH FARIES

The Diary of Hugh Faries

Introductory Note

It is by no means certain that the author of this anonymous diary was Hugh Faries; it may possibly have been written by another trader, Thomas McMurray. The Northwest Company's list of proprietors, clerks, and *engagés* for the year 1805 names the following clerks for the Rainy Lake district: Archibald McLellan, Thomas McMurray, Hugh Faries, William McCrae, Charles Charoux, Louis Chenette, and Louis Guilmont. The last three are included with the ordinary *engagés* and so almost certainly would not have had the authority that the author of this diary obviously had. Moreover, Chenette and Guilmont are often mentioned in the diary. McLellan, McCrae, and a certain "Thomas" are also mentioned, and hence it is hardly likely that any one of these is the author. It is uncertain whether the Thomas mentioned was Thomas McMurray or Thomas Tiosaragointé, apparently an Iroquois voyageur. The evidence seems to point slightly more to the Indian than to the Scotchman, but it is impossible to come to a definite conclusion because first and last names seldom appear together in the diary.

Little is known of either McMurray or Faries. In 1806 both men were still at the Rainy Lake post. A "Mr. Faries" was left by the great explorer Simon Fraser at his fort in the mountains when he set out in 1808 to investigate the course of the river that now bears his name. In 1816 a "Mr. Faries" was involved in the trouble between Lord Selkirk and the Northwest Company at the posts about the headwaters of the Mississippi. In 1817 Hubert Faille, a voyageur, reported in a sworn statement regarding this same trouble that he met "Messrs. Stuart, Fraser, Thomson, et Ferris" on this side of the Rat Portage. The similarity of sound between Ferris and Faries, especially in the mouth of a French Canadian, is striking. Indeed, Elliott Coues considers them one and the same name, for in his index to his *New Light on the Early History of the Greater Northwest* he reports that Hugh Feries or Ferris, " being probably Hugh Faries," was at Cumberland House with Mr. J. Thompson on June 12, 1812. In 1846 a Hugh Faries was the trader in charge of Fort George on the Fraser River.[1]

As for Thomas McMurray, a man of this name was also mentioned several times in the evidence presented at the trials resulting from the troubles between Lord Selkirk and the Northwest Company. After the death of Governor Semple it was Thomas McMurray, " a clerk of the North-West Company," who searched the trunks of the slain man at the direction of an enemy *bourgeois.* In other places in the same documents he is referred to as a partner of the Northwest Company. In 1830 a Thomas McMurray is listed as chief trader for the Hudson's Bay Company at Rainy Lake post; and in 1839 James Evans, a missionary to the Northwest Indians, found a Mr. McMurray in charge of Hudson's Bay Company's post at the Pic on the northern shore of Lake Superior.[2]

It matters little, however, who was the author, since he was obviously in charge only when his superior, McLellan, was absent. The latter had under his direction the posts of a wide

[1] For these references to Faries see Louis R. Masson, *Les bourgeois de la Compagnie du Nord-Ouest* (Quebec, 1889), 1:221; [John Halkett], *Statement Respecting the Earl of Selkirk's Settlement upon the Red River in North America: Its Destruction in 1815 and 1816; and the Massacre of Governor Semple and His Party* (London, 1817), p. 101; House of Commons, *Papers Relating to the Red River Settlement, 1815–1819* (London, 1819), p. 75; Father Pierre Jean de Smet, " Oregon Missions and Travels over the Rocky Mountains, in 1845–46," in Reuben G. Thwaites, *Early Western Travels,* Vol. 29 (Cleveland, 1906), p. 276.

[2] See *Papers Relating to the Red River Settlement,* pp. 195, 199, 239, 240; E. H. Oliver, ed., *The Canadian North-West, Its Early Development and Legislative Records* (Ottawa, 1914), p. 643. Copies of Evans' manuscripts are in the collections of the Minnesota Historical Society.

area, an area then hotly contested by the X. Y. Company and by the author's employers. This region included the main post, or depot, at Rainy Lake, and the sub-posts at Mille Lacs, Eagle Lake, Clay Lake, and the Dalles of the Winnipeg in Canada, as well as Vermilion Lake and Lake of the Woods on the boundary waters. Lake of the Woods was in turn divided into the post of that name and those of its west and east bays, then termed Lac Plat and Whitefish Lake.

The Rainy Lake post was of special significance, for it was here that the Athabasca brigades, famous among voyageurs as the hardiest of all Nor'westers, ended their journeys, the trip to Fort William and return being too long for a summer season. This explains the frequent references in the diary to the "Athabasca House," within the stockade. Special brigades of canoemen from Montreal also made the post the terminus of their voyage. Instead of returning to their city from Fort William, as did the other "pork-eaters" or summer men, these voyageurs carried their freight over the height of land and on to the Rainy Lake fort, where they exchanged it for the packs of beaver and other furs from the Athabasca posts.

The fort was situated on the north side of Rainy River, high above the stream, which in a series of falls and rapids forms the outlet of Rainy Lake. It was one of the oldest in the entire Northwest, a post having been continuously in the vicinity, so far as can be learned, since 1731, when La Vérendrye's men established a fort there. In 1804–05 it was a focus for the competition between the rival companies, the Northwest Company and the X. Y. Company. On January 12, 1805, as recorded in the diary entry for that day, a messenger arrived with news of the merging of the two companies. Before that time much of the activity at the fort was directed toward the capture of all possible furs from the rival fort, which was operating under the direction of one Lacombe at a point nearer the lake. The countryside along the entire course of Rainy River, eighty-five miles in length, has aroused exclamations of delight from travelers and traders since it was first opened to commerce by the white man. Thus an Englishman writing about fifteen years after the period of the diary says of Rainy River, "The Lapluie seems made for a pleasure excursion, all is serenity and beauty." [3]

The fort itself seems to have been a large one. The diary mentions several buildings within the picket stockade. Besides the Athabasca House there was a "new house," built during the course of the winter, small houses, a cooper's house, a stable, and an ice house. The quarters for the men were apparently comfortable, for there are references to an oven, and to beds in the buildings. Some idea of the defenses of the post has been given by Macdonell's reference to the bastions flanking the gates. Further details are given by Bigsby, who was there a few years later: "The fort is a set of timber dwelling-houses, stores, stabling, &c., forming a hollow square, protected by strong picketing and heavy gates. Near to these last is a small hole in the picket, through which to pass articles in unsafe times. High above all is a wooden platform, ascended by a ladder, and used as a look-out." [4] The gardens, and the use of domestic animals should also be noted.

Here some forty men were located at the time when the diary was written. Probably not more than thirty regarded it as their residence, however, for several *engagés* mentioned by the diarist seem to have been at the post only temporarily, usually as messengers from other forts. Besides the men there were Indian or half-breed women, partners of the clerks and men, and also younger members of the community, the offspring of these irregular unions. The author's consort presented him with a dusky daughter during the season covered by the diary, and at least one other birth is recorded.

From early days the fort had been the center of canoe-making for a wide area, for the canoe birch, which did not grow in all localities, was here abundant. One of the men,

[3] John J. Bigsby, *The Shoe and Canoe, or, Pictures of Travel in the Canadas* (London, 1850), 2:271.
[4] Bigsby, *Shoe and Canoe*, 2:272. See also page 104 above.

"old Amelle," was hired primarily, it would seem, to make canoes. The frames for ninety canoes were constructed by him, according to one entry in the diary. There were also a cooper and a carpenter among the men. Probably the cooper's main task was to prepare barrels for the wild rice gathered in the swamps and lakes and for the corn raised in the garden of the fort or brought in by Indians. Some may have been used for the fish caught in the river and lake. The fishery at the post is mentioned by numerous travelers, and its importance is revealed in the frequent references to it in the present journal.

Cutting, hauling, squaring, and sawing of lumber are often mentioned, for two new buildings and a stable were being erected. Horses were employed for hauling the logs, pitsaws were constructed, and other evidences of an economy that was fairly advanced for a wilderness settlement are to be found in the diary. Five thousand shingles were split, surely innovations, for fur-trading establishments ordinarily used great sheets of bark as "covering" for the roofs. Other products of this group of versatile men included fish seines, wooden canoes, dog or horse traineaux, wheelbarrows, traps, and snowshoes. The work was planned so that everyone was busy. Obviously the diarist was a good administrator.

The long days of work were relieved by diversions and amusements in which the voyageurs found whole-hearted enjoyment. Dances, frequently held on Sunday evenings, are mentioned again and again. There was a special celebration on New Year's Day, as was customary among French Canadians. Even feuds were forgotten during festivities; the deadly rivals of the two companies played together and their clerks dined together on Sundays, just as though they did not on other occasions use bodily violence to gain the ascendancy in the gathering of furs.

The Indians who came and went are mentioned not as objects of curiosity but as other men, customers with whom the clerk did business. About thirty are mentioned by name, and picturesque names they were: the Liar, the Pines, Big Rat, the young Toad, the Blackbird, the Dog's Head, the Devil, the Blacksmith. These and many others whose names are given only in French move through the pages of the diary. It is only contemporary narratives of this sort that give one any real understanding of the Indian. Endless descriptions produce but a pale image of the aborigine as compared with the colors that such a contemporary manuscript can bring out.

The journal is printed by courtesy of the Public Archives of Canada, where the original is deposited. No change has been made in the manuscript except that an occasional period has been added where inadvertently omitted by the author. The letter *d*. ("deleted") indicates words struck out by the diarist. Instead of annotating all the references to canoemen, guides, and interpreters, it has been thought better to reproduce two sheets of a list of employees of the Northwest Company in the Masson Papers in the McGill University Library.[5]

G. L. N.

[5] A few names on this list are not mentioned specifically in the diary. One of these is the fifth on the list, François Bonnin. It is interesting to note that after serving the Northwest Company for fifteen years, he settled near the fort on Rainy River, where he was living in 1817. He had a farm there, and from its produce he gave some potatoes to certain agents of the Hudson's Bay Company who were in dire want. This humane act aroused James Leith, a partner of the Northwest Company, who threatened to turn Bonnin out of his farm and to banish him to Montreal. *Papers Relating to the Red River Settlement*, p. 236.

The Diary

Sunday, July 29th 1804. About 2 oclock in the afternoon, after taking leave of the Gentlemen at Kamanitiquiac, M^r McLellan and I embarked for Lac La Pluie, passed the Swan River canoes who were encamp'd at the Petit Marais and at 8 oclock encamp'd at the foot of the Rapids.[1]

Monday 30th. In the morning the men returned from the Barrier where they had been up with a demie charge, we walked up to the Paresseux after Breakfast, which we reached at 12 oclock. the men came up with a demie charge a short

[1] Faries and his chief, Archibald McLellan, had just set off for Rainy Lake, where the latter served the Northwest Company as the principal clerk of the department. The traders had spent the early part of the summer participating in the business conferences and also in the feasting and *cameraderie* that always marked the annual gathering of the Northwesters at the company's inland headquarters on Lake Superior. Grand Portage had formerly been the seat of these festivities, but in later years the Canadian fur trade had been complicated by a threat that the United States government might collect customs at the lower end of the canoe trail, and the Canadian company had seen fit to remove its rendezvous in 1803 to a point on British soil. The new depot, soon to be called Fort William, was situated at the mouth of the Kaministiquia River, the terminus of an old French canoe route which had been rediscovered by Roderic Mackenzie in 1798 and which was being opened up and used in preference to the Grand Portage trail (which it joined at Lac la Croix) because it lay wholly within British territory. See above, page 102n. In August there was a general dispersion of traders and voyageurs from the rendezvous to their respective wintering posts.

Several days ahead of our two traders was Alexander Henry, Jr., whose account of the trip back to his Pembina post is found in Elliott Coues, *New Light on the Early History of the Greater Northwest: The Manuscript Journals of Alexander Henry and of David Thompson, 1799–1814* (New York, 1897), 1:247–250. The Fort des Prairies canoes and the Athabasca brigade were also on the trail and the Lake Winnipeg brigade was only a short distance ahead of the Rainy River canoes, some of which had been sent on in advance by their chief. The Swan River men traveled along with the Rainy River outfit, and the latter also encountered François Nolin and Lapointe of the Fort Dauphin department. While the wintering traders pushed north-

time after us.² they set off after dinner for the Barrier, and return'd about 8 oclock with the last demie charge. they saw the Swan River canoes, who were encamp'd one decharge below us. here we remain'd all night. Cloudy weather.

Tues-day 31st. About ½ after eight, the Swan River Canoes came up with us. our canoe arrived at the same time, having been up to the dead water, with a demie charge. After breakfast we walked up to the dead water — met a canoe with 4 men a little above the paresseux from Lac des chiens. they told us that the Lac Oui^e [Winnipeg] Canoes were at the Portage des chiens. we arrived at the dead water at ¾ past eleven. after we had dined & the canoe gummed we embarked the whole of the loading & proceeded about 1½ leagues. we then walked up to the Mountain which we reached by 5 oclock, and the canoe arrived at Six.³ La Verdure

ward into the interior, the pork-eaters prepared for their return voyage to Montreal, and Faries met groups of these men coming from Rainy Lake or Mille Lacs, as well as proprietors like the Mackenzies and other parties who were "coming out" from a sojourn in the Indian country. The canoe trail was far from being untraveled by white persons during the spring and summer seasons.

Faries' account of the journey to Rainy Lake resembles Macdonell's narrative in its frequent mention of the portages, which were then important landmarks along the trail. Such points include Paresseux (Lazy) Portage, Portage des Chiens (Dog Portage), Portage Ecarté (Lonely), and others mentioned by Garry and Belcourt. See " The Diary of Nicholas Garry, Deputy-Governor of the Hudson's Bay Company from 1822–1835," Proceedings and Transactions of the Royal Society of Canada, 1900, Section 2 (Second Series, Vol. 6), p. 118; and Georges A. Belcourt, Mon itinéraire du Lac des Deux-Montagnes à la Rivière Rouge (Bulletin de la Société Historique de Saint Boniface, Vol. 4, Montreal, 1913), pp. 34–37. A list is given at some length in William H. Keating, Narrative of an Expedition to the Source of St. Peter's River, Lake of the Woods, etc. (London, 1825), 2: 140–143. For details regarding McLellan's later career see Papers Relating to the Red River Settlement, especially pages 82, 90, 123, 239.

² A demi-charge was a part of the loading of a canoe. It was carried around a décharge while the canoe itself, thus lightened, was towed past the rapids. The water was unusually low in 1804, a fact which made the journey, always a difficult one, even more strenuous.

³ The Mountain Portage took the travelers past one of the finest waterfalls in the world, Kakabeka Falls. Long's party, passing that way in 1823, determined the height of the falls to be one hundred and thirty feet. See

arrived some time after having broken his canoe on the way up. the men set off again for the remainder of the Load. The Swan River canoes remain'd at the dead water. The water was remarkably low all along. What part of the loading was here the men took up the hill. Very fine weather.

Wednesday 1st August. At ½ past 7 oclock we went across the Portage, and breakfasted there. after breakfast we return'd and found Portelance & Lapointe quarrelling. it seems that La Pointe had insisted upon having the remainder of his load without an order, which the other refused, Mr Nolin being behind with the order.[4] they were near coming to blows, which probably would have been the case had not we arrived. M^r McLellan then told Portelance to give him what was necessary. We departed & proceeded to the Portage Ecarté. the men carried the canoe and Baggage over and we remain'd there the rest of the day to get the canoe mended. The Swan River canoes remain'd at this end of the mountain.

Thursday 2nd. Early in the morning we departed and proceeded to the Recollet which we reached at 7 oclock and breakfasted, then proceeded to the Portage de L'ile where the men made 3 Trips. it rain'd considerably for 1½ hours and then ceased. we proceeded to the Portage Plein Champ, & dined there. after dinner the men made 2 Trips up to the Portage des Couteaux, from thence 2 Trips to the next decharge, where we arrived at 5 oclock. the men were going up to the Roses [*décharge*] with a demie charge, but broke the canoe before they got up. they return'd & mended the canoe. We encamp'd here. it rain'd a little during the night.

Friday 3rd. Got all the Baggage up to the Roses and break-

Keating, *Narrative*, 2:134–136; also the map in David Thompson, *Narrative of Explorations in Western America* (edited by J. B. Tyrrell, Publications of the Champlain Society, Vol. 12, Toronto, 1916).

[4] One "Joseph Roy, *dit* Portelance," appears on Masson's list of voyageurs in 1804. He is assigned to the department of the Pic on the north shore of Lake Superior. François Nolin appears as a clerk in the Fort Dauphin department, and Joseph Lapointe is listed as a voyageur in the same district. Masson, *Bourgeois*, 1:404, 411.

fasted. from thence we proceeded to the 3rd Decharge where we encamp'd. Very fine weather.

Saturday 4. Left our encampment very early this morning. Foggy weather. about 8 oclock arrived at a small Portage where we breakfasted. Peignecon an indian came to us, from whom we got some Bark, we then proceeded to another small Portage, & then to Portage des chiens which we reach at 12 oclock. Met Mr St Germain with the Iroquois in the Portage.[5] he dined with us & then M^r McLellan wrote to Kam^a [Kaministiquia]. Exchanged canoes with the Iroquois. At Sunset the men had every thing across. Cloudy weather.

Sunday 5th. Embarked early this morning and proceeded about ½ way up the River des Chiens.

Monday 6th. Proceeded on our Voyage and about 4 oclock P M met a canoe from L. L. P. [Lac la Pluie] with Grease. we proceeded to the Portage above Jourdain's house and encamp'd. Rain during the night.[6]

Tues-day 7th. Set out early this morning, & shortly after it began to rain & rain'd all day. The canoe had about ½ fm Broken in the small river, and about 5 oclock arrived at the small Portage near La Prairie where we met Mr Roderick McKenzie & 2 other Gentlemen of the same Name. they took tea with us, and departed. We then proceeded to the P. La Prairie, and encamp'd at the Small lake where we overtook D. Jourdain — and met Paul's & Antaya's Brigades. Chenette was at the other end. Exchanged our canoe with Martin.[7] The weather cleared up towards evening.

[5] For notes on various persons named St. Germain, see Coues, *New Light*, 1:188n. It seems most probable that the person mentioned here was one Hy. (Hyacinthe or Hippolyte) St. Germain, who in 1798 had a trading house on Lake Superior, two days' journey from Grand Portage.

[6] Jourdain and Old Sincire, mentioned below, appear to have been free traders who maintained small independent trading posts of their own. See Alexander Henry's reference to such traders on the canoe route. Coues, *New Light*, 1:219.

[7] Roderic Mackenzie, cousin of Sir Alexander Mackenzie, had been active in the fur trade of the Northwest since 1785. He accompanied Alexander to the far West in 1786 and in 1788 established Fort Chipewyan on Lake

THE DIARY OF HUGH FARIES 199

Wednesday 8th. The men carried the Baggage across the Portage. at 6 oclock we embarked, and proceeded to the other end of the Portage du Milieu, where we encamp'd.[8] Fine Weather.

Thurs-day 9th. The men carried the Baggage across very early. then we proceeded to the Portage la Savanne, and breakfasted with Old Sincire, [?] we then went to the other end, where we overtook Chenette and Jourdin. they set out after dinner. some time after Majiaux Brigade 4 Canoes arrived. we exchanged our canoes once more and departed. it rain'd pretty hard for a quarter of an hour. we encamp'd about 2 leagues down the River having broke the canoe. Cloudy weather.

Athabasca, where he remained in charge during his cousin's expeditions of 1789 and 1793. It was he who in 1798 rediscovered the Kaministiquia canoe route, which the British began to use extensively about 1801. Probably the Mackenzie party was on its way to Montreal, where early in November the agreement was concluded that merged the interests of the Northwest Company and the X. Y. Company and brought to an end the period of competition and rivalry that had lasted for several years. For the text of the agreement see Masson, *Bourgeois,* 2:482–499. News of the merger reached the author of our diary on January 12, 1805.

A year or two later Roderic Mackenzie retired. He planned to write a history of the fur trade, based upon the observations and accounts of a number of traders, and in 1806 sent a printed circular and manuscript letter to several wintering partners and clerks of the Northwest Company requesting material. In reply he received a number of contemporary journals, among them four of the diaries reproduced in this volume. Mackenzie's history was never published, but much of his material was preserved in the Masson papers and is now in the Public Archives of Canada and in the McGill University Library. For a biographical sketch of Roderic Mackenzie see Lawrence J. Burpee, *Oxford Encyclopaedia of Canadian History* (Makers of Canada Series, Vol. 12, New York, 1926), p. 391. Martin, with whom Faries exchanged canoes, was with Mackenzie on the trail. See Coues, *New Light,* 1:442n. Another Roderic Mackenzie was a clerk in the Nipigon district in 1804. Masson, *Bourgeois,* 2:407.

Paul and Antaya are difficult to identify. Probably Faries met Joseph Paul of the English River department, one of the most famous guides of the Northwest. Louis Chenette was a clerk in the Rainy Lake department with Faries. Masson, *Bourgeois,* 1:179, 400, 412.

[8] The Portage du Milieu and the Portage la Savanne, crossing the height of land, lay across stretches of mud and swamp, which made the carrying of canoes difficult and dangerous. An effort was made to build some sort of

Friday 10th. Set out early in the morning and gummed twice before we reached the lake. we overtook Chenette and Jourdain, at the Pointe aux Sables. a little further met a Canoe of Pork-eaters returning from Mille Lacs. We arrived at Sunset at the house, and landed with Messrs Grant & Finlay from L. L. P. Mr Grant Junr was there also, who had been 26 days from Kam^a. We remain'd here for the night.[9]

Saturday 11th. There was an indian here who came for a trader to go in land. Mr Grant spoke to him, gave him some Rum and then departed. Chenette & Black set off at the same time.[10] we were obliged to remain here all day to get our canoe repaired. At night the indians got drunk, and the Cancre had his testicles pulled out by one of his wives, through jealousy. there was but a few fibres that held them, so that his life was almost despaired of. The men could not gum the canoe as the weather was cloudy and rainy.

Sunday 12th. The weather was still cloudy and did not clear up till after dinner. the men then gummed the canoe, and at ¾ past 3 oclock we embarked and proceeded to Clou-

log roadway, but walking remained perilous at best. Belcourt passed the grave of a voyageur who met his death here in a fall while portaging with a canoe. *Itinéraire,* p. 39–40; Garry, " Diary," Proceedings and Transactions of the Royal Society of Canada, 1900, Section 2, p. 121.

[9] In reviewing this volume in 1934, W. Stewart Wallace suggested that this reference is probably to James Grant, who was later the proprietor in charge at Fond du Lac. *Canadian Historical Review,* 15:76.
Bourgeois, 1:61, 66; Coues, *New Light,* 1:80n.

Mille Lacs was not the lake of that name in central Minnesota but the group of lakes on the new canoe route from Kaministiquia to Rainy Lake. The " house " or trading post mentioned by Faries was one of considerable importance. Most of the pork-eaters turned back after making the journey from Montreal to Kaministiquia, but some of them continued as far as Rainy Lake, where they exchanged their goods for the furs that had been brought down from the Athabasca area. Alexander Henry also mentions this group of *mangeurs du lard.* Coues, *New Light,* 1:248.

[10] The only references to a trader named Black seem to occur at the time of the struggle between Lord Selkirk and the Hudson's Bay Company on the one side and the Northwest Company on the other, especially between the years 1815 and 1817. See *Papers Relating to the Red River Settlement,* pp. 242, 243, for references to Samuel Black, a partner in the Northwest Company.

tiers Portage where we encamp'd.[11] M[r] Grant Jun[r] & D. Jourdain remain'd at Mille Lacs who were waiting for one of the canoes behind.

Monday 13th. Embarked early this morning and breakfasted at Portage la Pente, and proceeded to a small river where the Baggage was carried. proceeded to a small Portage where we dined. when we came to the rapids of the Portage des François, we unloaded the canoe and made 2 trips to the Portage, there remain'd one load more for to morrow.[12]

Tues-day 14th. Early this morning the men went for the last load. as soon as they arrived, there fell a violent shower of rain, accompanied, with thunder and lightning. we went to the other end of the Portage, and found Chenette and Jourdain there, who had not yet got their baggage across. our men got all across to-day but the canoe. Cloudy weather.

Wednes-day 15th. Jourdain set off very early, & the men went for our canoe. at 7 oclock we embarked and overtook him at Portage des Morts. we proceeded as far as the entrance of the Riviere aux Foins [Hay River], and encamp'd. Fine weather, & a westerly wind.

Thurs-day 16th. Proceeded to the bottom of the river and breakfasted there. the men carried every thing to the bottom of the river. At ½ past 9 oclock we embarked and met Old Cloutier at the entrance of Sturgeon Lake with 2 Canoes, 4 Men, and 1 Clerk. he told us that he had but 15 trading pieces, — we proceeded a good way down the River Lacroix and encamp'd. Very fine weather.

Friday 17th. Embarked this morning and proceeded down to Lake Lacroix, but it blew such a strong head wind, that

[11] In his index to Henry's journals, Coues gives the name of a Zacharie Cloutier who was in the service of the Northwest Company and who was at Grand Portage in 1799. *New Light,* 3:935; see also Masson, *Bourgeois,* 1:ii.

[12] According to Garry the Portage des François was a long one, passing over about two miles of beautifully wooded hills. See his "Diary," Proceedings and Transactions of the Royal Society of Canada, 1900, Section 2, p. 123.

we did not go far forward. we encamp'd between 4 & 5 oclock, where we overtook Black, who had been there since Morning. Strong wind and clear weather.

Saturday 18th. Early this morning we proceeded to the little portage La croix tho' it blew very hard a head.[13] at 1 oclock the men went down with a demie charge to the Pines. they return'd at Sunset having damaged their canoes. We remain here all night. Clear and windy weather.

Sunday 19th. We walked down to the Pines, which we reached a little after Sunrise. at 10 oclock the men arrived with the canoes. we went as far as the Grand Galais in Lac la Meccane and encamp'd.[14]

Monday 20th. Set out early this morning, & met Lambert & 3 other X. Y. men in the Detroit in Lac La Pluie, we supposed they were going to Vermillion Lake.[15] proceeded as far as the foot of the Grande Traverse, and encamp'd. It blew a strong side wind all day.

Tues-day 21st. Embarked early this morning. at the entrance of the River, found 3 indians drunk. we arrived at the

[13] Belcourt mentions three short portages by the name of Lacroix at the northern end of the route running through Lake la Croix. See his *Itinéraire*, p. 44.

[14] For a note on Lake Meccane see above, page 103n.

[15] There seem to have been two Vermilion Lakes to which Faries might have been referring. Alexander Henry, making the journey north from Grand Portage over the regular canoe route, noted a lake of that name lying on the trail between Lac la Croix and Lake Namakan. See Coues, *New Light*, 1:17. Another larger Vermilion Lake is situated some distance south of Lac la Croix, and could be reached by paddling up through Crane Lake and the Vermilion River. Almost certainly the many references in this diary are to the smaller lake. Dr. John McLoughlin was at a Vermilion Lake a few years later, and his "Description of the Indians from Fort William to Lake of the Woods," the original manuscript of which is among the Masson papers in the library of McGill University, leaves small reason to doubt that he was at the smaller lake. McLoughlin states that Mr. McCrae wintered at the lake the previous year — doubtless a reference to William McCrae, whose name is on the list of clerks in the Rainy Lake department in 1805. Bigsby also mentions a post on Lake Vermilion in *Shoe and Canoe*, 2:259. Furthermore, the maps in Thompson's *Narrative* and in *Shoe and Canoe* show only the smaller lake.

Fort at 12 oclock, and found Richard alone.[16] Sultry weather.

Wednes-day 22nd. In the morning the Liar & 2 other indians, whom we saw yesterday, came to the Fort. M^r McLellan dispatched the former off for Mille Lacs. Black prepared himself to set off for Lac des Bois [Lake of the Woods], & La France for Mille Lacs. M^r McLellan had a few words with Amelle concerning his equip^t. In the evening there fell a violent shower of rain, with thunder and lightning, and rain'd during the night.

Thurs-day 23rd. After breakfast Black set out for Lac des Bois, & La France with 4 men set out for Mille Lacs. Old Godin and Azure went down the river to make wooden canoes. Cloudy weather.

Friday 24th. Richard with 2 men and Mr Grant's Girl set out in search of indians. Chenette, Guilmont & Jourdain arrived about 9 oclock. we opened out the Bales, immediately, and made out an assortment for Eagle Lake. At 5 oclock P.M. Chenettes Girl was bro^t to bed of a daughter. Fine weather.[17]

Saturday 25th. This morning made up 5 Bales for Eagle Lake, and as many for the Lac des Bois. Old Godin came up for some Grease and a Saw. Cloudy weather.

[16] This no doubt refers to Richard Priket, one of the interpreters assigned to the Rainy Lake area. Masson, *Bourgeois*, 1:412.

[17] It was customary for the white traders to take Indian women for wives. Upon leaving the wilderness a trader ordinarily placed his wife and children under the protection of some honest man and provided a certain amount for their support. Daniel W. Harmon, *Journal of Voyages and Travels in the Interior of North America* (Trail Makers of Canada Series, Toronto, 1911), pp. 23, 39; George Bryce, *Remarkable History of the Hudson's Bay Company* (Toronto, 1900), p. 166. In 1806 it was decided that the practice of having these wives live in the forts at the company's expense placed too much of a burden on the concern, and a resolution was passed providing for its discontinuance. See the manuscript minutes of the Northwest Company, 1801–1811, p. 43.

Eagle Lake, which lies north of Rainy Lake, is the lower of two lakes of the same name in the region bounded by Rainy Lake, Lake Winnipeg, and the Winnipeg River. It was easily reached through one of the long northern arms of Rainy Lake as well as from Whitefish Lake.

List of the Men &ca. at the Lac La Pluie Departement For the Year 1805*

Names	Clerks	Guides	Interpreters	Foremen	Steersmen	Mid. Men	Summer Men	Years to Serve	Drs.	Crs.	Remarks
Pierre sans Soucie							1	0	1908 15		
Louis Cantarat		1					1	1	984 5		
Francois La Grave				1				3	1347 15		Guide & Foreman
Joseph Jourdain				1				1	1303 12		
Francois Bonnin						1		1	1177		
Louis Chenette	1					1		1	1460 8		Clerk & Interpreter
Louis Guilmont	1	0	1					3	912 8	1676	
Richard Pricket		0	1					1	15 9		
Antoine Azure						1	1	1	613 5		
Michel Boulanger					1			1	429 15		
Eustache Langlois				1		1		2			
Thomas Tiosaragointé						1		1	268	278 10	
François Duval						1		2			
Ignace Canawatiron								1		819 10	
Joseph Gayou					1			3	1230 11		

Name							
François Rossignol	6	2				1	1054 15
Joseph Rossignol					1	2	976 10
Jos. Sansfaçon					1	3	2312 15
Charles Charoux	1					3	1591 15
Charles Groux		1			1	2	922 2
Jacques Germain					1	2	859 16
Pierre Leclair			1			1	1299 10
Jos. Dagenais				1		5	2130 12
Benjamin La Bonté					1	1	1114 19	156 5
Hyacinthe Parisien			1	1		3	553 2
Louis Migneron						1	985 5
Louis Gaillard		1			1	2	884 5
Louis Delude					1	1	1636 5
Louis Démarais					1	1	
Archibald McLellan	1						
Ths. McMurray	1						
Hugh Faries	1						
Willm McCrae	1						
	6	3	5	5	13	5	27972 6	2930 5

* From a list of the employees of the Northwest Company, the original of which is in the Masson Papers in the McGill University Library and a photostatic copy in the possession of the Minnesota Historical Society.

Sunday 26th. About 8 oclock A. M. Chenette and Guilmont set off for Lac des Bois. In the afternoon, Mailloux & Amelle took a walk up to the X. Y. Fort, and saw a deserter there, from the Atha^a [Athabasca] River Brigade, named Gâyou. M^r McLellan sent Jourdain up with a note, desiring Lacombe to send him down.[18] he told him, he might go if he pleased, but the fellow would not come down. M^r McLellan went himself, & Richard and I followed him. the fellow made no resistance but came down immediately. M^r McLellan put him into a cellar swarming with fleas for the night. Richard brought a parcel of dried Meat, today, the Indians had not yet made any Oats.[19]

Monday 27th. Ammelle, with La Rocque & the Deserter went down the river for canoe wood. In the afternoon La Verdure arrived with 2 Canoes. he left Mr Grant in the River La Croix with his canoe broken to pieces. Cloudy weather.

Tues-day 28th. It rain'd a heavy shower before breakfast. Made up 5 more Bales for Lac des Bois. At 2 oclock P. M. The Swan River Brigade arrived. L heureux was near being killed by a fall carrying his canoe. he was senseless for some time. Lacombe came up at the time and bled him. Four men were obliged to carry him up the hill in a blanket. we gave him some turlington, and towards evening he was a little better.[20] Cloudy weather.

Wednes-day 29th. After breakfast Bonhomme set off with 4 men for Lac des Bois, with 15 Pieces. The S. R. [Swan River] Canoes remain'd here all day to repair. Plante one of their men fell sick, and remain'd here to embark with Ducharme.

[18] Lacombe was the chief of the opposition's post at the outlet of Rainy Lake. The fort of the X. Y. Company was nearer the falls than that of the Northwest Company.

[19] Wild rice was ordinarily called "oats" or "wild oats" by traders and voyageurs. It was gathered by Indian women in the late summer and was bartered by them for trade goods. Whenever it could be procured, "oats" served as a staple article in the traders' diet.

[20] By Turlington, Faries means Turlington's balsam, a medicinal tincture long famous as a remedy for bronchitis and apparently used to some extent as a general stimulant. It had a base of benzoin.

Thurs-day 30th. Early in the morning Mr McLellan set out for Lac des Bois in a small canoe with 4 Men, where he's to fit out the different Posts for the winter. The Swan River Brigade set out about 8 oclock. Grenier who had gone down with Bonhomme return'd sick. Old Godin came in the evening for provisions. he told us there was plenty of Sturgeon below. Mailloux went down with a Seine to try whether he could catch any. I gave Plante a vomit which did him much good. Fine Weather.

Friday 31st. In the morning Richard went up to the Petite Pêche to look for Hay.[21] he return'd about 9 oclock, and found a great deal. Old Azure had been up but could find none. Mailloux return'd to day but caught no Sturgeon. About 12 oclock Ducharme arrived. he had but one letter for Mr McLellan. he remain'd about an hour, and then set off. Plante embarked with him being a little better. In the afternoon I got a few things ready for Richard to go to the indians and late in the evening he set off with 3 Men but return'd soon after, to inform us that he had seen a small indian canoe at the Portage.[22]

Saturday 1st September. Mailloux went up to the Portage very early, and saw the indians returning home. he supposes them to be from Eagle lake. they told him they gave Lacombe 4 Bales dried meat & 4 Skins. About 2 oclock all the men return'd from below. In the evening Old Azure and his wife had a battle. he gave her a black eye. La Verdure being unwell I gave him a vomit, but it had no effect. An Xy Canoe arrived to day from the Grand Portage. Rain'd very hard during the night.

Sunday 2nd. Cloudy day. Rain throughout the night.

Monday 3rd. Early in the morning, I gave the men their provisions, and sent them off to work. Old Azure went a

---

[21] Bigsby refers to Little Peché River as near the western end of Rainy Lake. *Shoe and Canoe,* 2:269.

[22] "The portage," an expression often used in the diary, usually means the carrying place nearest the fort, that is, around the falls that obstructed the river between the fort and Rainy Lake.

mowing. La Verdure is still very unwell. A strong Westerly wind and clear wea[ther].

Tuesday 4th. I gave La Verdure a purge, which had more effect than the vomit. he was rather better than yesterday. I was busy since yesterday making a Seine. A strong S.W. wind which I suppose stops Richard.

Wednesday 5th. Azure return'd this morning, having mowed what hay there was below. I told him to go to the Petite Pêche, but he says he can not find out the place. he waits Richard's return. La Verdure no better than yesterday. Cloudy weather. Rain towards morning.

Thursday 6th. It rain'd the greatest part of the day. towards evening the sky cleared up. I finished the Seine & then began a Net. A S.W. Wind.

Friday 7th. Old Azure went off this morning to look for the Hay at the Petite Pêche. About 12 oclock Mailloux went up to the Portage & saw 2 men 2 Women, & 4 Children leaving the other end. they had been at the Xy's Fort. In the evening Azure return'd. he said he had mowed about 200 Bundles of fine Hay, & there was great abundance of it. La Verdure no better than usual. he eats only a little corn now and then. Fine weather.

Saturday 8th. In the forenoon Mailloux & I went up to the Portage in a canoe. we saw two of the Pines lying down drunk. they told us they had 10 Bags Oats, and were coming to the Fort with it, but Lacombe took it from them. In the evening the men return'd from below & I gave them each a dram. Cloudy weather.

Sunday 9th. In the forenoon I went up to the Portage with Amelle and Mailloux, and saw the indians that were there Yesterday. they told us they had more oats hidden a little way up the river. they then came down to the Fort, and in the dusk of the evening I sent 2 men with them for it. They return'd pretty late. The Mufle, his Brother and Son, arrived at the same time. I got but 3 Bags Oats from the former, and

1 from the latter. they kept me up the greatest part of the night.

Monday 10th. About 9 oclock Richard arrived. I sent the men who were here to go and help them across the Portage. they brought the canoe nearly full of Oats. I kept Joe here to go and help Azure to make hay while the weather is favourable. Ammelle went up the River to look for cedar as he says there is very little below, but did not succeed in finding any. The Mufle remain'd here all day.

Tuesday 11th. Azure, Godin & Grènier, went up to make hay, & Joe went to hew Logs. Amelle went off with his man to his old place below. about 9 oclock La France arrived from Mille Lacs. The Mufle went off in the afternoon. Jourdain went up as far as the lake to see if there were any indians coming down. Very fair weather.

Wednes-day 12th. Mailloux & La France with 2 men went down the river to Seine. they are to remain a night or two should there be a prospect of catching many. The 2 Verrats arrived to day, & brought a little dried Meat & took a few credits. About 1 oclock P. M. Mr McLellan arrived, with 15 Bags Oats and a few Rolls Bark. Very hazy weather.

Thurs-day 13th. This morning the Pines & Verrats went away, about 12 oclock Mailloux return'd with a few small fishes. We put up a few articles for White Fish Lake.[23] Richard got ready with 4 Men to go to the indians. Fine weather.

Friday 14th. Before day break, Richard set out, and some time after there fell a heavy shower of rain. Mailloux and La France went and cut wood for Casks. In the afternoon the large canoe came up from below, loaded with oats, & Bark. Rainy day.

Saturday 15th. In the afternoon the Verrat & his Brother

---

[23] When Faries refers to Whitefish Lake he is speaking of the northeastern member of the series of lakes which are collectively known as the Lake of the Woods.

in law, return'd again with a little dried Meat, which they traded. took a few debts, and then set off. Cloudy & Rainy weather.

Sunday 16th. This Morning Azure return'd with his wife from the hay. she brought a little Wattap. Gave the Sawers provisions for a fortnight. M^r McLellan bled old La Verdure, as he was not much better than usual. Rainy weather.

Monday 17th. Three men went down to Saw logs and 6 more to draw out canoe wood. Grènier went a chopping. The Cooper headed up Barrels to put Oats in. La Verdure was a little better today. Same weather as yesterday. We set a Net at Night.

Tues-day 18th. Jourdain went to the net, but caught only one Small fish. The Cooper headed up the rest of [the] Casks. Richard arrived about 10 oclock, with 15 Bags Oats. The Cedar also came with about 3 Skins. In the evening the Grue & another arrived. The weather cleared up.

Wednes-day 19th. Jourdain with 4 men went up to the Portage to pitch a Tent. The Grue got a large Keg of Rum and the cedar a Small one & then they set off. We filled up the remaining casks. there was 8 full of Oats, & 2 with corn. Very fine weather.

Thurs-day 20th. Young Jourdain & Thomas went down to help Amelle to get out his canoe wood. Lagrave went and cut wood for a stable. In the forenoon M^r McLellan went up to the Portage and met the Big Rat and Young Toad. he got a Skin from them. they came down to the Fort for what articles they wanted, & then went away. Azure & Coutu return'd, home, having made a sufficient quantity of Hay. A strong Westerly wind & clear weather.

Friday 21st. Azure set about drawing the wood for the stable. Lagrave was still chopping. About 11 oclock, Richard with Coutu set off for the bottom of the river, to watch Lacombe's proceedings, as he is to set off to day or to morrow. Jourdain sent Gouin down to inform us that there was an Xy. canoe setting off with 19 pieces. I then went up to the portage

THE DIARY OF HUGH FARIES 211

with 3 in a small canoe, and Jourdain, with Raboin and Ignace, went after them to see where they were going to. I remain'd there the rest of the day, and came home at Night. The 6 men who went down with Amelle came up to day with 2 Canoe loads of cedar. Azure went down with the horse to draw logs for the Sawers. Very fine weather.

Saturday 22nd. Four of the men who came up Yesterday went down again for more cedar. Lagrave went a chopping the remainder of the wood, for the stable. I went up to the Portage, and remain'd there all day. Amelle & the men who were with him came home in the evening. Clear weather.

Sunday 23rd. I went up to the Portage to day. About 5 oclock P. M. Jourdain return'd, he left the X. Y. Canoe in the little detroit. they were going to Vermillion lake. we got a few things packed up for Mr Grant, and a Keg of H[igh] W[ine]. Jourdain & Vallé got ready to set off to morrow for V. Lake. They took their canoe up to the Portage to night. La Grave came down to night, to inform us that 3 X. Y. men were gone off with 2 Squaws to the lake. M^r McLellan with 4 men, immediately got ready and set off in search. Lacombe set out for Lac des Bois in 2 Canoes. Very clear and warm weather.

Monday 24th. Jourdain set off about Sunrise, and Amelle with 3 men, went down again for cedar. Azure drawing the wood for a stable. Grenier is still chopping. Mailloux made a Case to put the remainder of the oats in. La Verdure is growing better every day. The Picotté, & his wife, came to the Fort, about 2 oclock. M^r McLellan arrived shortly after & kicked them both out of the Fort. (they had given all their oats to the X. Y. La Grave went up to the Portage to relieve Gouin. Clear weather.

Tues-day 25th. Three of the men who had been with M^r McLellan went down below and return'd, with 2 others, in the afternoon with a load of cedar. M^r McLellan spent the greatest part of the day at the portage & gave the Picotté and his wife a second drubbing. La Verdure went up there a fishing. In the evening Vaillant with 2 indians arrived from Eagle lake.

Wednesday 26th. La Grave, and Raboin got themselves ready to set off for Eagle Lake. La France, Jourd[a]in & the 2 Iroquois began building a stable. Mr McLellan wrote a few letters in the evening, & Raboin, & Lagrave went off in the night.

Thurs-day 27th. Vaillant went down to the Sawers to help them, but came up again as he could not saw. The 2 Indians went off today. The men finished the stable. L'abri du vent's wife was here today with one Beaver & a little meat. Richard arrived after dark, & brought 2 Bags Oats, with a few Skins. Cloudy weather.

Friday 28th. La France with 4 men went up to build a small house near the X.Y. Fort. Amelle went a chopping. La Grue's wife came here with some meat and a few Bustards.[24]

Saturday 29th. La France with 3 men working at the little house. The Iroquois pulled down a fence in the Garden. Coutu carted dung. In the afternoon the men came up from below. The Premier arrived, with 5 or 6 other indians. he brought his wife, who died last night, to have her buried. they got rum and drank all night. Clear weather & a N.E Wind.

Monday 1st October. La France and Gouin were at work at the house. In the morning Mr McLellan went up to see them. Lacombe told him he would throw down the house as it was built too near his fort. they disputed for some time, & then a scuffle ensued, but La France parted them. La Grue, and 3 other indians, brought a few ducks and Bustards. they took a few articles, got a large Keg Rum, & departed. In the evening Lambert & Dupuis arrived from Vermillion lake.

Tuesday 2nd. We got a few goods packed up for Mr

---

[24] The bustard or *bâtarde* is the Canada goose, classified by Sir John Richardson as *Anser canadensis*. Monseigneur Taché, *Sketch of the North-West of America* (translated by Captain D. R. Cameron, Montreal, 1870), p. 201.

Grant. The Premier and his band set off in the morning. In the afternoon, Amelle arrived with the remainder of his wood. Cloudy weather & a S. E. Wind.

Wednes-day 3rd. Lambert & Dupuis went off this morning. Mailloux, Coutu, and the 2 Iroquois went to cut hoops, & Keg Wood. La France with 3 men working at the little house. In the evening The Blackbird and Corneille's Son, arrived, with some Meat & a little Roll of Beaver.

Thurs-day 4th. Richard & I set off in a small canoe to go to the River Noire [Black River]. we went as far as the Big Forks, where we found Mailloux. we slept there. he had caught 3 Sturgeons to day. A Frosty Night.[25]

Friday 5th. We went down early to the River Noire & saw the Premier and his band. Old Le Clair whom we thought was there, was gone to W. F. L. [White Fish Lake]. Mailloux caught 5 Sturgeons this morning. we took 8 in our canoe, and arrived at the fort after dark. Jourdain Gouin and Gayou went down for a load of Planks. Cloudy weather.

Saturday 6th. Jourdain & Gayou pulled up 6 Kegs of Potatoes, but as there was appearance of rain, they went with Gouin to help La France.

Sunday 7th. In the evening the old Bras Court arrived with his Son and Michel Alarics wife. his Son went up to the Xy's shortly after.

Monday 8th. Richard, Jourdain & Gayou went down the river to L'abri du vent's lodge. Jourdain is to remain for the winter. The Bras Court took a few debts and departed. La France and Vaillant worked at the little house & the rest of the men dug up Potatoes. La Verdure was very Sick to day.

Tues-day 9th. Mailloux and Amelle went a chopping & the rest were employed as Yesterday. Clear weather.

Wednesday 10th. La France Coutu and the 2 Iroquois went

[25] The Big Fork River, long a famous route from Rainy Lake to the headwaters of the Mississippi, flows into Rainy River from the south several miles below the site of the Rainy Lake fort. Black River enters four miles farther down. Coues, *New Light*, 1:20.

for wood below, and took the Seine with them. Mailloux went a chopping. Ammele finished a small canoe he had begun a few days ago, & the rest pulled up Potatoes, till 12 oclock, when it began to rain. they then went up to finish the little house, at the X. Y. Fort. The Premier and Boiteux Son arrived, with some dried meat.

Thurs-day 11th. The Boiteux Son got what articles he wanted, & then set off. The Potatoes were all dug up by 12 oclock. the whole amounted to 150 Bushels. Mailloux & Amelle finished cutting their wood. La France & the 3 men, arrived with a load of wood & Hay, but no Sturgeon. La Verdure who had been some time in the lodge at the Portage removed into the little house. Lacombe & Mr McLellan agreed to send each a man to the Chaudiere to catch White Fish.[26] Mr McL. sent Gouin up to the X. Y. Fort to be ready to set off early in the morning. La France went up to stay with La Verdure.

Friday 12th. The men were employed making a chimney. Richard arrived in the afternoon. he brought a few Skins, and a little dried meat. Jourdain remain'd with L'abri-du-vent. Some time after, The Blackbird, and Frozen Foot arrived. they brought some meat & a few Bustards & set off again immediately. Grenier and Azure went a chopping.

Saturday 13th. Thomas went down with a Canoe for a load of Boards. he is to come up with the Sawers. The rest of the men plaistered their houses &c. The Sawers came up in the evening.

Sunday 14th. After Breakfast Mr McCrae & Amelle went a hunting in the lake. In the afternoon arrived l'homme Noir from Lac des Bois. he brought a few Muskrats. I am inform'd by him, that a number of Lac des Bois indians, are gone to winter in the River Ouinipic. Cloudy Day.

[26] The Chaudière or Kettle Falls, a short distance above the fort, was a scenic spot where the river tumbled over a series of cataracts in a drop of some thirty feet. It is mentioned in Garry, "Diary," Proceedings and Transactions of the Royal Society of Canada, 1900, Section 2, p. 125, and Bigsby, *Shoe and Canoe,* 2:271.

Monday 15th. The Sawers went off again for a fortnight. Azure & Grenier went a chopping. Gayou, Vaillant, & Coutu, finished plaistering the houses. L'homme Noir set off after he had taken what articles he wanted. Ammelle & I return'd in the evening having killed but one Bustard and a few Ducks. The Seines got ready to go a Seining tomorrow. Bras Court's Son brought us some fresh Meat. Fine Weather.

Tuesday 16th. Mailloux La France, and 2 Iroquois set off at ½ past one oclock A. M. to go a Seining, the Xy. having passed 2 hours before. Gayou and Vaillant went for a load of Boards. Coutu went a chopping with Azure & Grènier. Boulanger came home to day saying he [can] find no more Pines fit for logs. The Indians went away to day.

Wednesday 17th. Boulanger & Gayou went for a load of boards. Coutu brought the boards up the hill. The others at work as yesterday. In the evening, A Squaw came to the Fort for a few articles. La Grue and the young Cedar brought a little fresh Meat. Fine weather.

Thurs-day 18th. Vaillant & Coutu went down to the Seines for Sturgeon. Gayou brought the remainder of the Boards up the hill. Boulanger went a chopping, & Amelle began to prepare his canoe wood. Okaquanatifs arrived from the Chaudier. he came for men to go for meat, and a few Skins, he had. The men, that are fishing there, he says are very successfull, there being plenty of White fish. Very fine weather.

Friday 19th. At ½ past 5 oclock this morning Richard & Gayou set off with the indian to go to the Chaudiere. The rest of the men employed as Yesterday. In the evening Vaillant and Coutu return'd with 16^{lb} Sturgeons. Clear weather.

Saturday 20th. Vaillant & Boulanger made themselves a bed. Coutu mended his clothes. the others were chopping. Richard did not return as it blew a strong head wind all day.

Sunday 21st. Azure & Coutu went down to draw out logs for the Sawers.

Monday 22nd. The 3 men who remain'd here went a chopping. In the afternoon Boulanger went down to the Sawers, with the horses. Richard arrived at night with some meat, and a few white fishes. The men at the Chaudiere, had caught 1300. Cold Cloudy weather and a S. E. Wind.

Tues-day 23rd. Grênier and Vaillant went a chopping. Gayou went up to the X. y. Fort, to help them to mend a Canoe to go for the fish. Boulanger & Coutu came up in the afternoon. Guedon & Prospere arrived from White Fish Lake. Guilmont writes that he has 2½ Packs. they were 4 days on their way here. Very fine weather.

Wednes-day 24th. Early in the morning, Coutu Gayou & Grenier with 3 X. Y. Men set off to go to the Chaudiere for fish. Grenier is to remain there with the 2 others. Boulanger & Vaillant went down for Sturgeon. After Breakfast, the 2 men from White Fish lake set off. Azure came home in the afternoon having drawn out all the logs. Cloudy weather.

Thurs-day 25th. Azure went a chopping. In the afternoon 2 Women went past the Fort in a small canoe, going to the X. Y's. Mr McLellan & Richard went after them. they had nothing but a few empty Kegs which they took from them. A very strong S. W. wind all day and night.

Friday 26th. Azure finished chopping today. In the afternoon Boulanger and Vaillant, arrived. they brought 15 Sturgeons and a few small fishes.

Saturday 27th. Boulanger & Vaillant went down for a load of Boards, & Azure cut wood for flooring the stable. Fine weather.

Sunday 28th. Richard & I set off to go a hunting in the lake, & met, the men returning from the Chaudiere with 1050 White fish. In the evening the Fort was near catching fire, the wind blowing very hard from the S. W. and the country on fire all round us.

Monday 29th. We return'd this morning but killed nothing. Vaillant & Boulanger went a chopping. Azure cut the rest of the Stable Floor. The fire is still burning round the Fort.

Tues-day 30th. The Frozen Foot arrived with a few Skins, & dried meat. he remain'd about an hour and set off. Mr

McCrae and Richard set off about 12 oclock, in search of indians, that are in the Big Forks.²⁷ Boulanger & Vaillant went for a load of Planks.

Wednes-day 31st. The Men chopping fire Wood. Amelle mending a large canoe, to go for a load of White Fish at the Chaudiere. A little before dark, Mr Grant's Girl arrived from her Brother's lodge. In the night arrived 2 men, 1 from White fish lake, the other from River Oui^e. they are come to inform me of the X Y's being alone at the Dalles.

Thurs-day 1st Novr. The Corneille & Devil arrived with a few Skins & 4 Bales dried Meat. No work done today.

Friday 2nd. A little before breakfast, M^r McCrae & Richard arrived but saw nothing of the indians. The Corneille & Devil set off. About 12 oclock I sent M^r McCrae, with 3 men off to winter at the Dalles, along side of the X.Y. Early this morning, I sent 3 men with a large canoe, to the Chaudiere, for a load of fish.

Saturday 3rd Novr. Azure working at the stable & Amelle at his usual work. Mr Grant's Girl brought us 75 Bundles Wattap to day. S. W. wind all day.

Sunday 4th. Goddin paid us a visit to let us know that Joe is very Sick. I sent Goddin & Azure of directly with some Turlington for him. Azure is to remain with Goddin to finish the few logs they have yet to saw. Cloudy all day.

Monday 5th. About 9 oclock A. M. Joe came home and is still very sick. Easterly wind all day with rain.

Tues-day 6th. Joe is better to day. Wind as yesterday, & cold.

Wednes-day 7th. Joe began to work to day. Amelle at his usual work.

Thurs-day 8th. About 12 oclock Gouin arrived from the

²⁷ William McCrae was one of the clerks in the Rainy Lake department. His name was misspelled "McCrea" in Masson's list. See *Bourgeois*, 1:412. During the winter of 1804–05 he traded near the X.Y. people at the Dalles of the Winnipeg River, a spot just north of the Lake of the Woods, which was usually chosen for a post. The competition was keen, and McCrae was considered to have done well when he returned in the spring with three packs

Chaudiere, with 60 White Fish. In the evening arrived Jourdain with 2 others from V. Lake. Mr Grant sent them here as he has no provisions.

Friday 9th. I sent 2 men down for Sturgeon. In the evening the men with the large canoe, arrived from the Chaudiere with 1100 White Fish. The Seiners came home with 50 Sturgeons. The men who went off this morning, met them (at the little Forks. Very fine weather for the Season.

Saturday 10th. About 8 oclock arrived the Corneilles Sons with a few Beavers. they set off about 10 oclock. Two men went down for a load of Planks, and return'd in the afternoon. the rest of the men employed at different works. Azure and Godin came home. they have done sawing below. In the evening arrived the Grue, with 2 Bales Meat.

Sunday 11th. The Grue set off. I sent Jourdain with him to take care of his Skins. There fell a little Snow last night.

Monday 12th. Sent 4 Men off to Seine at the Manitou, & 2 with a large canoe for the remainder of the wood, (planks) the rest employed at different works.[28] In the evening the men arrived with the Planks.

Tues-day 13th. Got some logs squared to day for the new house. Goddin with 2 others renewing the pickets of the Fort. In the afternoon Young Jourdin arrived from Tapinawa's lodge with 27 Plus & left as many at the lodge. he is come for rum and a few articles they are in want of. The Seiners came home on foot & were obliged to leave the canoes at the Big Forks owing to the ice.

Wednes-day 14th. Very early this morning I sent La France to Tapinawa's lodge, & Richard with 2 men gone up the River Noire, where I suppose the X. Y. gone to. They have been

of furs. See page 241 below. A few years later McLoughlin reports him as wintering on Lake Vermilion. See above, page 202n. The Dalles are mentioned by Macdonell, above, page 104.

[28] The Manitou Rapid was a short pitch of about three feet in the Rainy River some thirty miles below the Rainy Lake fort. Warren Upham, *Minnesota Geographic Names* (Minnesota Historical Collections, Vol. 17, St. Paul, 1920), p. 284; Bigsby, *Shoe and Canoe*, 2:287.

missing since Friday last. Godin finish'd the front of the Fort. Azure drawing logs for the new house.

Thurs-day 15th. The men employed at different works. A very cold day.

Friday 16th. I gave a few parchment Skins, to the women to dress. The Cooper plaistering and White washing his house. Old Godin got wood home to make 2 traines.[29] No Logs were drawn to day as the horses could not be found. Weather cloudy.

Saturday 17th. The Horses not to be found. All the men at work. A strong Westerly wind, & fine weather.

Sunday 18th. Very fine calm weather.

Monday 19th. Three men squaring logs. Joe finished one of the traines. Azure looked for the horses all day but could not find them. Mailloux making Kegs. Amelle at his canoe wood, and the rest cutting fire wood. I was inform'd by Laverdure, that the X. Y. were preparing to go a deroûine. Accordingly I got Goods &c. ready to follow them & kept three men all night about their fort watching them.

Tues-day 20th. The above men came home & assured me that none of them came out of the fort all night. The men at the usual work, except old Azure. he is working with Goddin in stead of looking for the horses. A little after dark I sent a man across the river, & another to the point below the Fort, to watch the X. Y.

Wednes-day 21st. Azure hauling logs. In the evening arrived Richard with 27 Plus, that he mustered up among 8 or 9 indians. About 9 oclock he set off again to go up the Big Forks, with 3 Men &c. Very fine weather.

Thurs-day 22nd. All the men at work, except the 2 that arrived with Richard. The Peltries that were in the Shop, I got ty'd up. Say 3 Packs.

[29] A *traine*, or *traineau*, in the Northwest was a sledge or sleigh about seven feet in length, the front end of which was turned up in picturesque fashion to enable it to pass easily over bushes and low obstructions. These *traines* were usually drawn by dogs, but at this post horses were used.

Friday 23rd. Five men employed digging the turf to make another potatoe field in the Spring. Azure hauling logs. Joe made a Wheelbarrow to day.

Saturday 24th. The men still digging the turf. Very Cloudy with showers of rain. A little after dark arrived Jourdin & La France from the River aux Rapides with 42 Plus.[30]

Sunday 25th. Raining of and on all day. the men had a dance at night & bought a few pints Rum.

Monday 26th. I sent La France with 2 others up the Big Forks. I sent Coutu down for the wooden canoes. Azure hauling fire Wood, and the rest of the men digging, except the Canoe Maker, Carpenter, & Cooper. Rain'd all last night. Cloudy all day and a N. W. wind.

Tues-day 27th. The men at the usual work. Coutu arrived with the 2 wooden canoes.

Wednes-day 28th. Snowed very hard all day, very little work done out of doors, to day.

Thurs-day 29th. Snow'd all night. Azure drawing fire wood with the Traine.

Friday 30th. Snow'd best part of the day. The Water rose 2 Feet since Yesterday Morning. Got the canoe wood taken from the water Side.

Saturday 1st Decr. Got the snow taken out of the Fort. Godin & Boulanger squaring logs to saw. In the evening La France return'd without finding the indians. Three of the Xy men that set of three days before La France, return'd last night & had no better success than him.

Sunday 2nd. About 12 oclock last night, arrived 2 men with 33 Plus, that Richard sent. he remains with one of the Iroquois at the indians lodge. 2 of the X. Y. men remain'd likewise. Snowed very hard all day. In the evening had a visit from the X. Y.

Monday 3rd. A little before day, I sent off 3 men with

[30] The Rapid River, or Rivière aux Rapides, flows into Rainy River from the south about halfway between the Long Sault and Rainy Lake. It is shown on the map on page 70.

Rum, provisions &c to find Richard up the Big Forks. I got the snow thrown out of the Fort. Azure began to draw fire wood. Amelle making Snow Shoes.

[*d*. Tues-day 4th. About 12 oclock I sent La France with 2 others after the X. Y. who had been off last night]

Tues-day 4th. Amelle busy with the Snow Shoes. The rest of the men at different works.

Wednes-day 5th. About 12 oclock, I sent La France with 2 others after the X. y. who set off last night. Amelle finished the Snow Shoes.

Thurs-day 6th. In the evening, arrived the 2 men that set off with La France. they overtook the Xy at the Big Forks, who are waiting for indians there. La France then sent home the men that were with him, and remain'd alone with the X. Y. Snowed very hard all day.

Friday 7th. Got the Fort clean'd, & some logs and fire wood drawn.

Saturday 8th. Early this morning, I sent Jourdin off with a load of provisions, to remain with La France at the Big Forks. In the afternoon he came back with La France, & the X. Y. men. Azure finished hauling the logs. Got a few Cords wood drawn. Very Cold. The women netted 3 p[rs] Snow Shoes.

Sunday 9th. The X. Y. went past on their way to the Big Forks. Richard being with the indians I did not think it necessary to send after them. Very Cold. In the evening, arrived one of the Pines. he was starving. he was obliged to eat the few Skins he killed.

Monday 10th. I sent 4 men off to the Pêche d'hiver [winter fishing grounds], with Nets, to fish. One of them is to return to morrow. Joe & Godin sawing logs for the new house. Amelle at his canoe wood. In the afternoon arrived the young Pine, who was starving. Very cold.

Tues-day 11th. The Sawers were obliged to leave off sawing, being too cold. La France froze one of his toes coming from the Pêche d'hiver. In the evening Richard arrived accompanied with 4 of our men & 4 X. Y. men. they left the indians starving.

Wednesday 12th. Cantarat came from the Peche d'hiver. he is come for another lodge. they one they have being too small. Very cold.

Thurs-day 13th. Cantarat set off with a lodge. I sent Coutu with him in Mailloux Place. Not so cold as usual.

Friday 14th. Some of the men visiting and making traps. Godin caught a Martin. Very mild all day. I wrote a few letters for Lac des Bois, to night.

Saturday 15th. Very early I sent Young Jourdin and one of the Iroquois off to White Fish Lake and from there are to go to Lac Plat for the news.[31] In the evening, Mailloux arrived from the Peche d hiver with 2 Very large Pikes. Fell about 4 inches snow last night. The sawers sawed a few logs. The others clean'd the Fort.

Sunday 16th. Snowed during the day. In the evening La Verdure came down with 4 of the Xy men on a Visit. they danced till near 12 oclock. Gayou caught a martin.

Monday 17th. Old Godin caught 2 Martins. Got the Fort clean'd. Joe began another wheelbarrow.

Tues-day 18th. I sent Vallé to the Pêche d'hiver for fish. I got 2 p^{rs} Snow Shoes finished to day. Godin very unwell all day.

Wednes-day 19th. Godin and 2 others splitting shingles. Joe finished a new wheelbarrow. In the even^g arrived Vallé and Cantarat. they brought but 1 pike. Cantarat is come for provisions. The X. Y. went yesterday to the Pêche d'hiver to fish. A Strong S. Wind all day.

Thurs-day 20th. I sent Cantarat off with 6 Quarts Oats. I got another pair Snow Shoes turn'd today. Joe and Godin caught each a Martin. Godin at the same work as Yesterday. In the evening arrived Jourdain and Thomas — they met Bon-

[31] Lac Plat (Shoal Lake) is one of the group of lakes known collectively as Lake of the Woods. It lies to the west and slightly north of Whitefish Lake.

homme with an X.Y. man on their way from White Fish lake to this place. Guilmont sends Bonhomme here as he can get no good out of him.

Friday 21st. Very early Richard with 2 men and one of the Pines set off in search of the Queue de Porcèpic. I set Bonhomme to work with old Godin & wrote a few letters for Lac des Bois.

Saturday 22nd. La Verdure, Thomas, Young Jourdin & Vallé, set off for Lac des Bois. the latter is to remain at White fish lake. Jourdin goes from there to Eagle lake, & the 2 others to lac Plat. Amelle finished the lises of 90 Canoes.[32]

Sunday 23rd. Godin visited his traps and caught 2 Martins. In the evening our men went up to the X.Y's on a Visit.

Monday 24th. The Fishermen arrived with 7 Pikes. Cloudy all day.

Tues-day 25th. This morning I gave each of the men a dram. at breakfast they began to buy rum and drank untill 12 oclock at night. Some of the X.Y. men came down. Mr Lacombe came down at 1 oclock and went home about dusk. Richard arrived. he saw the Queue de Porcèpic but got nothing worth mentioning. Two of the X.Y. men went by yesterday morning. they are gone after La Verdure thinking he is gone to the indians.

Wednesday 26th. The best part of the men went up to the X.Y. but did not remain long. In the evening I engaged 4 men & gave them each a pint Rum. Snowed a little to day.

Thurs-day 27th. The men drank all last night and finished this morning about 9 oclock. Cloudy all day.

Friday 28th. The men at their usual work. I sent a man down to the Big Forks to see whether the X.Y. are gone up there or not. Fell some snow today.

Saturday 29th. About 12 oclock Cantarat came home & tells me that the X Y are following Laverdure. Cold and Cloudy weather.

Sunday 30th. Snowed today.

[32] The French expression for the ribs of a vessel is *lisses*.

Monday 31st. All the men at work. I sent for the shingles (say 5000). Coutu and Gouin arrived with 10 pikes.

Tues-day 1st Jany 1805. The men paid me a visit very early. I treated them as usual on such a day.[88] They went up to the X. Y's and came home to breakfast. All the X. Y. men came down to our house and remain'd all day. The men were very quarrelsome & had 4 or 5 battles.

Wednes-day 2nd. About 12 oclock arrived the eldest of the Pines with 12 Skins & 10 more belonging to Kashishwa who went to the X. Y's with his Brother. they gave the X. Y. about 20 Skins. Very cold all day.

Thurs-day 3rd. The Pine set off. he took a few debts. Azure's wife went with him for some Meat. Kashishwa came down for the payment of his Skins. I paid him & he took for 20 plus on credit. Very cold.

Friday 4th. The Cadet of the Pines set off to stay with his Brother. Snowed last night and part of the day. Mailloux & Godin making shingles.

Saturday 5th. Very little work done to day being too cold.

Sunday 6th. The Fishermen brought 10 Pikes. I dined with Lacombe to day.

Monday 7th. About 3 oclock in the afternoon arrived 2 of the X. Y. men from Lac Plat. My Girl was brought to bed of a daughter. Very cold.

Tues-day 8th. Still very cold.

Wednes-day 9th. Joe caught a Martin. As cold as usual.

Thurs-day 10th. Cantarat arrived from the Peche d'hiver. he is come for provisions, as they take no fish. Very cold.

Friday 11th. The men work'd till 12 oclock, & then went

---

[88] New Year's Day, *le jour de l'an,* was a day of celebration and frivolity among the French Canadians. Early in the morning the voyageurs made a ceremonial visit to the quarters of their *bourgeois* or clerk to give and receive the New Year's kiss and to claim a treat of wine or rum. After this the day might be spent in games and feasting, the evening in dancing and revelry. It is of interest to note that on such an occasion the men of the two rival posts exchanged visits and spent the day together, albeit not without some quarreling and fighting.

up to the X. y's, according to an invitation they got yesterday. they were 13 men of ours including Richard & Amelle.

Saturday 12th. This morning the men came home & the best part of them yet drunk. In the evening arrived Laverdure, with the news from Lac Plat, & White Fish Lake. in them 2 Posts we have 12 Packs & the X. Y. 1½. A little after dark arrived 2 men from Leech lake with letters from Montreal. I receiv'd one, and Lacombe 1, Sign'd by Messrs McTavish Frobisher & C° & Alex^r McKenzie & C°. we are informed that both companies are join'd. Very cold.[34]

Sunday 13th. In the evening Mr Lacombe made me a visit. Weather still very cold.

Monday 14th. Busy writing to White Fish Lake Eagle Lakes & to Mr Ranald Cameron, to the latter, I sent him a copy of the letter I rec'd from Montreal.[35] The men at different works. Not so cold as usual.

Tues-day 15th. Very early Bonhomme and one of Lacombe's men set off to Eagle lake. Likewise Guedon set off to White Fish Lake, with a few articles that Guilmont was in want of. Fell some snow to day. In the evening Azure's wife arrived from her Son's lodge with a load of meat.

Wednes-day 16th. The Fond du Lac men set out. I wrote a few lines to M^r McGillis.[36] The men at the usual work.

[34] Leech Lake in north-central Minnesota near the headwaters of the Mississippi River was for many years an important post of the Northwest Company. The Northwest Agreement between the Northwest Company and the X. Y. Company, mentioned on page 127n. above, was signed in Montreal on November 5, 1804.

[35] From Duncan Cameron's diary it would appear that Ranald Cameron was at Lac Seul during the winter of 1804–05. See the entry for August 28, 1804, in " Extracts from the Journal of D. Cameron, Esq.," Masson, *Bourgeois*, 2:275.

[36] Hugh McGillis, whom we have already met in the vicinity of Fort Alexandria and the Red Deer River (page 126), was in charge of the Fond du Lac department in 1804 and 1805, taking as his headquarters a post at Leech Lake. Here Lieutenant Zebulon M. Pike found him a year later, when the Pike expedition pushed northward to the upper Mississippi. The American explorer was most appreciative of the trader's hospitality, and his journal throws considerable light on McGillis' character. It is possible that the

Thurs-day 17th. I sent La Verdure with 2 others to Lac Plat, with a few Goods & letters to Mr McIntosh & Mr McCrae. One of Lacombe's men set off likewise to Lac Plat. Snowing & blowing, very hard all day. Joe Caught a fisher.

Friday 18th. I sent Cantarat off with one of Lacombes men to Vermillion lake. Old Godin finished splitting the shingles. Mailloux preparing wood for Kegs. Arrived 3 Indians at Lacombes. he sent for me to receive my debts. I only got 10 Skins for my Share, La Combe got about 50.

Saturday 19th. Gouin paid us a visit from the Pêche d'hiver. Godin went in search of Pines to saw.

Sunday 20th. Gouin return'd to the Fishery. I gave him a few Quarts Oats. In the afternoon I paid a visit to Lacombe.

Monday 21st. I sent 2 men to square more logs to Saw. the rest of the men at different works about the Fort. Young Jourdain is come from the peche d'hiver for provisions.

Tues-day 22nd. Jourdin set off with 8 Quarts Oats. Azure finished drawing the Shingles. Very mild weather.

Wednes-day 23rd. Richard gone to see the fishermen. Godin & Canada a sawing. The Toads Son arrived at the X. Y. with a few Martins and a Traine of meat. In the evening Richard and Young Jourdain came home. Very fine weather.

Thurs-day 24th. The men at their usual work. Weather the same as yesterday. The X. Y. built a small house Yesterday a little below us.

Friday 25th. Remarkable fine weather. the men at work as usual.

Saturday 26th. Weather the same as Yesterday.

Sunday 27th. A very strong S. W. wind all day & in the evening it began to snow. Gouin set off with more provisions.

Monday 28th. Snow'd very hard all last night. Got the Fort clean'd. Strong N W wind all day.

McIntosh whom Faries mentions in the next entry was Donald McIntosh, a clerk in the Lake Winnipeg district in 1799. Coues mentions a Mr. McIntosh located on the Winnipeg River in the summer of 1804. Masson, *Bourgeois*, 1:64; Coues, *New Light*, 3:979.

Tues-day 29th. I sent 7 men this morning to square logs. the rest of the men at the usual work. In the evening the men came home after squaring 18 logs. Very fine weather.

Wednes-day 30th. Sent 4 men to make a road to draw the logs to the water side. Godin & Canada Sawing. Remarkable fine weather.

Thurs-day 31st. Sent 4 men to square more logs, & Azure went to draw them to the water side, but soon return'd as he could not cross the river with the horse. Godin making shingles to day. Joe preparing wood to make a new table for the Athaⁿ House. A very strong N. E. wind all day.

Friday 1st Feby. Godin & Canada sawing planks. the others at different works. finish'd squaring logs. Cold all day. towards evening there fell some snow.

Saturday 2nd. Coutu arrived with 2 large Pikes. In the evening, arrived the 2 men that were with Laverdure. The Latter remains at Lac Plat, to wait for the news of the river Ouinipic. The men left off work to day earlier than usual. An easterly wind.

Sunday 3rd. I sent Boulanger, & Coutu to the Pêche. In the evening Cantarat arrived from V. Lake with 2 of Mr Grant's men. they are come for a Keg of H. W. & Goods. Mr Grant writes me that he has 8 Packs Beaver and all appearances that he will make very well out. The men tells me that Mr Grant drinks very hard. The men had a dance & bought some rum. Godin caught a Martin.

Monday 4th. The men danced till this morning. Very little work done to day. In the evening Lacombe's men arrived from Eagle lake. Bonhomme is gone to Lac la Glaize with Black.[87] Remarkable fine weather.

Tues-day 5th. Got a few goods put up for Vermillion lake. All hands at work, except old Godin, who is unwell. Very fine weather.

Wednes-day 6th. Very early this morning Mr Grant's men

---

[87] Lac la Glaize (Glaise) is probably Clay Lake, just north of Rainy Lake and close to Eagle Lake.

set off very heavy loaden, with Goods Rum &c. I sent a man with them to help them to day & is to be back tomorrow. 3 men cutting more fire wood. the rest of the men working about the Fort. Old Godin began to work a little to day. I had a visit from Mr Lacombe. Weather as yesterday.

Thurs-day 7th. The man that set off yesterday return'd this morning at 1 oclock. he went as far as the Detroit. The men cutting fire wood. Godin & Canada sawing. La France finished a traine to day. Very fine weather. Joe caught 4 Martins.

Friday 8th. I sent 5 men to make a Saw Pit, & to draw the logs to it.[38] the others at work about the Fort. About 12 oclock arrived 2 men from White Fish Lake for provisions. they saw an indian about 2 days march from this, that has seen nobody since last fall. About 10 oclock I sent Richard & Thomas off to the above indians lodge.

Saturday 9th. I sent Cantarat to the Fishery for fish. he return'd in the evening without any. Gouin came with him for provisions. the men work'd as usual. A very strong South wind to day.

Sunday 10th. Gouin set off with 10 Quarts Oats. Mr Lacombe invited me to dinner. I made an agreement with him, as follows, he gave me 996 Plus of debts, and he is not to trade or receive a single skin from any indian — for which I am to give him 6½ Packs Beaver, 15 fine & 5 common Otters & to finish the ½ Pack with Martins & Muskrats. In the evening it began to Snow.

Monday 11th. Snowed all night, and did not cease till this evening. About 12 oclock Mr Lacombe came down for part

---

[38] It was customary in the Indian country to saw boards by means of a frame pit saw. "The log is cut and hewed on two opposite sides to the thickness of 9 inches or a foot. . . . Lines are then struck as near to each other as the thickness of the board requires, which the saw is made to follow. One man stands upon the sticks to be sawed, and manages one end of a saw 5 or six feet in length . . . while a second stands under it and manages the other." Letter of Sherman Hall to Aaron Hall, Jr., September 30, 1832, a photostat of which is in the collections of the Minnesota Historical Society.

of his payment. I gave him 1½ Packs Beaver. The rest I will pay by degrees. Got no work done out of doors to day.

Tues-day 12th. I set 5 men at work to fill the Ice-house. the rest at the usual work. In the afternoon La France came down with 2 Young lads, that went to Lacombes. they brought a few Skins, 2 Bags Oats, and a little fresh bear's Meat. I gave them each a Gallon Keg, & they went to sleep at Lacombes.

Wednesday 13th. The men at work as usual. Cloudy weather all day. About 8 oclock at night, arrived old Laverdure from Lac Plat. he brought me a letter from M^r McIntosh and another from M^r McCrae. the former writes me, he has 10 Packs, & his neighbour 5. M^r McCrae has 2 Packs.

Thurs-day 14th. About 12 oclock, the men finished filling the ice house. Richard arrived with 22 plus. Very fine weather.

Friday 15th. The Sawers finished sawing the logs that were at the Fort. I sent 29½^{lbs} Beaver up to Mr Lacombe per Lefevre. Rather cold to day.

Saturday 16th. The Sawers went to saw in the woods to day. La France & one of the X. Y. men set off to make traps, are to be absent 8 days. About 12 oclock arrived 2 indians from the River Noire. they are come for men, to fetch the few skins they have.

Sunday 17th. The above indians set off. I sent Richard & 2 men with them, to fetch the Skins & some Meat. Coutu paid us a visit to day. he is come for provisions.

Monday 18th. Coutu set off. I gave the sawers provisions for a week, as they are to remain in the woods to saw. Bonhomme arrived from Eagle lake guided by an indian. Very fine weather.

Tues-day 19th. I sent 4 men in the woods, to carry the boards that are sawed to the water side. the rest of the men at the usual work about the Fort. Weather the same as Yesterday.

Wednesday 20th. The Indian that guided Bonhomme, set off this morning. I wrote a few lines to Mr Aeneas McDonell, by him.[39] In the afternoon Richard arrived with 65 Plus, & some dry'd Meat. Weather remarkably fine.

Thursday 21st. I sent 4 men to make another Saw pit, & the rest of the men employed about the Fort. I sent 72^{lb} Beaver to Mr Lacombe per his Canoe Maker. In the evening Gouin arrived from the Pêche d'hiver for provisions. Weather as fine as Yesterday.

Friday 22nd. Joe with 3 others began to work at the new house. the rest of the men employed at different works. La France & Lefevre, came home Yesterday with 4 Martins. they made 180 Martin traps. Very fine weather.

Saturday 23rd. Gouin set off to the Pêche d'hiver with 3 Quarts Oats. About 12 oclock it began to snow very hard for about 2 hours, & the remainder of the day it rain'd. Very little work done out of doors to day, owing to the bad weather. In the evening Boulanger came home from the Pêche d'hiver.

Sunday 24th. In the evening Mr Lacombe paid me a visit. the men had a frolick, and kept up till 3 oclock in the morning. I engaged three men today. Very fine weather.

Monday 25th. I sent Guilmonts men off loaded with provisions, & Bonhomme set off with them to come back with Young Mumpherville. Very little work done to day. About 12 oclock arrived the Black legs & little Chief. they are come for men to go for their skins & Meat. weather the same as Yesterday.

Tuesday 26th. Richard & 4 men set off with the above indians. About 10 oclock arrived the Queue de Porcèpic's Nephew, with a little bear's Grease. I gave him a few pints rum & he set off. Weather as fine as usual. La France & Le Fevre gone to visit their traps. Old Azure unwell to day. The rest of the men working.

---

[39] Eneas McDonell was a clerk at Lac Seul in 1807. According to his own statement he had been in that vicinity since 1803. See Davidson, *North West Company*, p. 224n.

Wednes-day 27th. The men at their usual work. I bled old Azure to day. Very fine weather.

Thurs-day 28th. About 10 oclock La France & Le Fevre arrived. they caught 13 Martins. The men at the usual work.

Friday March 1st. About 3 oclock arrived the Handsome-Pine, from Lac des Bois with only 1 otter. he is encamp'd at the River Noire with the Chief. Azure still sick. Very fine weather.

Saturday 2nd. Gouin arrived. he brought 2 very large Pikes. The Pine set off. The men at their usual work. Godin came home. he has left off sawing. Very fine weather.

Sunday 3rd. I took a walk up to Lacombes to day. A very strong South wind all day.

Monday 4th. Godin &c. began to take down the Athabasca House. About 12 oclock Richard arrived from the Rapid River, with near 2 Packs & some meat. had a few showers of rain to day.

Tues-day 5th. I sent 68^{lbs} Beaver to Mr Lacombe per Le Clair. The men at work as usual. Very fine weather. La France & Le Fevre gone to visit their Traps.

Wednes-day 6th. Very fine weather. the men at work as usual.

Thurs-day 7th. Very cold all day and a strong North wind. Fell a little snow last night. the work going on as usual. La France caught 3 Martins.

Friday 8th. No work done to day. A very cold N. E. Wind. About 12 oclock arrived Bonhomme from White Fish lake. Guilmont writes me that Mr Lacombe has not dealt fairly with me, that he wrote to Mr Monk to trade the debts I bought from him, & moreover that some of his people of Lac des Bois is to come and pass the Spring in the river.[40] I sent for Mr Lacombe & spoke to him about all this, but he says it is false,

---

[40] George Henry Monk was a clerk of the Northwest Company. He is listed as being in the Fond du Lac department in 1806, and he left an account of Leech Lake in 1807. This narrative appears together with an explanatory preface by Grace Lee Nute in *Minnesota History Bulletin*, 5: 28–39.

however, I shall not depend on him; I will send Richard off as soon as possible to know more about it. Godin is very sick.

Saturday 9th. Snowing & blowing very hard all day, the wind the same as Yesterday. No work done out of doors to day.

Sunday 10th. Weather rather worse than yesterday. Best part of the roof of the Atha[a] house was blown off. I sent 102[lbs] Beaver to M[r] Lacombe per Lefevre.

Monday 11th. Richard, Jourdin & Lefevre, set off for White Fish lake. I wrote a few lines to Mr Monk, concerning my agreement with Mr Lacombe. I got the roof of the Atha[a] Store mended, & the Fort cleaned. Very fine weather.

Tues-day 12th. No work done out of doors. Weather colder than usual. I sent 2 men to the Pêche d'hiver to be back to morrow or next day. Old Godin is getting better.

Wednes-day 13th. About 12 oclock arrived the Corneille's Son. he is come for men to go for his Skins. One of the men, who set off yesterday return'd this evening with 12 Carps. Very Strong & Cold N W wind.

Thurs-day 14th. I sent 2 men off with the Corneilles Son. Little or no work done to day. In the evening arrived Gouin & Boulanger loaded with fish.

Friday 15th. Boulanger & Gouin set off to the fishery. the latter is to be back in the evening. Godin working at the Atha[a] House. In the afternoon arrived 3 indians from the Big Forks. Very fine weather.

Saturday 16th. La France & Thomas set off with the above indians for their Skins. Weather the same as Yesterday.

Sunday 17th. In the evening La France arrived with 50[lbs] Beaver & a few dress'd Skins. Godin caught one Martin. fine weather.

Monday 18th. I sent 50[lbs] Beaver to Mr Lacombe per Le Clair. The Cedar arrived. he is come for men to fetch his & the Queue de Porcèpic's Skins. arrived likewise 2 men from the Pierre a Calumet. In the evening Bonhomme arrived with

63 Plus. the men working at the Athabasca House & others carrying planks, from the other side the river, to the Fort. Azure & his woman set off, to the Little Forks to make Sugar.[41]

Tues-day 19th. I sent 31^{lbs} Beaver to Mr Lacombe per Le Clair. La France, Thomas & one of Lacombes men, set off with the Cedar, & 2 others with the 2 young indians. I sent Bonhomme to stay at Mr Lacombe's, to watch the indians, in case they should wish to give Skins away privately.

Wednes-day 20th. It began to snow last night & continued all day, with a very strong Easterly wind. About 1 oclock arrived 2 of the men who set off Yesterday with 20 plus, mostly in Martins.

Thurs-day 21st. About 12 oclock arrived La France with 35^{lbs} Beaver, & a few Martins & Otters, with a Bale of Meat. I sent ½ Pack peltries & 35^{lbs} Beaver to La Combe. I have yet 63^{lbs} Beaver to give him. Six men busy throwing the Snow out of the Fort. Remarkable fine weather all day.

Friday 22nd. Jourdain arrived with the Grue, & his Young Men. they brought 110 Plus. they are encamped at the Pêche d'hiver. I gave them a large Keg Rum & 2 f^{ms} Tobacco. they set off in the afternoon with only ½ a keg & left the other en cache.

Saturday 23rd. I sent 2 men to the Fishery for Fish. I sent Mr Lacombe the remainder of the Furs that I agreed to give him. I have at present about 3 Packs remaining, exclusive of dress'd Skins. Richard arrived from W.F.L. nothing very particular. The 2 men arrived loaded with fish.

Sunday 24th. The Grue sent 2 Boys for the remainder of his Rum. they remain'd about an hour and set off. The Grue & Blacksmith's wives, paid us a visit. Very fine weather.

Monday 25th. Very early this morning I was disturbed by the men of the Fishery. they & the X. y. Men ran off from

[41] For other references to the making of maple sugar see pages 32 and 270. The Little Fork River flows into the Rainy River from the southeast about six miles above the Big Fork.

the Pêche d'hiver, & as they Say the indians that encamp'd there wanted to kill them. I set off directly with Richard to know the reason of all this. About 10 oclock we arrived at the lodges,—but it seems that the men had a false alarm. About 3 oclock we got home again & found the Queue de Porcèpics Nephew at the house waiting for me. he brought nothing at all. he came to beg a little rum. I gave a 2 Gallon Keg Mix'd rum between him & his uncle & he set off to the Pêche d'hiver. The men were very busy to day making themselves Huts, out of doors, as I intend getting the old house taken down this week. very fine weather. In the evening the Seiners went to the Fall to Seine, but caught nothing.

Tues-day 26th. I sent 40 Bushels of Potatoes up to Mr Lacombe's cellar, having no place for them here. Began to take the old house down. Very fine weather.

Wednesday 27th. Very early this morning I put myself in one of the little houses. The Grue paid me a visit. he set off about 2 oclock. I gave him a 2 Gall^n Keg of Rum. Assamac the chief arrived with his Uncle. they brought a few Skins. The men working about the old house, &c. Very fine weather.

Thursday 28th. The Chief & his uncle set off. I gave the chief a 2 Gallon Keg Rum, & his uncle a large Keg. Mr Grants girl set off to make Sugar. The men at the usual work. Two men arrived with Fish. A very strong South wind all day.

Friday 29th. The Young Cedar arrived he kill'd 2 Orignals. I traded one of them & sent 4 men for it, but they return'd without finding it. We saw Bustards to day for the first time. The Queue de Porcepic's Nehpew paid us a visit. he brought nothing. Wind the same as Yesterday.

Saturday 30th. Arrived 2 men with fish. Jourdain set off yesterday to help Mr Grant's Girl to carry her things to the little Forks. A very strong South wind. I sent 2 men off to the fishery to be back tomorrow.

Sunday 31st. Arrived 2 men with Fish. In the evening had a visit from the X. Y. people & M[rs] Lacombe. they danced till near 12 oclock. Very fine weather.

Monday 1st April. Rain'd very hard all night & had a few showers to day. Joe began to raise the new house. Jourdain arrived in the evening.

Tues-day 2nd. I sent 4 men off to the Seines. Richard with 2 others, set off to the Rapid River, with ammunition for the indians, that are there. Young Jourdain refusing to do his duty I turn'd him out of the Fort. Rain'd during the day. of course very little work done, out of doors. In the evening arrived 2 men loaded with fish. The old Toad arrived with one of his Sons. they bro[t] 50 plus.

Wednes-day 3rd. The old Toad & his Son, set off with about 3 Gall[s] mix'd rum & some ammunition. About 1 oclock, A. M. arrived the Corneille's Son and the Eagle. they brought 26 plus in Martins and Otters. they took a little ammunition & set off again. Coutu came home from the Fishery. I sent Cantarat in his place. Old Godin began to raise the Atha[a] house. Remarkable fine weather. Yesterday I receiv'd 150 Gun Flints from Lacombe.

Thurs-day 4th. Coutu began to make a chimney in the new house. Joe finished covering the house. Godin busy covering the Atha[a] house. I rec'd 39[lbs] of Nails assorted from M[r] La Combe. Strong South wind all day. Cantarat brought a load of fish and return'd directly.

Friday 5th. The men at work as usual about the buildings. Cloudy weather all day. A little after breakfast arrived the Queue de Porcèpic with 4 dress'd Skins. after taking a few necessaries, & the Rum I gave him, he set off. In the evening arrived one of the Queue de Porcèpics Nephew's & family. he is going a piece down the river to work Beaver. Canada is lame of one hand.

Saturday 6th. Fell about 4 inches snow last night. I sent 4 men to the Fishery for fish, & to tell the 2 men that are there to come home to morrow. Wabikekek, & another indian and family arrived. they brought me a little fresh Caribou meat, for which, I gave them a Gallon mixt rum. they encamp'd a little below the Fort. In the evening the men return'd from the Fishery, with only 8 fish.

Sunday 7th. Boulanger & Cantarat came home from the Fishery, with the nets & Baggage. Mr Lacombe paid me a visit to day. Very fine weather. In the evening, I sent Duval & Young Umpherville to the little Forks, to get me some sugar, if there was any made.

Monday 8th. A little before day, it began to rain & Snow very hard, till about 12 oclock. I got the inside of the new house plaistered to day. Wabikekek brought me the meat of a young Orignal. I paid him with rum & he set off directly. In the evening Duval arrived. he brought me about 10^{lbs} Sugar, that old Azure sent me.

Tues-day 9th. This morning I had a few words with Grènier, for not working as he ought. he set off, & past the remainder of the day at Lacombe's. About 2 oclock, arrived Richard with a few Skins and a little Sugar. In the evening Grenier came home for his things, to set off, for good and all. I hindered him from going. Very fine weather. Mailloux hurt his hand to day.

Wednes-day 10th. When I mustered the men up to their work, I found Grenier absent. the men tells me that he set off in the night. About 12 oclock arrived the Frozen Foot with the Blackbirds brother. they brought only 23 Plus. I gave them a small Keg, and some ammunition and they set off.

Thurs-day 11th. Godin finished covering the Athabasca house. Joe busy making the Floor in the new house. the rest of the men working at the chimnies. About 12 oclock, I sent Richard & Young Umpherville, to the Big Forks to trade Sugar. Very fine weather.

Friday 12th. Godin began the flooring in the Atha^a house. the others at work as yesterday. Mailloux making kegs. Canada's hand is still very bad. Remarkable fine weather.

Saturday 13th. The men finished the chimnies to day.

Amelle has finished preparing his wood &c. for the canoes. he only waits for fine weather to begin his canoes.

Sunday 14th. Arrived 3 young men from the Grue's lodge, with a few Bustards. I paid them with rum & they set off. About 12 oclock arrived the Queue de Porcepic's nephew with 7 Beavers & the Meat of 2. I gave him a 2 Gall^n Keg & he set off. Mr Lacombe breakfasted with me this morning. Very fine weather.

Monday 15th. The men working as usual except Canada, whose hand is still Sore. Amelle and I dined with Mr Lacombe. Weather as fine as Yesterday.

Tues-day 16th. This morning Amelle began to make a canoe, of 3½ f^{ms} long, for voyaging. about 12 oclock, Richard came home. he traded about 1½ Kegs Sugar. Richard saw Grenier at the Big Forks with the Seiners, and told him to come home, but he refused, saying, he would rather die than return.

Wednes-day 17th. Old Azure arrived with Mr Grants girl. Azure brought me about 60^{lbs} Sugar. The Cedar brought us 4 Bustards and an Otter. he took ammunition on credit for Bustards. I gave him a gallon Keg Rum. The men at work as usual & they go on very well.

Thurs-day 18th. I sent Mailloux & Coutu down to the Seiners. the former is to stay there a few days to Seine. Richard & Young Umpherville gone a hunting in the lake. I sowed for garden Seeds to day. In the evening, Mr Lacombe's wife arrived from below making Sugar. She brought me 2 Small Sturgeons, that the Seiners sent me by her. they are the first that we got from them since they left this. Mr Grant's Girl traded about 30^{lbs} Sugar to day for Rum.

Friday 19th. About 12 oclock it began to rain and rain'd all day. In the evening Mailloux & Coutu arrived with 14 Sturgeons. Richard arrived. he killed only 1 Bustard & 1 Duck.

Saturday 20th. Raining all day. I got the inside of the new house plaistered to day.

Sunday 21st. Fell a little snow last night, & had some showers of rain to day. I sent Boulanger to the Manitou, for white earth, to White wash the houses.[42]

Monday 22nd. Amelle began to make a large canoe, but was obliged to leave off, as it was too cold. The Grue & the Blackbird arrived, the latter paid me 22 Skins on his credit, & the Grue gave me 30 Bustards, with 3 Bales dried Meat. I gave them a large Keg between them.

Tues-day 23rd. Jourdain arrived with 9 Sturgeons. Kept two men all day, digging in the garden. Very fine weather. I lent 65 Bundles Wattap, to Mr Lacombe.

Wednes-day 24th. Jourdain set off again to the Seine. About 12 oclock arrived the Young Pine & Tems Clair's Son in Law, with about 30^{lbs} Sugar. I paid them in Rum, and they took a few debts for gum & Wattap. In the evening arrived Laverdure. A little after dark Boulanger arrived, with 3 Bags white earth.

Thurs-day 25th. Rain'd very hard all night. the work going on as well as can be expected. I sowed a few more garden seeds.

Friday 26th. A little before breakfast, arrived L'homme Noire with 77 Plus, that he paid on his credit. he has 70 yet at his lodge. I gave him a large Keg & he set off about 12 oclock. I sent Richard with him for his Skins. In the afternoon arrived two women from the Big Forks, with 20 Skins in Beaver & 60 Bundles Wattap.

Saturday 27th. Very cold all day & had some showers of rain.

Sunday 28th. About 12 oclock arrived one of the Sainers with 7 Sturgeons. In the evening, the X. Y. men and Madame Lacombe paid us a visit. they danced untill near 12 oclock.

Monday 29th. The Sainer set off. I sent old Azure with him to fetch the horses up. The Corneille arrived with 2 young men. they bought a few orignal Skins, & 4 Bales dry'd

---

[43] A kind of clay was used for plastering the houses in the fur country, and a white earth was made to serve as whitewash.

Meat. I gave them 2 Small Kegs Rum, & they set off directly. Mr Lacombe paid me a visit. In the evening Azure return'd without the horses. Grenier bro^t us 10 Sturgeons.

Tues-day 30th. Grênier set off again to the little Forks with the Sainers. Amelle finished the small canoe. Snowed for about 3 hours this morning. Very little work done out of doors. Canada is at last got well.

Wednes-day 1st May. Richard arrived from the Rapid River with 2 Packs Furs. The men made a new oven & plaistered the outside of the new house. I got a small assortment made out for the [Lake] Meccane.

Thurs-day 2nd. Richard with 3 men and one of Mr Lacombe's men, set off very early for the Meccane, to endeavour to draw in my debts &c. with the indians of that place. One of the X. y. Men arrived from the little Forks with sturgeon. he brought Six for us. Arrived 2 young lads with 4 Bales dry'd meat. I gave them a 2 Gall^n Keg of Rum & they set off directly. Amelle began another large canoe to day.

Friday 3rd. Mr Grant's girl set off to stay with her Brother. About 12 oclock arrived one of the Toad's Sons with 20 plus, and a Bale dry'd Meat. I gave him a 2 Gall^n Keg Mix'd Rum & he set off. Very cold all day, and a strong N. W. wind.

Saturday 4th. I sent up to Mr Lacombes for the Potatoes, that I put there for seed. Amelle not able to work at the canoes being too cold.

Sunday 5th. Mailloux set off in a small canoe to cut hoops at the Big Forks. I past the afternoon at Mr Lacombes. Very fine weather. a little after dark, I was surprised at the return of Mailloux with one of the Sainers, to inform me that Chenette was arrived at the little Forks; & that the X. y. was coming behind, and might probably trade along the river. I embark'd in a small Sauteux canoe, with 2 men, & arrived at the Little Fork at 9 oclock at night. I sent Jourdain & Young Umpherville, to the Long Sault, to remain there till all the Lac des Bois people were past.

Monday 6th. I embark'd with Chenette, & got at the Fort at 8 oclock. on my arrival, I sent Mailloux & Azure to the Saine, in place of the other Sainers. I removed into the new house to day. In the evening arrived one of the Bras Court's Son's with 32 plus. I gave him a 2 Gall^n Keg Rum, & he set off directly.

Tues-day 7th. The men cutting potatoes for seed. Joe cut his foot very badly to day, squaring a log.

Wednes-day 8th. I got 6 Bushels potatoes sowed to day. I sent 2 men to the Little Forks for Sturgeons. they return'd in the evening with 16. Very cold all day.

Thurs-day 9th. At 1 oclock in the morning I set off to see the indians at the Big Forks. we got there at 5 oclock, & after searching in all the lodges, I found only one Beaver & a quantity of Wattap. at 10 oclock, we embark'd on our way home, at the Little Forks, en passant we got 18 Sturgeons from the Sainers. In the evening, arrived the Devil with only 2 dress'd Skins. Tapinawa likewise arrived from the Long Sault.

Friday 10th. The Tapinawa set off. he took a few debts. I gave him a large Keg Mix'd Rum. The Devil set off. I gave him ½ keg of rum, & a few goods, with 45 plus that he owed me for his daughter. Jourdain arrived from the Long Sault with 20 plus. on his arrival I gave him the Devil's daughter, for 500^{lb} G P C [Grand Portage Currency].

Saturday 11th. A little before breakfast arriv'd the Young premier. he is come for a few debts, to pay in Bark & Wattap. on his departure I gave him ½ keg Rum. About 12 oclock arrived the Picotte's Band. they are going into the lake. The Cedar arrived with a Bear Skin, a little Grease & some Meat.

Sunday 12th. We had a visit from Mr Lacombe & his wife. the latter remain'd untill about 12 oclock at night dancing. Very fine Weather.

Monday 13th. The Sainers brought 40 Sturgeons. I got a few Packs made to day. Remarkable fine weather.

Tues-day 14th. Lambert of the X. Y. arrived from the Xy

Lac des Bois, with 3 Packs. I got 23 Packs press'd to day. Godin making a gallery to the Atha^n house.

Wednes-day 15th. About 12 oclock, arrived Richard with 12 packs Furs, and a little Oats. In the evening Mr Grant arrived from Vermillion lake, with 16 Packs of 96^{lb} each.

Thurs-day 16th. Busy making Packs. I sent for Bonhomme to come home, from the X. Y. The Big Rat's Son arrived, he brought only 1 drest Skin.

Friday 17th. About 12 oclock arrived M^r M Crae with 3 men in a Sauteux Canoe. he brought 3 Packs which is well, considering the place he wintered at, & the disadvantage he had under his neighbour. four of the X. Y. Clerks, & as many of their men paid us a visit. they danced with our people till near day light.

Saturday 18th. About 7 oclock this morning I sent 2 Canoes off to Kamanitiquiac with 31 Packs. My Girl embark'd in one of them, to see her daughter. had a shower of rain in the evening.

Sunday 19th. Rain'd very hard all night, & had several showers of rain to day with a strong N. W. wind. The Dogs Head arrived with a few Beavers, & some Wattap. I gave him 3 Gall^s Rum & he set off. The Sonnant arrived, & en-camp'd at the Fort.

THE DIARY
OF THOMAS CONNOR

The Diary of Thomas Connor

Introductory Note

Less is known about the author of this interesting diary than about any of the others in this volume. It appears probable that the journal was written by one Thomas Connor, but little is known of his character or the facts of his life. A manuscript record book of pioneer settlers of the St. Croix Valley enrolls him as an Englishman by birth. The list of Northwest Company employees in the Fond du Lac department in 1805 includes his name and a notation of his being indebted to the company to the extent of £1,026.3. His status at that time is a matter of uncertainty; Masson lists him as a voyageur, but the diary leads one to the conclusion that he held a position of higher rank.

The journal, now in the possession of the Public Archives of Canada, covers the winter of 1804–05, which the author spent in the region of Cross Lake and the Snake River. Of especial interest is his narrative of the building of his trading post. We see the young trader meeting his Indians at Cross Lake and discussing with them the site of his winter quarters. He finds a suitable place on the Snake River, and the men are soon busy clearing ground for a shop and a store, also for living quarters for traders and men. The work proceeds rapidly, the men spurred on by the promise of receiving a dram each morning and evening if they exert themselves. (See page 255.) In less than a week the store is finished, and provisions and goods are under lock and key. Two weeks more and the buildings are covered, floored, and plastered, and Connor has moved into his dwelling house. By the fifth of November the men have moved into their quarters and the Indians begin to appear, bringing in skins to pay off their debts and taking new credits for the coming season's hunt. Having completed the houses, the men turn to the cutting and raising of stockades, and on November 20 Connor reports that "the Doors of the Fort where [*sic*] fixed & Shut this Evening." (See page 259.) The next day the finishing touches are put on the post, and a flagstaff is erected, from which the British colors will float in the heart of the wilderness. The diarist wastes no words, yet the picture he draws is clear and distinct in outline.

The activities at the post during the winter are recorded with a precision comparable to that of Faries and McLeod — the ceaseless coming and going of Indians and of employees, the trading of skins, the hunting expeditions for meat. One party is sent out to the Indians of the Sandy Lake department, five men taking goods and rum worth 163 skins to their lodges. Some of the men make sledges or repair canoes; the women collect gum for the canoes and, in the early spring, busy themselves boiling and working sap into maple sugar. The frequent mention of "oats," or wild rice, for which the St. Croix Valley was famous, shows how important a commodity it was in the trader's stock of supplies. The Indians of the upper St. Croix were called Folle Avoine or "Wild Rice Makers," and the harvest they gathered each year was a staple product in the trade of the region.

Life in Connor's camp is not without danger and excitement. The Indians are a troublesome lot, and on several occasions it is necessary to set guards for defense. More than once Connor himself intervenes when disorder threatens. The Snake River area, it will be recalled, presented special difficulties because it was hotly contested between the Sioux and the Chippewa tribes. Much of the trouble, however, was due to the generous use of liquor in the trade, and to the fierce competition between the Northwest Company and the X. Y. Company, a struggle revealed throughout the pages of the diary. It is interesting to note the author's reaction to the agreement signed by the competing companies, news of which reaches him just before New Year's Day. Although this agreement provides that the X. Y. traders shall share the fur trade to the extent of twenty-five per cent of the stock, Connor seems to regard it as marking the destruction of the rival concern. Accordingly he redoubles his efforts to prevent the Indians from taking furs to his competitors, a policy hardly to be reconciled with the plans of cooperation which the partners had in mind.

Of Connor's later life little can be said. He appears to have continued in the trade at Pokegama for some years after the diary was written. After 1816 the British were excluded from the fur trade south of the Great Lakes, and Connor became affiliated with the American Fur Company, a concern controlled by John Jacob Astor. His trading house was apparently well known among the natives in the vicinity, for Jedediah Stevens, a Protestant missionary who stopped there in January, 1830, notes that "the house was ful of Indians all the evning." Connor also handled supplies sent in for the missionaries at the Pokegama Mission, established in 1836 by the American Board of Foreign Missions. Being a Catholic, the trader was not over-tolerant of the Protestant zealots, although he was willing to listen to what they had to say. Stevens did his best to impress his host with the divine truth as revealed in the Gospel of St. John and "endeavored to commend them [Connor and his family] to God." He made little progress, however, and the trader continued in his own way of life, unable to enjoy the blessings that Stevens possessed in such full measure. Frederic Ayer, who was at the Pokegama Mission in 1837, reported that the trader withdrew his children from the mission school, fearing lest they should be led away from the Catholic faith. For the most part, however, his relations with his customers were friendly enough, and at one time he went so far as to offer the use of his trading house for mission meetings.

Connor took an Indian woman for his wife, and the couple had several children, of whom the oldest daughter, described by Ayer as intelligent, pious, and industrious, was married to an Indian convert of the mission. The census of St. Croix

County, Wisconsin, for the year 1840 shows that Connor was between fifty and sixty years old at that time and that there were nine other persons in his household. As time went on the family separated; in 1847 William Folsom found the old man and his wife living in a bark shanty on the St. Croix. The traveler was given the best entertainment that Connor's humble circumstances could afford, and he appears to have spent a pleasant evening listening to the trader's stories of the valley and his many trading experiences. The following year Connor left the St. Croix. The rest of his life he spent at Lake Superior, and he gave his name to Connor's Point in West Superior.[1]

The diarist frequently — one might almost say habitually — runs his sentences together without punctuation or capitalization. To facilitate reading, periods have been inserted where required, but no changes have been made in capitalization. Words struck out by the diarist have been included within brackets and preceded by *d.*, signifying " deleted."

C. M. G.

[1] See William H. C. Folsom, *Fifty Years in the Northwest* (St. Paul, 1888), pp. 47, 262; also the diary of Jedediah Stevens, letters of Frederic Ayer, and the manuscript volume, "Obituary Record, St. Croix Valley Old Settlers' Assoc'on," all in the manuscript collections of the Minnesota Historical Society.

The Diary

Lake St Croix Saturday 15th Septr 1804.¹ At 6 A M. Embark'd under a very heavy rain. arrived at Noon at Namaiocawagun, the place where La Prairie pass'd the summer. I found him & Seraphin with 2 Men here. they had no provisions having left all their Oats in Cache. La Prairie made only 4 Small packs during the Summer. the Goods I had forwarded by M^r La Mare was in excellent Condition. Mr Reaume has been absent 20 days trading provisions at Paguégamant. we apprehend some Accident has befallen him.²

Sunday 16th. Fine Weather blows a Gale S W. took a Statement of my Goods & put an Assortment apart to send by La Prairie tomorrow, in pursuit of my Opponent & watch his Motions.

---

¹ Connor is here referring to the Upper St. Croix Lake, which is virtually the source of the St. Croix River. From the head of this lake a two-mile portage led to the upper waters of the Bois Brûlé River, which flows north into Lake Superior near what is now Superior, Wisconsin. The route by way of the Bois Brûlé and Upper St. Croix Lake was the one commonly used to reach the St. Croix River and the Mississippi.

² Seraphin Lamarre appears on Masson's list as a clerk in the Fond du Lac department. See Louis R. Masson, *Les bourgeois de la Compagnie du Nord-Ouest* (Quebec, 1889), 1: 409. It is difficult to know from Connor's use of the two names whether he is referring to one or two persons. Little seems to be known of La Prairie except that he was a clerk of the Northwest Company who had been trading the year before in opposition to Michel Curot of the X. Y. Company. See "A Wisconsin Fur-Trader's Journal" (Curot's journal) in Wisconsin Historical Collections, 20:396–471. Joseph Réaume was an experienced trader who had been at Red Lake as early as 1785; in 1792 he made an expedition to the source of the Mississippi River, and in 1799 and the years following he traded for the Northwest Company in the Fond du Lac region. During the winter of 1804–05 he was stationed, according to Connor, at Namai Kowagon. See page 400n. and the entries for September 19 and 20.

Namaicowagun is undoubtedly the Namai Kowagon mentioned by School-

Monday 17th. Cold & Stormy wind N. at 9 A M La Prairie & family departed after Chenier with 12 Galls H[igh] W[ine], Tobacco & powder.³ wait Reaumes Arrival to deliver him the Equipment of La Prairies.

Namaiocowagun St Croix River 18 Septr 1804. A fine Day wind S W. this afternoon Mr Reaume made his Appearance from Serpent River where he had traded 42 Bags of Oats shortly after the 2 Canoes I left behind in River Brulé. ordered each Man a Dram. towards Evenening [*sic*] there fell a heavy Shower of Rain.

Wednesday 19th Septr. Warm & Calm. gave La Prairies assortm^t in Charge of Mr Reaum. Orderd the Canoes to be in repair to depart tomorrow.

Thursday 20th. Fine Weather. wind S E. was prevented from departing untill the Afternoon my Men being all Drunk, owing to Mr Seraphins Neglectfullness. Camp'd at 4 P M below the big rapid to repair 2 of the Canoes they got broke. left Mr Reaume alone to take care of Lapraires Equip^{mt}.

Friday 21st. At 6 A M I went off with 2 Canoes to search for Gum. left Seraphin in Charge of the 3 Others. at 10 A M Camped at the Grand Gallé & dispatched all the Women to gather Gum. at 4 P M they returned with only 4^{lbs}.⁴

Saturday 22nd. fine & Calm. at 7 departed. Camp'd at 11

---

craft. It was the site of a flourishing Indian village situated on the St. Croix ten or eleven leagues below the head of Lake St. Croix. See Henry R. Schoolcraft, *Narrative of an Expedition through the Upper Mississippi to Itasca Lake* (New York, 1834), p. 138. "Paguégamant" is one of a variety of ways in which Connor spells Pokegama, the Indian word for the Serpent or, to give it its modern name, the Snake River. This stream is a branch of the St. Croix flowing from the uplands east of Mille Lacs southward through the present Kanabec County, Minnesota, thence eastward through Pine County, joining the St. Croix directly east of Cross Lake. See below, page 254.

³ Shortly after 1800 William Morrison went into the region west and south of Fond du Lac, trading for the X. Y. Company, then under the leadership of Sir Alexander Mackenzie. Among the members of his party were two brothers of the name Cheniers, Michel and Antoine. One of these was apparently competing with Connor in 1804. Minnesota Historical Collections, 7:123.

⁴ A "galet" in the Northwest usually meant a gravel bank. Here the Grand Galet and Little Galet were taken as landmarks along the route. See

A M above the little Gallet where I remaind to get Gum. Orderd the other Canoes to proceed on to the Portage of the Gallet. Women returnd this afternoon with near 30^{lbs} of Gum.

River St Croix Sunday 23 Septr 1804. Charming Weather. at 6 A M Embark'd. arrived at Yellow River at 1 P M where I found La Prairie with 10 Indians the principals of this Village all the others were off with Chenier.[5] it is not known to any Certainty which River he intends to fix himself for the Winter. I was receivd with Shouts and several Volleys of Small Arms in hopes of getting a Drink. I referr'd them however till the Morrow. Wrote imediately a letter to Mr Reaumes with Orders how to Act.

Monday 24. fine & Calm. Gave 3 Kegs Rum to the Indians. at 7 A M Dispatchd 2 Canoes to bring the Effects in Mr Reaumes Charge & departed imediatly in pursuit of Chenier at 4 P M. near Serpent River met an old Indian & family who begged of me to put ashore & Camp & I Complied. he inform'd me that Chenier was up the Rapids of Kettle River where he was Building his Winter house & that tomorrow he Chenier was to go down St Croix River near the fall to gather the Hunt of 16 Indians who have been absent these 10 days past.[6] if he gets the start of me he will be a Conjurer.

Tuesday 25. Cloudy at 4 P M Orderd 3 Kegs of Indian to be put in my Canoe & paid the old Indian 4 Gall^s rum due him on a Canoe. took my departure in Quest of Chenier. Hunters at 3 P M came up with them. they had made a Poor Hunt. 3 Indians were Absent & not Expected for 10 Days to come. traded 6 Deers in Meat 10 Deer Skins & 3 Beavers a little Tallow the whole they had which cost me a Keg of Rum.

Curot, "Journal," Wisconsin Historical Collections, 20:409. These are now known as the Big and Little Yellow Banks.

[5] The Yellow River is a tributary of the St. Croix, entering it from the south about midway between the Namakagon and the Snake rivers. It flows through what is now Burnett County, Wisconsin.

[6] The Kettle River follows a southerly course through present Pine County, Minnesota, joining the St. Croix some distance above the Snake. The falls were probably those located at the present village of St. Croix Falls, Wis.

left the rest for Chenier. Indians insolent & threatnd to take my Rum but did not put it in Execution. got no Sleep.

St Croix's River Wednesday 26 Septr 1804. At 8 A M left the Drunken Indians as they had nothing more to Trade. they were very importunate & insolent, which determind me not to give them a Single Dram. at Noon met Chenier with 3 Men going to his Indians. he stared with a gastly look at seeing me turnd pale & passd without uttering a Syllable. at 5 P M arrived at my Encampment where I had left the Old Indians. during my Absence my Men had traded 3 Bags of Oats.

Thursday 27th. Fine Weather. remaind till 2 P M to get Gum made & repair our Canoes dry our Meat &c after which we departed. On entring Serpent River found the Water so low I orderd the Men to make 2 trips. We made about One league head Way & Campd at 4 P M to repair the Canoes. here I buried under Ground 3 bags Oats & 60^{lb} flour in case of Necessity the Ensueing Spring.

Friday 28th. Cloudy Weather. at 7 A M sent of the Canoes with half a Load. I remaind behind to take care of the Baggage. at Noon the Men came for the remainder of their Loading. Camped at 4 P M. near the still Water. in the Night had a false Alarm which kept us all Night under Arms. the Fool & family Joind us here. got 2 Kettles on Credit.

Saturday 29 Septr. A Rainy Morning which prevented our Departure till 1 P M when we Embarkd & got up 3 long Rapids. the Men returnd for their half Load. arrived at 6 P M. here we remain for this Night.

Riviére aux Serpent 30th Septr 1804. A very Cold Morning. at 9 A M left our Camp. at 4 P M arriv'd at the Head of the Still waters with all our Loading. shortly After, the Old La Pon arrived with a Beaver. Gave him 2 Gal^s HW & sent him back with Orders to invite all the Squaws to make Gum, being destitute of that Article.

Monday 1st Octo^r. Weather as Yesterday. it froze Considerably last Night. at 10 A M embarkd & at 3 P M arrived at Cross Lake where I found 3 Squaws makeing Gum.[7] shortly after all the principal Men came here to fix on a place for my Winters abode. Gave them a Keg of 9 Gal^s H Wines & they went away to drink at their Lodges.

Tuesday 2nd. Cloudy Stormy Weather. we remaind here all Day to repair our Canoes. this forenoon, the Outarde brot me a Small Deer. gave him 1 Gal. H Wines and engaged him as my Hunter for the Winter he being accounted the best of all the Indians of this Department.

Cross Lake Wednesday 3rd October 1804. Cloudy with thunder & rain at 9 A M. Embarkd after hiding 10 Kegs H W & a Bale of Carrot Tobacco. at 11 arrived at Paguayaman River to search for a Spot to build upon. shortly after all the Indians arrived with 5 Bags Oats. gave them another Keg H W to get rid of them.

Thursday 4th. Cold & Cloudy. Men Employd handling their Axes a few Sober Indians came & got Credit. they intend to go to their Hunting Ground tomorrow.

Friday 5th. Charming Weather this Morning traded 5 Bags of Oats for Rum. Indians still Drunk. gave Debts to a few.

Saturday 6th. Weather as Yesterday. dispatchd 2 Canoes to fetch the Oats Mr Reaume had traded. gave More Debts to the Indians. traded a few Skins for Rum.

Sunday 7th. Fine Weather. Compleated all the Indian Credits & gave them 2 large Kegs being in 2 seperate Bands to encourage them to Hunt well. went with 2 Men in a Canoe in search of a More Convenient place to Build. found a more eligable Spot about a Mile up the River. this evening the Men returnd with 42 Bags of Oats 10 which were Spoiled not eatable.

Serpent or Paguaygamant River Monday 8 Octr 1804. Stormy Weather this Morning. went & Camped where I intend passing the Winter. traded 2 Bags of Oats a few Skins for Rum.

[7] Cross Lake is a fair-sized body of water through which the Snake River flows. Pine City, Minnesota, is situated at the southern end of the lake.

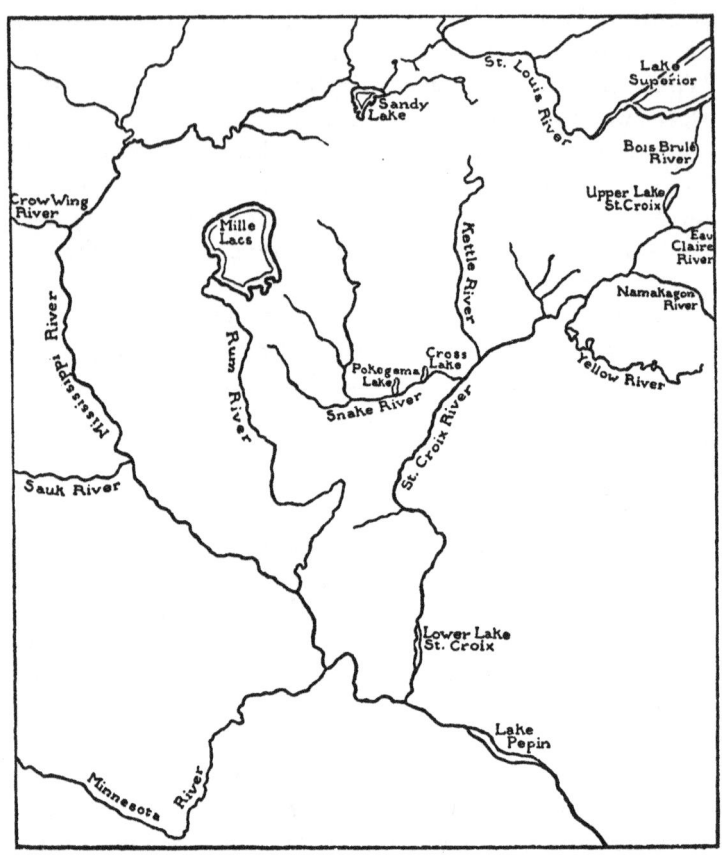

THE TRADING REGION OF THE ST. CROIX RIVER

Tuesday 9 Octr. Fine Weather. Men Employd Clearing a Spot to build upon having perform'd a great Days Work gave them ½ Gall^n H W. Orderd the Sturgeon Net in the Water.

Wednesday 10th. Rainy Day which prevents the Men Working. took a Pike of 37^{lb} Weight in our Net the largest I ever yet saw.

THE DIARY OF THOMAS CONNOR 255

Thursday 11th. Weather as above which keeps all hands Idle. my Hunter brot: the Meat of 2 Deers & 60 fine fat Ducks.

Friday 12th. Clear Weather wind N E. the Court Oreille [Ottawa] & my Hunter are off for 2 Days. men perform'd a great Days Work. gave them each a Dram morning & Evening & promised to do the same till our Buildings are Compleated provided the[y] exert themselves.

Saturday 13. Charming Weather. Men as Yesterday. Pierro gave me 30 Large Ducks.

Winter Quarters Sunday 14 Octr 1804. Cloudy with rain. Men Employ'd at the Shop & Store. the little Horns lame Wife & family Camped here. my Hunters brot me 1½ Deer. gave them 1 Gallon H W. they requested more but I refused & they were Sulky.

Monday 15th. Weather as Yesterday. Men finishd the Store & put all the provisions & Goods under Lock & Key a happy Circumstance in time of Danger.

Tuesday 16th. Fine Calm Weather. Men hard at Work Covering the Houses. gave them ½ Gall: Rum. my Hunter & Pierro gave me 30 large Ducks.

Wednesday 17. Weather as Yesterday. Men Employd at the Chemnies. took 3 large Piconoes in our Net.[8]

Thursday 18th. Stormy with rain at intervals. Men Compleated the Masonry of 4 Chimneys. took one Sturgeon & 3 piconoes in our Net. Piero gave me 1 Outarde & 12 large Ducks.

Friday 19th. Charming Weather. Men finished 2 Chimnies. got 100 Rats from Piero & 12 large Ducks.

Winter Quarters Saturday 20th Octr 1804. Lovely Weather. Men Compleated the remaining 2 Chimnies.

[8] The traders were dependent on fish as well as on game and wild fowl for their food. Connor's "piconoes" should be *piconou*, listed by Taché as the *Cyprinus (Catastomus) sueurii*. It is a fish belonging to the family of carp. Monseigneur Taché, *Sketch of the North-West of America*, translated by Captain D. R. Cameron (Montreal, 1870), p. 208.

Sunday 21st. Stormy with rain at intervals. Men began to floor the Houses.

Monday 22nd. Cold Wind N E with a fall of Snow 10 Inches Deep. Pierro gave me 15 large Ducks. no Work done this day.

Tuesday 23. Clear & Warm which causes the Snow to melt apace. Men at Work flooring the Houses.

Wednesday 24th. Cold Wind N. the Court Oreille came in quest of 3 Men to fetch 10 Beavers he has Killd also 10 Deers. Pierro gave me 26 Ducks & 4 Geese.

Thursday 25th. Cold Weather blows a Gale S W. My Hunter Came with 24 Ducks of difft. Kinds 2 Deers & 3 ps dry Meat pierro 16 Ducks 1 Goose & 30 Rats. Men finishd plastering my House.

Friday 26th. Charming Weather. sent 3 more Men for the Meat of the Court Orell gave me. my Hunter brot 30 Ducks 3 Geese. Pierro 18 Ducks. Men finishd plaistering my Rooms.

Winter Quarters Saturday 27 October 1804. Warm Weather Men finishd Covering all the Buildings. my Hunter gave me 14 large Ducks & 1 Goose. 3 Men came back with each a load of Meat from the Court Oreilles Lodge.

Sunday 28th. Weather as Yesterday. the fixtures of my Shop Compleated and the Goods in Order. my Hunter gave me 11 large Ducks. Piero 14 the Court Oreille 1 Beaver in Meat.

Monday 29th. Charming Weather. put 25 Bags of Oats under Ground and the provision Store in Order. gave La Pon my Hunter & Pierro each 2 Galls Rum. this evening enterd my dwelling House.

Tuesday 30th. Weather as Yesterday. Indians Drunk & troublesome. Men Employ'd finishing their rooms.

Wednesday 31st. A Sultry Day & Calm. found myself indisposed. took an Emetick which did me much Service. Men finishd my Bed Room.

Winter Quarters Thursday 1st Novr 1804. Enchanting Weather. this Day being all Saints gave my Men 1 Galln

Rum. they did no Work of course.[9] this afternoon Monsr Marin [d. & Father] Arrived with a Capital Beaver Hunt. gave him 4 Gall^s Rum.

Friday 2 Novr. Weather as above. Indians Drunk & those that were here prior to Marin the Chief arrival were very insolent but he behaved Manfully & deserves every attention.

Saturday 3 Novr. Cloudy & rain. at 5 P M all the Beaver Hunters arrived brot 200 Skins & paid their Debts Nobely. gave them 2 Kegs Rum & 3 fath: Tobacco. they drank all Night very peaceably.

Sunday 5th [sic]. Pleasant Weather. Indians Drunk & peaceable except the Court Oreille who behaved himself so ill that I was forced to drub him. my Men entered their dwellings.

Monday 5th. Fine Weather. Indians still Drunk & troublesome. they came the whole Band to perform their Warr Dance Marin at the Head but said it was against his inclination. to please them gave 4 Gall Rum ¼ Vermillion & 1 fath[om] Tobacco.[10]

Winter Quarters Tuesday 6th Novr 1804. Cloudy Day. Orderd my Canoes to be put up for the Winter. the Chief called little Horn made me a present of a handsome pipe & Tomahawk, or warr club with which the Sioux Kill'd the Peaux D'oursons [Bearskins] family. Indians still drunk & insufferably troublesome. it was with much difficulty, I put a stop to their Drinking.

Wednesday 7th. Cold Weather. Men Employd Cutting stockades to build a Fort. the Plat [Plate] went off to Mr Reaumes Quarters. Wrote a letter of advice by him.[11]

[9] All Saints' Day was a great holiday among the French Canadians. Even at the small trading posts of the interior the voyageurs contrived some celebration of this festive occasion.

[10] Vermilion and painters' colors were commonly used by the whites in trading with the Indians. Harold A. Innis, *The Fur Trade in Canada* (New Haven, 1930), p. 169; also a note by Thwaites in Wisconsin Historical Collections, 19:217n.

[11] An Indian by the name of Le Plat or Plat Coté was a celebrated chief of the Lac du Flambeau band who in 1804 was trading in the interests of

Thursday 8th. Weather as Yesterday. this forenoon the whole of the Indians assembled & requested me to give them a Keg of Rum to take a parting drink before they disperse for their respective Hunting Grounds. policy induced me to Comply. this is the 6 Keg they have expended for Nothing since the 2nd inst:

Friday 9th. Stormy Wind N. Men employd bringing up the Stockades. this afternoon the Tete Jaune [Yellow Head] & Son came from hunting. Beaver made an indifferent Hunt. paid their Debts. gave them 6 Gall^s Rum. they drank peaceably & gave me no Manner of trouble.

Winter Quarters Saturday 10 Novr 1804. Cloudy Wind N E. the River froze over which prevents the Indians decamping. Men employd as Yesterday.

Sunday 11th. Cold Wind N E. this Morning the 2 Chiefs Marin & little Horn took their Departure to hunt Deer.

Monday 12th. Weather as Yesterday. gave Credit to several Indians that are to depart tomorrow. Men Employ'd bringing up Stockades.

Tuesday 13th. Mild & Cloudy. Men began raising the Stockades. Old La Pon & family took their departure to Hunt Beaver.

Wednesday 14th. Cold Wind S W. Men as Yesterday. nothing else Material.

Thursday 15th. Weather as Yesterday. the Court Oreille brot: 2 Deers for which he got Rum which caused a drinking bout. he was troublesome as Usual. got 10 Beavers for Rum. Men as Yesterday.

Friday 16th. Very Cold wind N. Indians still Drunk. Men as Yesterday.

Saturday 17th. Fine Weather. Court Oreille went back to his Lodge. Pierro & the Six went to Hunt Beaver.

Winter Quarters Sunday 18th Novr 1804. Cloudy appearance of Rain. this forenoon one of Marins Naphews arrived.

the X. Y. Company. See Curot, " Journal," Wisconsin Historical Collections, 20:425n.

tells me there is no Deer where they are encamped, which determines the Indians, to go a considerable distance in search of Beaver. sent 4 Galls H W to the chiefs. this afternoon my Hunter made a demand of all my Men to fetch 10 Deers.

Monday 19th. Charming Weather. sent 4 Men to my Hunters Lodge. dispatchd Mr Seraphin with a Man to examine a Cache of 10 Kegs of H W to know if all are safe. he came back at Noon. found the whole in good Order. towards evening I was surprised to see 2 of the X Y Men Arrive with an Indian. luckily all my Indians are absent yet I apprehend they will poison the Minds of the Women by offering to sell Cheaper than I do.

Tuesday 20th. Weather as Yesterday. My Men arrivd with the Meat of 7 Deers. X Y Men & Guide returnd to their Quarters. the Doors of the Fort where [*sic*] fixd & Shut this Evening.

Wednesday 21st. Warm Day. this forenoon my Men Erected a Flag Staff. gave them a Gallⁿ Rum. towards Evening Pierro & the Six arrived. brot 5 large & 6 Small Beavers.

Thursday 22. a Summers Day. this Afternoon the Peaux Dourson came back & Camped here again occassiond by Hunger. I scolded them. they promise to depart again in 2 or 3 Days hence.

Winter Quarters Friday 23 Novr 1804. Fine Weather. sent 5 Men to my Hunter for Meat. this afternoon X Y Chenier with 4 Men came here with Goods & a trifling Quantity of Rum in hopes of getting a few Skins. the Event was they returnd as they came except their Rum, which my Indians very Politely drank off a leur Santé.[12]

Saturday 24th. Cloudy with rain. at daylight the X Y Men returnd home. fired a Voley & abused Seraphin. he made no reply. Men came back with the meat of 1 Bear Only. my Hunters have been alarm'd by the Sioux which prevents their Hunt.

[12] *A leur santé* may be freely translated " with toasts to their good health."

Sunday 25th. Cloudy Rainy unpleasant. the River being free of Ice sent 2 Men for the 10 Kegs H W. they returnd a 4 P M. this Evening Girard arrived with a Sick Indian on his Back. I do not expect he will survive.[13]

Monday 26th. It raind all last Night & this Day without intermission. my Indians made several Applications for Liquor which I refused owing to the Brochet [Pike] & Rognion [Kidney] 2 of Cheniers Chiefs that are here & I am determind they shall not taste my Liquor without payment.

Tuesday 27th. Clear weather wind N W. the Brochét took his departure. the Rognion remaind here unwell. my Indians made another Effort for Rum to no purpose. during this Night a fall of 8 Inches Snow.

Winter Quarters Wednesday 28th Novr 1804. Snowy Weather wind N E. all the Indians out a Hunting Killd 5 Deers. gave them 2 Kegs Rum.

Thursday 29th. Cold Weather Indians Drunk & troublesome. threaten to leave me if I refuse them Rum. put them to a defiance. they flew to Arms. we prepared to receive them & they thought proper to be peaceable.

Friday 30th. Unpleasant Snowy Weather. Indians out a Deer hunting. my Hunter was the only one that Killd any.

Saturday 1st December. Weather as Yesterday. sent Bouché for a Deer my Hunter Killd.[14] the Rascally Indians have agreed to make their Mittay Ceremony & beg'd Rum which I refused & abused them as they deserve.[15]

Sunday 2nd. Cloudy unpleasant weather. nothing Material Occurred.

[13] Joseph Girard was a voyageur in the Fond du Lac department in 1804. Masson, *Bourgeois*, 1:410.

[14] François Boucher was an interpreter in the Fond du Lac department in 1804. Masson, *Bourgeois*, 1:410.

[15] The rites of the Midewiwin or Grand Medicine Society, perhaps the most important religious ceremonies of the Chippewa Indians, have been perpetuated to the present day among the Indians of Minnesota. Frances Densmore gives a description in her work on *Chippewa Customs* (Bureau of American Ethnology Bulletin 86, Washington, 1929), pp. 86–93.

Monday 3rd. Fine Warm weather. sent Le Blanc for the Meat of a Deer. Men began cutting Chord Wood.

Winter Quarters Tuesday 4th Decer 1804. Cloudy weather wind S W. Indians performd the superstitious Mittay Ceremony, which continued the whole Day.

Wednesday 5th. Cloudy & Snow. all the Indians on a Hunting excursion. they will be 3 days absent.

Thursday 6th. Weather as Yesterday. nothing Material Occurred.

Friday 7th. Cold Day wind N. thermometer 10 Degrs below freezing.

Saturday 8th. Weather as Yesterday. Employd Pierro to Make snow Shoes.

Sunday 9th. Cold at 20 degrs below Freezing. my Hunter sent for 4 Men to fetch Meat.

Monday 10th. Mild Weather. the Peaux Dourson came for 2 Men to fetch the Meat of a Deer & a small Bear. gave him 2 Galls Rum in payment.

Winter Quarters Tuesday 11th Decer 1804. Cold very Severe 30 Degrs below freezing pt. all my Men absent amongst the Indians. they have Killd 2 Bears & several Deers. this evening Men came back with each a load.

Wednesday 12th. Weather as Yesterday. sent 3 Men to the Court Orellies Lodge for the meat of a Bear.

Thursday 13th. Cold increased. thermotr stands at 35 degrs. the severity of the Weather obliged all the Hunters to desist. they came back having Killd 9 Deers & 4 Bears for which I paid ½ Keg of Rum. they were very Quarelsome amongst themselves. I was obliged to interfere to prevent Murder being Committd.

Friday 14th. Mild with a fall of Melting Snow. Indians still Drunk & troublesome. I was obliged to Protect the Court Oreille & family in the Fort & Mount Guard all Night. the Peaux Dourson attempted Stabbing me. luckily I had a Stick with which I disarmd him & drove him into his hut.

Saturday 15th. Weather as Yesterday. Indians still Drunk.

traded Meat & Grease for Rum. Court Oreille still under my Protection. in the Course of the Day a fall of 14 Inches Snow.

Winter Quarters Sunday 16 Dece^r 1804. Cold Weather at 10 below freez: p^t. nothing Occurr'd worth noting.

Monday 17th. Cold as Yesterday. one of the Chimneys took fire but soon Extinguish'd. Men employ'd repairing it.

Tuesday 18th. Cold very intense 30 deg^{rs} below F.P. [freezing point]. this forenoon the Peaux Dourson the Fool & families off to Hunt. are not to come & Camp here before the Middle of February.

Wednesday 19th. the Cold diminishd stands at F P. sent Bellaire to remain with the Peaux Dourson.[16]

Thursday 20th. Cloudy appearance of Snow. nothing Occurred of Note.

Friday 21st. Warm Weather. thermo^{tr} up at temperate. all the Indians decamped to Hunt for the Winter Season.

Saturday 22. Very Mild Appearance of Snow. got a Bear Skin from the Borgne [One-eyed] for Medecines. Adminsterd him poor Wretch. I apprehend he will shortly prove a Corpse.

Winter Quarters Sunday 23rd Dece^r 1804. Weather as Yesterday. Nothing of Consequence Occurred this Day.

Monday 24th. A Mild Calm Day. this forenoon Bouché & Le Blanc came with a load of Bears Meat from Pierros Band. they have Killd 4 Bears, every appearance of their making a Good Hunt.

Tuesday 25th. Cloudy with Snow. at 10 A M La Prairie came & paid me a Visit. good Accts from his post. this being Christmas Day gave a treat of Rum &c to my Men which occasiond several Battles. Bellaire brot 2 Deers from Peaux Dourson.

Wednesday 26th. Weather as Yesterday. at 10 A M La

---

[16] On the list of men employed in the Fond du Lac department in 1805 appear the names of two men, father and son, called Louis Belair. Apparently Connor's Bellaire was one of them. See photostats of lists of men in the various departments of the Northwest Company in 1805 in the collections of the Minnesota Historical Society.

Prairie returnd to his Post with a small supply of Goods &c. at same time Mr Seraphin with 2 Men went to Visit Pierro in Order to get their Bear Skins. the 2 Men have Orders to remain there to take care of their Skins being apprehensive the X Y Banditti may pay them a Visit.

Thursday 27th. Cloudy unpleasant Weather this Morning went back to the Peaux Doursons Lodge.

Friday 28. Snowy Day. this forenoon Mr Seraphin came back with only 1 Bear Skin. the others were not Stretchd. Wrote a letter of advise to Mr Reaume by an Indian that is gone to his Quarters.

Winter Quarters Saturday 29th Decem^r 1804. Weather as Yesterday. this afternoon the little River one of La Prairies Indians passd bye on his Way to Join his brother. made a short stay.

Sunday 30th. Cold day. Wind N. Bellaire came from the Peaux Doursons Lodge. Complains of Hunger, says the Indians Kill nothing.

Monday 31st. A Cloudy Mild Day. at 9 A M to my Amazement I was Saluted by Mr Bellaux from Montreal.[17] I remaind speechless for a few Seconds & after recovering from my Astonishment I cou'd scarsely put trust to sight. he gave me the Melancholy intelligence of M^r McTavish's Death, & by him I receivd a letter advising me of a Settlement having taken place between the 2 parties trading to the N W which puts a Stop to Opposition.[18] this evening Le Blanc & Bouché brot some Meat & 3 Bears Skins from Pierro & C°.

Tuesday 1st Jany 1805. Weather as Yesterday. my Men paid me the usual Complts of the Day. gave them a treat of Rum &c & each ½ Carrot Tobacco. after Breakfast sent the

---

[17] A man by the name of Belleau was in charge of a post on Snake Creek, between the Swan and the Assiniboine rivers, in 1797. It is possible that he was the man who made the journey from Montreal to Cross Lake in 1804. See Gordon C. Davidson, *The North West Company* (University of California Publications in History, Vol. 7, Berkeley, 1918), p. 93; David Thompson, *Narrative of Explorations in Western America* (edited by J. B. Tyrrell, publications of the Champlain Society, Vol. 12, Toronto, 1916), p. lxxiii.

[18] See above, pages 127n. and 225n.

Men to Pierros Band with 5 Gal^s H W. with Orders to inform all the Indians of the X Y C^o destruction.

Winter Quarters 2 January Wednesday 1805. Cold & Cloudy thermo^{tr} 20 Deg^{rs} below F P. sent Bellaire to the Hunters to encourage them to kill Deer.

Thursday 3rd. Cold 10 deg^{rs} more than Yesterday. at sun rise despatch'd Mr Seraphin & 2 Men with a letter to X Y Chenier in order to discover what was going forward at same time to deter the Indians giving any more Skins. Mr Bellaux took an Inventory of the Shop.

Friday 4th. Cold as Yesterday. Nothing Material Occurred.

Saturday 5th. Cold as Above. this afternoon Bouché came with 2 Bears from Pierros Band. they complain of Hunger. Pierro is on his Way to Camp here.

Sunday 6th. Cold Wind S E. this forenoon Pierro & family camped here. they say this is the 2nd day that has been without victuals.

Monday 7th. Cold 25 deg^{rs} below f.p. Nothing Material Occurred.

Winter Quarters Tuesday 8th Jan. 1805. Calm Mild Snowy Day. at 2 P M Mr Seraphin with X Y Chenier arrived. in the course of the evening made a settlement with him respecting his future Conduct with the Indians. he agreed to every thing I proposed with much good Nature. this Evening Bellaire & my Hunter came with a Deer & 4 ps Meat.

Wednesday 9th. Cold 30 deg^{rs} below F P. after Breakfast Chenier & Man returnd to his Quarters much discouraged. paid my Hunter for 7 deers 2 Gall^s H W & 1 Qt Rum to the Tete Jaune.

Thursday 10th. Cold at 35 deg^{rs}. at sunrise dispatchd Déseve to the little Horns band to inform them of what had taken place between Chenier & me at same time forbid them to go near or trade a single skin with him. at sun sett Girard & Bellaire brot 3 Deers from the Hunters Lodge.

Friday 12th. Cold excissive at 40 deg^{rs}. at 4 P M Deseve came back. he tells me it was Apropos that I sent him as the Indians had an inclination of paying Chenier a Visit. at present they alter their Course & hunt in a different Direction.

Winter Quarters Saturday 12 Jany 1805. Temperate. sent Mallet to the Hunters for a Deer the Men left behind.

Sunday 13th. Sharp Weather wind S W. at sun set Mallet came back with the Deer I sent him for Yesterday.

Monday 14. Weather as Yesterday. sent 2 Men to the Hunters to encourage them to kill Deer being scarce of Meat. Bouché arrived with the meat of a Bear. this Day a fall of 4 Inches Snow.

Tuesday 15th. Mild Weather thermo^{tr} 20 deg^{rs} below F P. sent Bouché back to the Lodges with Amunition. at 3 P M Wabetais Brother one of Cheniers Indians arrived brot: nothing. his arrival gives me a certain Satisfaction.

Wednesday 16th. Charming Weather thermo^r up at Temperate. this Morning Wabitais Brother returnd to his Lodge. gave him ½ fath: Tobacco for his Brother, forbidding him giving any more Skins to Chenier.

Thursday 17th. A Very Stormy Cold Day. wind N. with a thick drift of Snow. this Afternoon came with a Deer from the Hunters Lodge. Bellaire remaind to take care of 8 More that remains on the Scaffold.

Winter Quarters Friday 18th January 1805. A Cold Day 20 dg^{rs} below F P. Orderd 3 Men to be ready to start at Sun rise to fetch Deers Meat from the Hunters Lodge. gave them 10 Measures powder with 200 Ball.

Saturday 19th. A Snowy Mild Day at Sun rise Deseve Girard & Mallet went to the Hunters for Meat. Pierro went also to dig up grand River Root.

Sunday 20th. Cold at 35 below F P. Mr Bellaux & Seraphin obliged to draw fire Wood. a large Billet fell on my foot & sadly bruised one of my Toes.

Monday 21st. Cold as Yesterday. this Afternoon my Men came home with 6 Deers. there remains 9 more on a Scaffold.

Tuesday 22nd. A Mild Cloudy Day. Men employed makeing Sledges. took up 12 Bags of Oats from the Cache. nothing else Material Occurred. 2 Men went back to the Hunters.

Wednesday 23rd. Cloudy & Mild. Mr Bellaux Makeing a Sledge &c. nothing of Notice Occurred.

Winter Quarters Thursday 24 Jany 1805. A Mild Calm & Cloudy Day. at 2 P M to my great Satisfaction Mr Marin a respectable Chief with Father & family made their appearance after an Absence of 2½ Month. I apprehended the Sioux had killed them. they have upwards of 100 Beavers &c. shortly After the Beggarly Band of Hunters arrived. gave a Keg of Rum to the Chief & Father & another to the Hunters for 15 Deers. they drank very peaceably.

Friday 25th. Cloudy Weather. Indians still Drunk & Quarelsome amongst themselves. 2 got Stabbd but not dangerous.

Saturday 26. Clear Mild Weather. Indians at length sober again.

Sunday 27th. Very fine Weather. this Afternoon the Téte Jaunes Son expired after a long & painfull Malady of upwards of three Months. his Death costs me a Keg of Rum to content his relatives. he was a most excellent Indian. desired his Father to pay his Debt & to be attentive to the White people. this Afternoon, Wabitai one of Cheniers Indians came here in search of his Son that ran Away unknown to him.

Winter Quarters Monday 28th Jany 1805. Cloudy Mild Day. therm^{tr} at F P at 10 A M the Dead Indian was buried. Coverd him with a Flag & Shirt & gave a Small Keg Rum & ¼^{lb} Vermilion. Wabitai was nearly Killd three diff^t times. at length he escaped by running into my House.

Tuesday 29th. A fine Clear Day. early this morning Wabitai with his Son return'd to his Lodge. at 3 P M the little Horn M^r R: Chief with all the Beggarly band Camped here. paid a few Skins. gave them 2 Kegs Rum.

Wednesday 30th. Cloudy Mild weather. thermo^{tr} up 10 Deg^{rs} above F P. Indians are very peaceable. traded 6 Beavers for Rum & gave old La Pon a small Keg after paying the whole of his Debt. expended one more Keg in the Course of the Day for Grease & other rubbish. after Sun set it raind a heavy Shower after which a Squall of Hail & in the Night a Storm of Snow. the Platt an Indian from Cheniers Quarter camped here. brot: Nothing.

Winter Quarters Thursday 31st Jany 1805. A very unpleasant Stormy snowy Day. Indians still Drunk. traded 2 Kegs of Rum chiefly for Beaver at 10 Skins pr Keg. in the Course of the day there fell upwards of 6 Inches of Snow.

Friday 1st February. A fine Clear Day rather cold. traded a 9 Galln Keg of Bears Grease for Rum. Indians still drunk but very peaceable. Wrote a letter to Mr Reaume to know what is passing in his Quarters.

Saturday 2nd. A Cold Stormy Day with a considerable drift of Snow. at sun rise sent Girard & Bellaire with a letter to Mr Reaume. dont expect them back before a fortnight. this Afternoon I was attackd with a Violent inflamation in my left Eye.

Friday 8th. I have been confined to my room since the 2nd Inst: owing to the inflamation of my Eye during which interval nothing of any Note Occurred. this Day all the Indians decamp to Hunt Deer to leave their families to make Sugar & the Men are to go to the Beaver Country. gave them 1 Keg Rum.

Winter Quarters 9th Feby 1805. Fine Mild Weather thermtr at Temperate. this forenoon 2 Young Lads arrived from the Drunkards Lodgs & report that the Indians were near Killing each other. at same time requested a Small Keg of Rum which I refused them.

Sunday 10th. Weather as Yesterday. attended with a Considerable thaw. nothing Material occurred.

Monday 11th. A Cold Day but clear Sky. Wishaima & family took their departure to hunt.

Tuesday 12th. Weather as Yesterday. this forenoon 2 Women Came for Amunition & at 2 P M they returnd to their Lodges.

Wednesday 13th. A Cloudy Stormy Day Wind N E with a fall of Snow of 6 Inches that did not Cease till after sun sett.

Winter Quarters Thursday 14 Feby 1805. A Cold Day wind N. at 11 A M Mr Reaume with 3 Men came from Laprairies Quarters. it appears that the same extragance as usual has taken place notwithstanding my positive orders to La Prairie to avoid giving large Credits.

Friday 15th. fine Clear Weather. this afternoon the Plat & Brother arrived on their Way to Cheniers for his Beaver traps he left there.

Saturday 16th. pleasant Weather. Wrote a letter to Chenier & the Plat requesting he wou'd supply me with an Origniale Skin for pack Cords.

Sunday 17th. Charming day. at sun rise Mr Reaume returnd to his Quarters. sent 3 Men for 5 Deers that Pierro & Co have Killd. after Sun set a Woman from La Prairies Quarters arrived. she met M^r R & reports that he walks with great difficulty owing to a sore Leg.

Winter Quarters Monday 18 Feby 1805. Very pleasant Weather. this evening my Men came home with the Meat of 5 Deers. the Plat brot a letter from Chenier.

Tuesday 19th. Charming Weather. this Morning an Indian came from the little Horns Lodge requesting Rum to make a Feast in hopes to save the life of one of his Daughters that is very unwell. policy induced me to Consent & sent him a Gallon of H W. the Plat & his Brother followed the Keg. sent a man to Pierro & Co for meat.

Wednesday 20th. A Lovely Day. therm^{tr} up at Summer Heat. of course a Considerable thaw. this afternoon Déseve arrived with 2 Beavers & the Meat from Pierro & Co. at same time 4 Indians passd bye on their Way to the Indians of M^r Rs: dept^{nt} I suppose to invite their relations to Warr.

Winter Quarters Thursday 21 Feby 1805. Weather as Yesterday. at sun rise Mrs [Messrs.] Bellaux & Seraphin with 1 Man went to pay a Visit to Chenier of L. P. at same time to get a Moose Skin and probably will pay a Visit to Laprairie. Piero arrived afternoon brot only 1 Beaver.

Friday 22nd. A Cloudy Day attended with a great thaw. at 1 P M to my great Surprise 2 Indians of Sandy Lake Depart^{nt} made their Appearance in quest of Rum &c to fetch a Quantity of Beaver they have at their Huts.

Saturday 23. Charming Weather Wind S W. thermom^{tr} at Summer Heat. this forenoon Deseve arrived with the Moose Skin shortly after the little Horn Mr Reaumes Chief with 4 Squaws & a Dead Child which my Men interred. put apart Goods & Rum &c to the Amt: of 163 Skins to send to Trade with Sandy Lake Indians.

Winter Quarters Sunday 24th Feby 1805. A very pleasant Warm Day. Wind S W. the snow Melts fast. this Morning the little Horn returnd to his Hut. gave him a Gall^n H W to bewail the Death of his Child & coverd the Corpse with a small Blkt pay [sic] N W. this afternoon the Six & family Camped here. they gave me a little Deers Meat & requested Liquor which I refused. shortly after Miquouanance One of Cheniers Chiefs with 5 Other Indians of my Depart^{nt} made their Appearance & one of them brot a Note from Laprairie for a Gallon of H W on his Acct but I refused to Consent.

Monday 25th. Weather as Yesterday. this forenoon little Reaume came with a letter from Mr J. Reaume. he informs me that Messrs Bellaux & Seraphin were still at La Prairies. the same Day Deseve with 4 Men went with the Sandy Lake Indians to Trade at their Huts.

Winter Quarters Tuesday 26 Feby 1805. Warm Weather. this forenoon Mr Bellaux & Seraphin arrived. they slept at Cheniers last Night. Cheniers Chief & Son went back to their Huts. gave him a Carrot of Tobacco.

Wednesday 27th. Weather as Yesterday. at day light sent to Monse Marin the Chief for a Load of Meat but did not risque to send Liquor before I Knew what Quantity he had.

he was very displeased & threatend to send to Cheniers in Future. at 2 p m the Men came back with the Meat of 4½ Deers.

Thursday 28th. Weather continues Warm. at day light Mr Seraphin with 2 Men returnd to the Chiefs Lodge with 10 Galls Rum. Orderd them to repremand the Chief for his threatning Message. at 2 P M Seraphin came back. he left all the Indians in a good Humour.

Winter Quarters Friday 1 March 1805. Warm Day. thermtr up at Summer Heat. the 2 Men that went Yesterday with Mr Seraphin to Lodges arrived before day light with the Meat of 6 Deers. this forenoon all the Squaws went off to their Sugar Huts.[19]

Saturday 2nd. Sharp Weather. wind N. sent back the 2 Men to the Hunters for more Meat. nothing Material Occurred.

Sunday 3rd. Cloudy with a Strong S E Wind. thermt at Temperate. at Sun rise the Men that went for Meat came back. prepared a Net to set as soon as the Navigation will admit.

Monday 4th. A Cloudy Day with a Smart Shower of Rain after which a fall of Melting Snow. at 11 A M Henrie with Good returns brot: near one pack of Beaver & other Good furrs nearly 1½ pack in Value. shortly after the Grand Coquin & Brother appeard much intoxictated with Cheniers Rum. made a demand for more Liquour which I refused.

Winter Quarters Tuesday 5 March 1805. Mild & Calm. after Sun sett the Indians of Yesterday took their Departure. made a request of Goods which I refused. Wrote Mr Reaume to send by one of the Men tomorrow at same time a Note to X Y Chenier in quest of Tea. my Squaw brot about 4lb Sugar.

[19] The annual departure to the sugar bush was an important and enjoyable event in the life of the Indians. Each group of relatives or friends had its own section of the forest known as its sugar bush, where the sap was collected, boiled down, and worked into sugar. See page 32n. above; also Densmore, *Chippewa Customs*, p. 122.

Wednesday 6th. A Cloudy Day with a N E Wind & a small Snow Storm. this Morning Reaume took his Departure to return to his Quarters.

Thursday 7th. Cloudy & Cold. packed up all my Peltries in Number 13 Packs all Good. a Squaw Calld the Chiene came & traded 4 Rats for Oats.

Friday 8th. A Stormy Cloudy Snowy Day which laid upwards of 6 Inches on the Ground. this forenoon 2 Messengers arrived from the 2 Chiefs Marin & little Horn makeing a humble request for Rum before they depart for their Beaver Hunt.

Winter Quarters Saturday 9th March 1805. A Blows a Tempest from the N E with a heavy fall of Snow. the drift is so thick that the Indians dare not venture to return to their Lodges. gave 10 Quarts of H W to send off tomorrow to the 2 Chiefs & their Band with 3 Men to encourage their Hunt. gave each of my Men 1 Measure of Powder 30 Ball & 2 p^r of Mokesons. the Six with several Squaws arrived here from the Sugar Bush owing to the Stormy Weather. this is most Boisterous day we have had during the Winter.

Sunday 10th. Weather as Yesterday Snows without intermission the whole [day]. There is upwards of a foot of new fallen Snow on the Ground. sent 3 Men to Join the Beaver Hunters to encourage them to Hunt & assist them with 10 Gall^s H W.

Monday 11. Fine Clear Weather with a Sharp N Wind. sent 2 Men for a load of Meat left at the Lodges by the Indians on their Departure.

Winter Quarters Tuesday 12 March 1805. Cloudy Weather Wind N. sent Bellair to assist to make Sugar. nothing Material Occurred.

Wednesday 13th. Clear day wind N W, with a trifeling thaw. this Afternoon one of Monsomanains Brothers in Law came in Quest of a Gallon of H W. three of my men being in the Lodges induced me to Comply & shortly after he took his Departure.

Thursday 14. Cloudy Weather. wind S attended with a Considerable thaw. this forenoon 2 Squaws arrived from the Sugar Huts intoxicated & informed me that the Indians of Yesterday had deceived me & took the Rum to their Lodges which kept them Drunk all the Night.

Friday 15th. A Cloudy dull lonesome Day. Mild Weather with a Considerable thaw. this Afternoon Messrs Bellaux Seraphin & one of my Men put a Net under the Ice. sent Déseve with a Bag of Oats to my Sugar Makers.

Winter Quarters Saturday 16 March 1805. A fine Summers Day. thermo^{tr} at Summer Heat. took a Pike of 10 ^{lb} in the Net set Yesterday. towards Evening it began to rain & Continued the most part of the Night.

Sunday 17th. Cloudy & foggy part of the forenoon. afterwards a Clear Sky. thermo^{tr} 10 Dg^{rs} above summer heat. fishermen took a Small Carp in the Net which was greatly injured by floating trees. they took it up & this afternoon set a new one. this evening Chacobai shot a Duck the first of this Year.

Monday 18th. A Mild Day with a Considerable thaw. Cloudy weather. fishermen found their Net broke in half. of Course no fish. this Afternoon saw a large Flock of Shell Drakes pass bye. Bellaire came from the Sugar Lodges. reports that the Maple Trees give no Juise. at Midnight it began to rain.

Winter Quarters Tuesday 19 March 1805. A Rainy unpleasant Day Wind N E. Hail & Snow at intervals. sent one of my Men with a Canoe to set a Net where the River is free from Ice. he returnd without Success. this afternoon Margoe & Brother came with a little Sugar. they slept here.

Wednesday 20th. A Stormy Day with a thick fall of Snow that Continued till 2 in the Afternoon. wind N. after the Storm ceased Margoe & Brother returnd to their Lodge.

Thursday 21st. Fine Clear weather attended with a considerable thaw. this Afternoon the Court Oreille with Bouche arrived with the Value of 10 Skins difft Kinds for Rum.

Friday 22ⁿᵈ. A Cloudy Day with Snow & cold which continued the Whole Day. this Morning the Court Oreille & Bouché returnd to the Lodges with 3 Galls H Wines. towards Evening Margoe arrived for provisions. the Maple trees are quite dry.

Winter Quarters Saturday 23 March 1805. Cloudy Mild weather with a great thaw. the Maple Trees gave an inmence Quantity of Juise.

Sunday 24ᵗʰ. A Cloudy Day. wind N E. the Maples gave a Surprising Quantity of Water.

Monday 25ᵗʰ. Clear & Cold. wind as Yesterday. Men set a Net. Mʳ Bellaux Shot 2 Shell Drakes the first Ducks we got this Year. Margoe sent a Mocock Sugar 70 ᵗᵇ Net.[20]

Tuesday 26. Weather as Yesterday with a trifeling thaw. took a small Pike & a Pickerel in the Net. nothing else Material Occurred.

Wednesday 27ᵗʰ. A fine Mild Day. light Airs from the N E attended with a great thaw. 2 Small fish in our Net. this Afternoon the Six sent me a Wild Goose & Margoe 14 ᵗᵇ Sugar.

Thursday 28ᵗʰ March 1805. Hot Weather. thermotʳ at 110. Mʳ Belleau went to Hunt wild fowl. saw a Wolf that devoured a Deer. ran up & started the Wolf. brought the Deer which makes us an excellent Feast.

Friday 29ᵗʰ. Weather nearly as Warm as yesterday. the River broke up & a Quantity of Ice drives down. Men took no fish in their Nets. at Sunset the Weather Cloudy & raind all the Night.

Saturday 30. A Cloudy Mild Morning. after Sun rise the Mist Cleard away & in the Afternoon the River was freed of the Ice. Pierro & Margoe came here brought 60ᵗᵇ Sugar. gave the Old fellow 1 Gallon H W. fishermen took a pike in their Nets.

---

[20] A mocock, or makuk, was a large vessel made of birch bark into which maple sugar was packed. The amount of sugar in a single such container varied from thirty to eighty pounds. See page 32n. above.

Sunday 31st. A Cloudy Stormy Day. the River is entirely freed of Ice. Mr Bellaux very unwell & Seraphin in the same Situation. Blooded him which gave him great relief. towards sun set the Téte Jaune & Son arrived. their Errand is for their Canoes. reports that none of the Indians are gone of for their Beaver Hunt owing to overflow of the River.

Winter Quarters Monday 1st April 1805. A Very Stormy Day. wind S W. a vast Quantity of Large Pines were rooted up by the Violence of the Wind. the Téte Jaune remaind here to repair his Canoe. this Afternoon the Six & family came here for his Canoe. they remaind here all the Day. the Waters rose upwards of 1 foot perpendicular.

Tuesday 2nd. A Tempestiouse Day. wind S W. this Morning the Tete Jaune & Six returnd to their Huts. not a single Fish in the Nets this evening. Orderd the Sturgeon Net in the Water. Henrie shot 2 Wild Geese & a Duck. gave me one of the Geese.

Wednesday 3rd. A fine Warm Day. Moderate Winds S W. no fish in the Nets. Messrs Bellaux & Seraphin out a Fowling. Mr B. came with 10 Ducks & Mr S with 2. Henries Squaw & family Came from the Sugar Bush. they say that the Maples give no more Water.

Winter Quarters 4th April Thursday. A Warm Stormy Day. wind S. towards the Afternoon a light Shower of rain. at 5 P M Mr Marain his father La Pon the Peaux Dourson & Court Oreille with my Hunter Girard & Le Blanc made their appearance. their Errand is for their Canoes. shortly after they presented 10 Beavers & made a Demand of Rum which I refused without hesitation upbraiding them of Neglecting their Hunt & paying their Debts. they hung their Heads & made a grumbling reply not pleased with my reasoning. Margoe & family Camped here. gave up Sugar Makeing. the Maple Juice is turnd quite Bitter.

Winter Quarters Friday 5 April 1805. Cloudy & Cold. this forenoon all the Indians returnd to their Huts with 4 Gallons of H W. Pierro Camped here this afternoon. nothing else Material Occurred.

Saturday 6th. A Cold Cloudy Day with a light fall of Snow. at 6 P M sent 2 Men to fetch 3 Bags of Oats & ½ Bag of Flour that was hid under Ground last fall in Serpentine River. at Noon the little Horn one of the [MS illegible] Chiefs arrived with some Peltries.

Sunday 7th. At 8 A M the little Horn returnd to his Hut. at miday the Six & family arrived with Bark sufficient to make a Canoe. at 3 P M he returnd to his Lodge with 2 Gallˢ H W. Pierro & Family accompanied him in Quest of Bark & Gum.

Winter Quarters Monday 8 April 1805. The most tempestious Day we have experiendust this Year. the Pines with number of other Trees fell near the Fort. before Noon the Men that Went for the provisions I hid last fall arrived. they lost the flour & had a narrow escape of their lives. their Canoe overset & they lost their Blankets Guns &c. the Canoe met with the same fate. Compassion prevailed & ordained me to give them each a Blanket they having nothing to Cover themselves. no fish in our Nets.

Tuesday 9th. A Charming mild Calm Day. sent 2 Men to Join the Indians to raise Bark & Gum. they came Back at Noon owing to the Indians having taken their Departure Yestarday. no fish in our Nets.

Winter Quarters Wednesday 10 April 1804 [*sic*]. A Stormy Warm Day. thermotr at Blood heat. blows a Gale S. no Fish in our Nets.

Thursday 11th. A Sultry Calm Day. heat as Yesterday. no Fish in the Nets. the little Horns Family Camped here. report that the Beaver Hunters with their Wives in Generl went off 3 Days past from which reason I expect a Capital Hunt. the Six & Pierro got 3 Galls Rum for Canoe Bark.

Friday 12th. A Very Hot Day. thermotr at 105. took 3

fish in our Nets. Mr Bellaux shot a Goose & a small Duck. Indians Drunk traded more Bark & a Keg of Sugar.

Saturday 13. Warm Weather. wind N E. 2 fish in our Nets. this Afternoon 2 of X Y Cheniers Men made their Appearan[ce] in a Small Canoe with a small Pack of Goods & Silver Works in hopes of trading some Beavers with my Hunters. its my look out to prevent their Success. at same time brot: a very Simple letter to which I made a similar Answer.

Sunday 14th April Easter Day 1805. Very Hot Weather. thermo^{tr} at 108. this Morning the 2 X Y Men returnd with my letter to their Quarters. in the Afternoon the Peaux Dourson Wishaima & little River made their Appearance empty Handed. after Scolding them they took their Departure. Mr Seraphin with Déseve were sent off prior to their Arrival & returnd with them as they report it an impossibility to meet the Beaver Hunters. each Band takes a Different rout.

Monday 15. Charming Weather. Orderd the Men to fetch the Canoes in order to get them repaird. took 4 fish in the Nets. the X Y Men have not as yet returnd. I hope my Ans^r to Cheniers letter had the desird Effect.

Winter Quarters Tuesday 16 April 1805. A Very Hot Day. therm^{tr} at 110 Deg^{rs}. this afternoon sent Mr Seraphin with Deseve to the Lodges to Trade Gum & Sugar. gave them 9 Galls Indian Rum & a fath^m Tobacco. Pierro & Shacobay hard at Work Mending my Canoes.

Wednesday 17th. Weather as Yesterday. at 7 A M Mr Seraphin made his Appearance in a Shamefull plight. brot about 3/5th Keg of Gum 1½ ^{lb} Sugar 1 Bag Ooats & 1 Otter with a fisher. expended ¾ of the Rum which put me out of Humour. the Indians Compleated 2 Canoes.

Thursday 18th. A Cloudy Sultry Day. thermo^{tr} 2 deg^{rs} above summer Heat. my Canoe Menders at work for themselves. headed 5 Kegs Sugar. put 4 in a hole under the fire place of my Chimney. this afternoon Mr Reaume with 2 Men came with 2 Kegs H W. report that Chenier is Camped with them. of Course my letter had its desired Effect. Indians repairing my Canoe.

Winter Quarters 19th April 1805. A Cloudy Rainy Day. wind N E which prevents Mr Reaumes departure also the Canoe Menders to Continue their Work.

Saturday 20th. Weather as Yesterday. Mr Reaume however took his departure knowing that we are scarse of Provisions. this Afternoon the little Horn & the Plat with Bouché & Le Blanc arrived. brot: only 25 Beavers in Value which does not pay their Debts. they however requested Rum which I refused. the little Horn after several Harangues went off in the Dumps.

Sunday 21st. A Stormy Cold Day with flying Showers. wind N W. Pierro & Shawcobai how [ev]er, finishd repairing my last Canoe. the Plat gave me 10 Beavers in payment & expects the Value in which he will find himself mistaken.

Winter Quarters Monday 22nd April 1805. A Warm pleasant Day. Pierro finishd repairing the Canoes. the little Horn gave me the Meat of a Deer. it came very Apropos. our provisions begins to be very Scarse. this Afternoon all the Beaver Hunters Arrived. they made a pitifull Hunt. nevertheless they expect a large present of Rum. I reffurred them till tomorrow. gave a Silver Medal to Mr Marin. he is [a] realy deserving Character.

Tuesday 23rd. A Cloudy Day. Wind N W. the remainder of the Hunters made their Appearance towards Evening. requested rum to which I did not agree.

Wednesday 24th. Charming Weather & Calm. all the Chiefs & Youngsters made their Appearance. 3 Chiefs say Old La Pon his Son & little Horn gave 5 Kegs M. R 3. Carrots Tobacco & 2 fath^s twist. requird abot 60 Skins in payment of their Debts.

Winter Quarters Thursday 25 Ap^l 1805. A Cold rainy Day with intervals of Snow. Yesterday Evening the Indians began their usual Custom of Stabbing. no less than 7 got wounded: 2 of them I beleive are Mortally so. they are still Drunk but peaceable & very attentive to us.

Friday 26th. A Stormy Cold Day. wind N. dispatch'd Deseve & Bouche with 10 packs & 3 Kegs H Wines. made up the remai[n]d[e]r of our Peltries. Indians still Drunk.

Saturday 27th. A pleasant Day. pack'd up all our Baggage & at 2 P M embark'd. Camped at 4 at Cross Lake w[h]ere I found the Men that went away Yesterday.

INDEX

Index

ABERCROMBY, GEN. JAMES, 20, 23
Agriculture, at Rainy Lake post, 212, 213, 214, 220, 234, 237, 238, 239, 240; on Rainy River, 194n. *See also* Red River Settlement
Alaric, Michel, 213
Albany, N.Y., 28, 47; in French and Indian Wars, 19, 20, 24, 27n.
Albany River, 91n.
Allary, Michel (Mitchel), clerk, 157n., 161, 163, 164, 173
Allumettes Portage, 78, 87
Amelle, ———, canoe maker, 193, 203, 206, 208–217, 219, 221, 223, 225, 237, 238, 239
American Board of Foreign Missions, 247
American Fur Co., 158n., 247
Amherst, Gen. Jeffrey, 26, 27
Anse à la Bouteille, 90
Anse au Sable, 101
Anse aux Perches, 81
Anse aux Pieres, 112
Anse aux Tourtes. *See* Pigeon River
Antaya, 198, 199n.
Arechea, Yankton chief, 54, 56
Argy Portage, 75, 76n., 87
Assamac, Indian chief, 234
Assiniboine Indians, 57, 112, 123, 125n., 172n.; customs, 114, 179; Stone band, 130, 134, 135, 139, 140, 143, 147, 155, 163, 167, 168, 169, 172, 174, 177; census, 150n.
Assiniboine (Upper Red) River, 6; posts and traders, 38n., 63, 64, 97, 106n., 123, 125n., 145n., 158n., 172n.; name, 97n.; Macdonell on, 108–116; fish, 116. *See also* Fort Alexandria
Astor, John J., 247
Astoria, 142n., 160n.

"Athabasca," 89n., 94
Athabasca House, Rainy Lake, 191, 192, 227; building of, 230–241
Athabasca region, traders, 12, 13, 14, 16, 64, 96n., 98n., 99n., 101n., 123, 124, 142, 149, 198n.; brigades, 191, 195n., 206
Augé, ———, 102, 114
Ayer, Frederic, missionary, 247
Azure, Antoine, at Rainy Lake post, 203, 204, 207–211, 214–221, 224–227, 230–233, 236–240

BADGER, 116, 152, 167
Baldwin, Capt. David, 18, 19n., 20n.
Bann, ———, 141, 159
Bas de la Rivière. *See* Fort Alexander
Basswood Portage, 101, 102n., 117
Batard Anglois, Indian, 150, 168
Batême, ———, 99, 100
Batteau, building, 165–175, 178
Beans, 32, 35, 40
Bear, 41, 116; as food, 44, 55, 102, 111, 141, 229, 259, 261, 262, 264, 265; skins, 148, 157, 240, 262, 263. *See also* Grease
Beaulieu, ———, 170
Beaver, 59, 125n., 150, 155, 159; skins, 45, 55, 130, 133, 136, 138, 139, 140, 143, 145, 148, 157, 173, 180, 183, 212, 213, 218, 227, 228, 229, 230, 231, 232, 233, 237, 238, 240, 241, 251, 252, 257, 258, 266, 267, 269, 270, 274, 277; blankets, 52, 53; unit of value, 151, 154, 161, 162; Indian hunts, 178, 180, 235, 237, 251, 256, 258, 259, 268, 269, 271, 274, 275, 276, 277
"Beaver," 89n., 94
Beaver Hill, 125n., 148
Beggué, ———, 180, 184

281

Belair, Louis, 262–265, 267, 271, 272
Belleau (Belleaux), ———, 263–266, 268, 269, 272–276
Belleau, Pierre, 172
Bellile, ———, 134, 168, 169, 174, 175, 176, 181
Bennet, Capt. John, 89n., 96
Berthier, ———, 67, 68
Big Fork River, route, 213n., 217–221, 223, 237, 239; Indians on, 232, 236, 238, 240
Big Rat, Indian, 194, 210, 241
Birchbark, for canoes, 39n., 71, 111, 182, 183, 198; traded, 209, 240, 275, 276
Bird Mountain. See Montagne des Oiseaux
Black, Samuel?, 200, 202, 203, 227
Blackbird, Indian, 194, 213, 214, 236, 238
Black River, 213, 218, 229, 231
Blacksmith, Indian, 143, 149, 150, 169, 194, 233
Blankets, as trade goods, 132, 133, 144, 159, 167, 169, 173, 176
Blegen, Theodore B., 17, 65n.
Blondeau, Maurice, 29n., 110n.
Blood Indians, 123, 155
Boeuf Blanc, Indian, 150, 151
Bois Blanc. See Basswood
Bois Brûlé River, 6, 249n., 250
Boiselle, ———, 153, 154, 182, 184, 185
Bonhomme, ———, 206, 207, 222, 225, 227, 229–233, 241
Bonnet Portage, 106, 117
Bonnin, François, 194n., 204
Bottle Portage, 102, 117
Boucher, François, 260–265, 272, 273, 277, 278
Boulanger, Michel, 204, 215–217, 220, 227, 230, 232, 236, 238
Bourgeois, 7, 97, 100, 101n., 123, 137n.; defined, 4
Bow River, 142n.
Braddock, Gen. Edward, 18
Bras Court, Indian, 161, 162, 174–176, 213; sons, 173, 215, 240

British, in fur trade, 3, 247. See also various companies and traders
Brochet (Pike), Indian chief, 260
Broduck, General. See Prideaux
Brulé, defined, 77n.
Brule River. See Bois Brûlé River
Buffalo, 53, 56, 141; hunted, 58, 110, 113, 115, 125n., 130, 139, 144, 146, 149, 150–156, 160; robes and skins, 135, 165, 166, 168, 169, 174, 175; pounds, 140, 151, 159, 161
Bull, ———, 25
Bustards. See Geese
Butte des Morts, battle, 35n.

Cachin, ———, 164
Cadieu, ———, 153, 154, 174
Cadotte, ———, 130, 143, 149, 156–159, 162, 166, 175
Cadotte, Jean B., 12
Calumet, 35, 76; pipestone, 51, 52
Cameron, Duncan, 91n., 115n.
Cameron, Ranald, 115, 225
Campion Portage, 87
Canada, ———, 226–228, 235–237, 239
Canawatiron, Ignace, 204, 211
Cancre, ———, 200
Canoes, 51, 82, 184, 241; Montreal, 5, 67n., 68, 88n., 96, 97, 98n.; capacity, 30, 46, 67n., 68, 88; broken and mended, 39, 52, 54, 71, 75, 76, 79, 84, 109, 111, 182, 196, 197, 198, 199, 200, 202, 206, 216, 217, 246, 250, 252, 253, 275, 276, 277; making, 39n., 104, 182, 183, 192, 203, 206, 210, 214, 215, 219, 221, 223, 237, 238, 239, 275, 276; brigade travel, 67, 68, 72, 80, 85, 88, 90, 98, 103, 195n., 206, 207; North, 88n., 97, 98n.; skin, 162, 166, 174, 178, 181, 182. See also Birchbark, Gum
Cantarat, Louis, 204, 222–224, 226–228, 235, 236
Cardin, ———, 112, 145, 157, 158, 173
Caribou, 235

INDEX

Caribou Portage, 98, 117
Cariole, 152, 154
Carp, 116, 181, 183, 232, 255, 272
Carp Portage, 101, 117
Carrillon Rapids, 71, 72
Carron, ———, 133–136, 159, 169, 171
Carver, Jonathan, explorations, 15, 38, 39, 40n., 45
Catfish, 43, 116
Cave Portage, 73, 87
Cedar, Indian, 210, 215, 232–234, 237, 240
Chaboillez, Charles, 137, 141, 158, 170, 171
Chacobai. *See* Six
Charoux, Charles, 189, 205
Chaudière. *See* Kettle Falls
Chauvin, ———, 144, 149, 150, 153, 160, 162, 175
Chef des Canards, Indian, 172, 174, 175, 176; relatives, 176, 178, 179
Chênes Portage, 74n.
Chenette, Louis, 157, 189, 198–201, 203–206, 239
Cheniers, Antoine or Michel, 250, 251, 252, 259, 264–270, 276, 277
Cheval de Bois. *See* Wooden Horse
Chiene, Indian squaw, 271
Chiens Portage, 74
Chippewa, 8, 40n., 106n., 123, 161, 162, 257n., 269; warfare, 7, 47, 48, 50, 85, 246, 259, 266; canoes, 239, 241; Snake River band, 251–278; Mide ceremonies, 260, 264
Churchill River, 6, 68n., 99n.
Chute à Blondeau, 71, 87
Chute à Jacqueau, 105, 106n., 117
Chute aux Esclaves, 106, 117
Clay, as whitewash, 238
Clay Lake, 191, 227
Cloutier, Zacharie, 201
Collin, Joseph, 129, 130n., 133, 136, 144, 148–150, 155–163, 166, 171, 180, 183
Columbia River, 142n.
Connecticut, 11, 16, 17, 19n., 20n., 24. *See also* Milford

Connor, Thomas, 123; post, 6, 7, 245, 247, 253–259; diary, 6, 245, 248, 249–278; sketch, 245, 247
Connor's Point, name, 248
Cook, Capt. James, 13
Corn, raised by Indians, 32, 33, 35, 40, 56, 193; traders' food, 95, 108, 208, 210
Corneille and son, Indians, 213, 217, 218, 232, 235, 238
Cotté, Gabriel, 90
Cotté, Nicholas, 90n.
Court Oreille, an Indian, 255–258, 261, 262, 272–274
Couteau Portage, 101, 117, 197
Couteaux. *See* Knife Lake
Coutu, ———, 210, 212, 213, 215, 216, 220, 222, 224, 227, 229, 235, 237
Crane Lake, 202n.
Crapaud. *See* Toad
Cree Indians, 109n., 111n., 123, 169, 172n.; near Fort Alexandria, 125n., 140, 150, 156, 165, 167, 168, 172, 174, 177, 178, 180
Croche Portage, 83
Crooked Lake (Lac Croche), 102, 117
Cross Lake, Connor's post, 6, 245–247, 249–278; Indian village, 253
Crown Point, N.Y., 18
Crows, 116
Cumberland House, traders, 12, 126n., 190
Curot, Michel, 249n.
Cut Finger, Indian, 174, 177, 178, 184
Cut Lip, Indian, 136; widow, 168, 169

DAGENAIS, JOSEPH, 205
Dakota Indians. *See* Sioux
Dalles, of French River, 85; of Winnipeg River, 104, 105n., 191, 217
Dannis, ———, 71, 88; at Fort Alexandria, 133, 143, 144, 152, 156, 157, 159, 163–165, 182, 183
Dauphiné, ———, 130, 134, 169, 174, 178, 179

Day Child, Indian, 163, 171–176, 178, 179, 180
Dead River, name, 109n.
Death River, name, 109n.
Décharge, defined, 196n.
Deer, 32, 35, 37, 41, 44, 56, 115, 116; traded, 30, 45, 258, 266; as food, 111, 132, 133, 135, 139, 141, 143, 146, 180, 253, 255, 256, 259, 260, 261, 264, 265, 268, 269, 270, 273, 277
Deer Portage. See Fowl Portage
Degrade, defined, 103n.
Delude, Louis, 205
Démarais, Louis, 139, 140, 166–169, 174, 178, 205
Demi-charge, defined, 196n.
De Peyster, Capt. Arent S., 47n., 49
Derraud's Rapid, 84
Déseve, ———, 264, 265, 268, 269, 272, 276, 278
Detour Point, 86, 87n.
Detroit, Mich., 34, 35n., 42, 89; fur trade center, 11, 27, 29, 86, 87
Devil, Indian, 194, 217, 240
Disease and sickness, among traders, 55, 130, 131, 133, 135, 157, 167n., 169, 177, 178, 206, 207, 208, 211, 213, 217, 222, 231, 232, 256, 274; among Indians, 112, 155, 167, 168, 172, 174, 175, 176, 200, 260, 262, 266. See also Medicines
Dog Lake, 196
Dog Portage, 196n., 198
Dog Rib Indians, 57n.
Dog River, 102n., 198
Dogs, among Indians, 42, 58, 114; used by traders, 102, 103, 150, 151, 154, 162, 164, 179
Dog's Head, Indian, 194, 241
Ducharme, ———, 206, 207
Ducharme, Etiénne, 130, 133, 146, 148, 153, 154, 156, 160, 161, 164
Ducharme, H., 133
Ducharme, N., 144, 146, 149, 153, 154, 160, 171
Ducks, 36, 38, 44, 110, 116, 212, 215, 237, 255–257, 272–274, 276

Du Jaunay, Father Pierre, 31n.
Dupuis, ———, 212, 213
Duval, François, 204, 236

Eagle, Indian, 235
Eagle Lake, post and traders, 191, 203, 207, 212, 223, 225, 227, 229
Eagles, 116, 164
Eaux qui Remuent (Troubled Waters) Portage, 107, 117
Ecarté Portage, 196n., 197
Elbow (Recoude), post, 106n., 125n., 126, 133, 136, 139, 146, 147, 151, 159, 163–165, 172–178
Elk, 110, 111, 115, 125n., 130
Enfant Prodigue, Indian, 138
English River, 99n., 105n., 142n., 158n.
Escalier Portage. See Stairway
Evans, James, missionary, 190
Evans, John, 113n.

Faignan, Joseph, 68
Faille, Hubert, 189
Falcon, Pierre, 137, 159, 165, 167, 168
Fall Indians, 123, 172, 177, 178, 180, 183
Fallardeau, Joseph, 168, 171, 174
Faries, Hugh, 123, 205; diary, 6, 7, 189, 195–241, 246; sketch, 189
Fausille Portage, 83, 87
Ferguson, ——— (Alexander Ferguson?), 141, 144, 147, 157, 158, 163, 164, 173, 185
Fidler, Peter, 126n.
Finlay, Jacquo, 136, 137, 138, 154, 156
Finlay, James, 137n.
Finlay, John, 98, 200
First Connecticut Regiment, 19n.
Fish and fishing, 107, 181, 182, 183; hook and line, 32, 73, 110, 115; kinds listed, 33, 41, 43, 56, 116; spearing, 82; obtained from Indians, 83, 108; commercial, 89; nets and seines, 193, 207–210, 214–216, 218, 221, 234–240, 254, 255, 270, 272–276. See also various kinds of fish

INDEX

Fisher, 116, 226, 276
Flacon. *See* Bottle Portage
Flour, 107, 108, 110, 169, 252, 275
Folle Avoine, Indians, 246
Fond du Lac, route, 6, 7; department, 95n., 225, 231n., 245, 249n., 250n., 260n., 262n.
Fool, Indian, 252, 262
Forsier, ———, 166, 168, 175, 178, 179
Forsyth Richardson & Co., 90
Fort à la Corne, 98n.
Fort Albany, 105n., 134n.
Fort Alexander, 107n., 108n., 110, 138n.
Fort Alexandria, 225n.; McLeod at, 69n., 123, 125-185; described, 125n., 135n.; other traders, 126, 127n., 130n.; pemmican supply, 132n., 138, 160, 161, 162; food requirements, 132n.; defenses, 172n., 178, 183
Fort Augustus, 98n., 142n.
Fort Charlotte, 92n., 96, 97
Fort Chipewyan, 12, 96n., 124, 198n.
Fort Coulonge, 76n., 77, 78n.
Fort Dauphin, routes to, 111, 112n., 125n., 147, 184, 185; traders and voyageurs, 112n., 123, 127, 129n., 130, 134n., 135n., 141n., 144, 145, 151, 157, 158, 163, 164, 173, 184, 185, 195n.
Fort des Prairies, 155, 157, 180; locations, 98n.; traders, 100, 101n., 129n., 137n., 141, 142, 144, 147, 148, 149, 151, 152, 162, 168, 169, 172, 174, 195n.; lower, 129n., 141, 142, 157, 162, 169, 170, 172n., 174; upper, 142, 155
Fort des Trembles, 111n., 112
Fort Douglas, 124
Fort Duquesne, 18
Fort Edward, 19, 20, 21, 24
Fort Erie, 26n., 28
Fort Espérance, 96n., 100n.
Fort Garry, 109n.
Fort George, on Lake George, 19n.; on Saskatchewan River, 98n., 100n.;
at Astoria, 142n.; on Fraser River, 190
Fort Gibraltar, 109n.
Fort la Reine, 38n., 111
Fort Lévis, 26n., 27
Fort Maurepas, 107n.
Fort Niagara, 24, 27, 28; captured, 25
Fort Ontario, 24n., 26
Fort Pelly, 106n.
Fort Pitt, 18n.
Fort Qu'appelle, 96n.
Fort Rouge, 109n.
Fort Schlosser, 28
Fort Stanwix, 28
Fort Vermilion, 98n.
Fort Wedderburn, 124
Fort William, 198, 241; Northwest Co. headquarters, 5, 93n., 195n.; routes from, 102n., 191; traders, 124, 142n.
Fort William Henry, 19, 20
Fowl Portage, 98n., 117
Fox, 32, 116; skins traded, 135, 148, 150
Fox Indians, 34, 35n., 42
Fox River, route, 6, 33-35, 37
Franchère, Gabriel, 64, 76n.
François Portage, 201
Fraser, Simon, explorer, 99, 189
Fraser River, 99n., 190
French, posts and traders, 3, 4, 38n., 45, 91n., 94n., 98n., 107n., 109n., 111n., 191
French and Indian Wars, described by Pond, 11, 18-27; forts, 18, 19, 20, 21, 24, 25, 26, 27
French River, route, 5, 30, 67n., 83-88; portages listed, 87
Frêne, Indian, 130, 131, 132, 172, 177
Frisé, ———, 130, 131, 135, 137, 141, 152-155, 158, 159, 171, 176
Frobisher, Benjamin, 12, 29n.
Frobisher, Joseph, 12, 68, 88, 99n., 104, 109n.
Frobisher, Thomas, 12
Frosier, ———, 166, 168
Frozen Foot, Indian, 214, 216, 236

Fur trade, significance and extent, 3, 4, 6, 8, 12, 29n., 82, 112n., 113n.; ranks of employees, 4, 7, 33n., 67n., 72n., 93, 97, 204, 260n.; organization and methods, 5, 7, 72n., 107, 131n., 144n., 145n., 149n., 219; packs, 88, 91n., 92n.; independent traders, 90, 109, 198n., 199. *See also* Canoes, Trade goods, various companies

GAILLARD, LOUIS, 205
Galet (galais), defined, 105n., 250n.
Gayou, Joseph, 204, 206, 213, 215, 216, 222
Geese, 44, 110, 116, 171, 212, 214, 215, 234, 237, 238, 255, 256, 273, 274, 276
George, Pennesha, 38n.
Germain, Jacques, 205
Gervais, ———, 157, 158
Gibault (Jibault), ———, 154, 156
Gibault, Father Pierre, 31n.
Girard, Joseph, 260, 264, 265, 267, 274
Girardin, ———, 133, 150, 155, 156, 157, 161–163, 180
Godin, ———, 203, 207, 209, 217–224, 226–228, 231, 232, 235, 236, 241
Goodwin, Robert, 134
Gouin, ———, 210–214, 217, 224, 226, 228, 230–232
Graham, Felix, Pond's partner, 29, 46
Grand Calumet, 75–78, 79, 81, 87, 98
Grand Coquin, Indian, 270
Grand Décharge, 105
Grand des Cerise Portages. *See* Great Cherry Portage
Grand Marais, 108; defined, 77n.
Grand Medicine Society. *See* Midewiwin
Grand Portage, 12, 65, 68n., 88, 108, 149, 153, 202, 207; post, 5, 7, 67n., 89n., 92–96, 195n.; route, 6, 13, 97–104, 117, 195–203; traders, 69n., 92, 94, 95, 99n., 158n., 184, 201n.; trail, 92n., 96; currency, 93, 94n., 132, 240
Grand Portage (new), 99, 117
Grand Récollet, 84, 87
Grand River. *See* Ottawa River
Grand Traverse, 103, 108, 202
Grant, Cuthbert, 96, 100, 102, 106, 112, 114
Grant, David, 94, 95n., 100n., 115n.
Grant, James?, 200, 201, 206, 211, 213, 218, 227, 241; Indian wife, 203, 217, 234, 237, 239
Grant, Peter, 100n., 115, 158; at Grand Portage, 94, 95n.
Grant, Robert, 95, 96n., 112, 115
Grease, 95, 203; bear, 30, 37, 230, 240, 267; traded, 130, 148, 150, 155, 156, 158–166, 169, 171, 175, 179, 183, 184, 198, 203, 234, 262, 263, 267. *See also* Pemmican
Great Cherry Portage, 99n., 117
Green Bay, 3, 33
Grenier, ———, 207, 209–211, 214–216, 236, 237, 239
Gros Cap, 85, 89
Groux, Charles, 205
Grue, Indian, 210, 212, 215, 218, 233, 234, 237, 238
Guedon, ———, 216, 225
Guilmont, Louis, 189, 203, 204, 206, 216, 223, 225, 230, 231
Gum, for canoes, 39n., 40n., 71, 75, 76, 170, 171, 196, 200; traded, 238; gathered, 246, 250–253, 275
Gunflint Lake, 100n.
Gunflints, 235
Guns, 8, 134; traded, 107, 153, 156, 159, 164, 167, 170, 173, 178

HAGE, MRS. ANNE A., 17
Haldimand, Col. Frederick, 24
Halero, James, 117
Half-Moon, 19n.
Hambro lines, 75
Hamickonitt, Indian, 166
Hare, 32, 116
Harmon, Daniel W., 86n., 100n.; at Fort Alexandria, 125n., 132n., 133, 136, 137n., 138, 143, 151, 152, 156,

INDEX 287

158, 162, 164, 169, 170, 174–176, 181–185; sketch, 126n.
Harrison, Edward, 126, 127n., 170, 184
Hat Point, 92
Hawks, 116
Haymaking, at posts, 32, 207–210, 214
Hearne, Samuel, 11
Height of land, 81n., 99, 117, 199n.
Hell Gate (Porte du l'enfer), 80
Henry, Alexander, the elder, 12, 13, 68n., 76n.
Henry Alexander, the younger, 150n., 160n., 195n.
Herring, 33
High wines. See Liquor
Hill River, portages, 118
Hivernants. See Winterers
Holmquist, Mrs. June D., 17
Hoole, ———, 148, 149
Horses, 34; Spanish, 41, 113; Indian, 52, 58, 114, 143, 150, 151, 163, 167; use at posts, 112, 114, 125n., 129, 130, 132, 136, 138, 145, 150, 151, 153, 157, 162, 167, 168, 170, 171, 173–177, 179, 180, 181, 182, 193, 211, 219, 238, 239
Howe, Gen. George, death, 21
Howes, ———, 142
Howse Pass, 101n.
Hudson, ———, trader, 91
Hudson Bay, 100, 109n.
Hudson's Bay Co., competition, 4, 91n., 99n., 123, 139, 141, 142n., 194n.; merger with Northwest Co., 4, 103n., 124, 158n.; posts, 11, 12, 90, 91n., 99n., 105n., 107n., 124, 125n., 134n., 141, 190; routes, 101n., 105n., 117–119; traders, 105, 106, 108, 109, 117, 126, 133, 134n., 138, 141, 142, 190, 194n. See also Elbow, other posts and traders
Hudson River, 19n.
Hull, Que., 73n.
Huneau, François, 68
Hunters and hunting, at posts, 110n., 111, 130, 131n., 132, 133, 135, 136, 138, 139, 141, 143, 144, 146, 148–150, 152–155, 160, 161; Indian, 154, 253, 255, 256, 259, 260, 261, 264. See also Buffalo, other animals and birds

ILE PERRÔT, 68n.
Indians. See various tribes
Innis, Harold A., 15
Ireland, Bazil, 96
Iroquis Indians, warfare, 71n., 85; at Fort Alexandria, 140, 141, 143, 148–154, 157, 158, 160, 183, 184, 185; employed by Northwest Co., 184, 189, 198, 212, 213, 215, 220, 222
Isle à la Crosse, post, 64
Isle à la Mort, 183, 184
Isle Portage, 105, 117, 197

JACCO, Indian, 172, 177, 178, 180
Jack River, portages, 118
Jacob's Falls, 106n.
Jessaume, René, 112, 113n.
Joachim Portage, 79, 87
Johnson, Sir William, 25, 26n., 27n.
Johnstone, Col. John, 24, 25n.
Jollifour, ———, 157, 158
Joncquard, Chrysostome, 113n.
Jourdain, D., 201
Jourdain, Joseph, 198n., 199–200, 203, 204, 206, 209–214, 218, 222, 233, 235, 238–240
Jour d'Enfant. See Day Child
Jourdin, "Young," 218, 221–223, 226, 232, 236
Jussomme. See Jessaume

KAKABEKA FALLS, 196n.
Kaministiquia River, route, 102n., 195–202. See also Fort William
Kane, Lucile M., 17
Kashishwa, Indian, 224
Kettle Falls, Ottawa River, 73, 74, 87; French River, 83, 87; Rainy River, 104, 117, 214–218
Kettle River, 251n.
King, James, 142, 143, 160, 172

Kingston, Ont., 76
Knife Lake, 101n.
Knox, Henry, 14

LA BONTÉ, BENJAMIN, 205
La Boune, Jacques (Maron), 130, 132, 136, 138, 139, 157, 169, 170, 175, 178, 180
L'abri du Vent, Indian, 212, 213, 214
Lac Coulonge, 78
Lac des Allumettes, 78, 79n.
Lac des Bois. *See* Lake of the Woods
Lac des Chats, 75n., 77; portage, 74
Lac des Chaudières, 74
Lac des Chiens. *See* Dog Lake
Lac des Couteaux. *See* Knife Lake
Lac du Boeuf, 85
Lac du Bonnet, 106
Lac du Flambeau, 137n.; Indians, 257n.
Lac la Croix, 102, 195n., 201, 206; portage, 117, 202n.
Lac la Glaise. *See* Clay Lake
Lac la Pluie. *See* Rainy Lake
Lac Plat, post, 191, 222n., 223–227, 229. *See also* Lake of the Woods
Lac Seul, traders, 225n., 230n.
Lachine, 29, 67, 69, 117
Lacombe, ———, X. Y. trader, 191, 206–208, 210–212, 214, 223–240
Lacombe, Mrs. ———, 235, 237, 238, 240
La Comble, ———, 130, 143, 153, 157, 158, 173, 176 180
La Couture, ———, 148, 149, 173
La France, ———, 203, 209, 212–215, 218–221, 228–233
La France, Baptiste, 135, 146, 153, 154, 164, 174, 176
La France, Baptiste, murdered, 142, 168
La France, Joseph, 103n.
La Frenière, ———, 149, 153, 154, 166, 168, 178
Lafrênieres, Titiche, 79
La Grave, François, 204, 210, 211, 212
Lahontan, Baron Louis A., 15, 32
Lake Athabasca, posts and traders, 12, 13, 14, 198n.
Lake Champlain, 21, 29
Lake Dauphin, 12. *See also* Fort Dauphin
Lake Erie, 28
Lake George, 29; in French and Indian Wars, 19, 21–24, 111n.
Lake Huron, 82; fur route, 5, 29, 30, 67n., 85–87
Lake Manitoba, 111, 112n.
Lake Michigan, 3, 29; fur route, 5, 6, 33
Lake Nipigon, posts, 90, 91n., 100n., 115n.
Lake Nipissing, 30, 67n., 82, 83, 106
Lake of the Two Mountains, 30, 69, 72
Lake of the Woods, 13, 107, 108n., 222; posts and traders, 6, 191, 203, 206, 207, 211, 223, 231, 239, 241; Indians, 48, 214, 231; size, 104. *See also* Lac Plat, Whitefish Lake
Lake Ontario, 24, 28, 76
Lake St. Clair, 29
Lake Superior, 67n., 85, 91, 100, 117; posts and traders, 5, 6, 47, 48, 50, 190, 198n., 248; described, 89–92, 95; sailing vessels, 89, 94. *See also* Grand Portage, other posts and traders
Lake Temiscaming, 72, 79
Lake Winnipeg, 6, 107, 108, 109, 117; traders, 123, 158n., 195n., 196
Lalonde, ———, 68, 69n., 79
Lamarre, Seraphin, 249n. *See also* Seraphin
Lambert, ———, 145, 146, 170, 202, 212, 213, 240
Langlois, Eustache, 204
La Plante, ———, 147, 157, 173
Lapointe, Joseph, 157, 195n., 197
La Pon, Indian, 252, 256, 258, 266, 274, 277
La Prairie, ———, clerk, 249, 250, 251, 262, 268, 269
La Présentation, mission, 26n.
La Rose, Baptiste, 129, 130, 132, 133, 134, 135, 136, 159, 171

INDEX 289

La Tourelle, Joseph, 67
La Verdure, ———, 126, 157, 170, 171, 182, 196, 206–211, 213, 214, 219, 222–229, 238
La Vérendrye, sieur de, 94n.; posts, 38n., 107n., 109n., 111n., 191
La Voye, ———, 134, 136, 138, 140, 144, 149, 159, 166, 178
League, defined, 72n.
Le Blanc, ———, 261–263, 274, 277
Leclair, Pierre, 205, 213, 231–233
Leech Lake, posts, 95n., 225, 231n.
Le Fevre, ———, 229, 230–232; the younger, 143, 144, 157, 160, 170, 171, 175, 176, 181; the elder, 168, 169, 170, 171
Le Franc, Father Marie Louis, 31n.
Le Gardeur, Jacques, sieur de St. Pierre, 111
Leith, James, 194n.
Le Mire, ———, 134, 136, 148, 162, 171
Le Moine, ———, 69, 88, 89
Le Sieur, Toussaint, 107, 108
Lesser Slave Lake, post, 64
Le Sueur, Pierre, 52n., 57n.
L'Heureux, François, 130, 134, 152, 206
L'Homme Noir, Indian, 214, 215, 238
Liar, Indian, 194, 203
Liquor, 44, 45, 89; rum, 35, 50, 86, 101, 103, 130, 133, 135, 137, 138, 140, 143, 144, 146, 148, 150–152, 155–157, 159, 162, 163, 166, 169, 170, 172, 173, 175, 176, 183, 200, 210, 212, 218, 220, 221, 223, 224, 227, 228, 230, 233–241, 246, 251–253, 256–258, 260, 261, 263, 264, 266, 267, 269, 270–272, 275–277; use in trade, 126, 127, 130, 133, 134n., 137, 139, 141, 146, 149, 158, 163, 165, 169, 170, 174, 208, 229, 246; high wines, 135n., 137, 144, 145, 147, 148, 153, 156, 157, 163, 164, 171, 173, 185, 211, 227, 250–255, 259, 260, 264, 268, 269, 271, 273, 275, 277, 278

Little Fork River, fishing, 218, 239, 240; maple sugar camp, 233, 234, 236
Little Horn, Indian chief, 255, 257, 258, 264, 266, 268, 269, 271, 275, 277
Little River, Indian, 263, 276
Little River. See Mattawa River
Lobstick, 102n.
Long Island, N. Y., 24
Longmoore, ———, 142
Long Sault, Ottawa River, 64, 69, 71, 72, 87, 88; Rainy Lake, 239, 240
L'Orient, ———, 171
Luke, John, 154
Lynx ("cats"), 116, 130, 143, 145, 148, 150, 161; skinning, 145n.

McCrae, William, 189, 202n., 205, 214, 217, 226, 229, 241; sketch, 217n.
MacDonald, John, 142, 160, 172; sketch, 142n.
McDonnell, Eneas, 230n.
Macdonell, John, 38n., 123, 127n., 192, 196n.; diary, 6, 7, 63, 65, 67–119; family, 63, 64, 65; career 64; marriage 65n.; mentioned by McLeod, 137, 141, 145, 146, 147, 150, 151, 154, 157, 158, 160, 168, 170, 171, 172, 173
Macdonell, Mrs. John, 64, 65
Macdonell, Miles, 65
McGill, James, 29n.
McGill University, 29n., 63, 124, 194
McGillis, Hugh, 126, 127n., 143–146, 154–156, 169, 170, 173, 175, 183–185; sketch, 225n.
McGillivray, Duncan, 86n., 100, 142, 147, 149, 158, 160; sketch, 142n.
McGillivray, William, 14, 96n., 101n., 124
McIntosh, Donald, 226, 229
McKay, Donald, 106, 107, 109
McKay, George, 137, 170
McKay, Neil, 100, 111
McKay, William, 99, 158

Mackenzie, Sir Alexander, 14, 127n., 198n., 225, 250n.
McKenzie, Daniel, 101
McKenzie, Henry, 158
McKenzie, Kenneth, 158
Mackenzie River, explored, 13, 14, 16
Mackenzie, Roderic, trader, 63, 195n., 198, 199n.; sketch, 198n.
Mackenzie, Roderic, clerk, 199n.
Mackinac. *See* Michilimackinac
McLellan, Archibald, at Rainy Lake, 189, 190, 195, 197, 198, 203, 205–216
McLeod, Alexander, 69n., 95, 96n., 158
McLeod, Archibald N., diary, 6, 7, 123, 125–185, 246; Macdonell's companion, 69, 71, 73, 88, 89, 92; career, 69n., 123
McLeod, Normand, 69n.
McLeod Lake, 99n., 126n.
McMurray, Thomas, 189, 190, 205
McTavish, Frobisher, & Co., 12, 124, 225
McTavish, McGillivrays, & Co., 124, 158n.
McTavish, Simon, 101n.; death, 127n., 263
Magic, among Indians, 40, 50
Mailloux, ———, 206–209, 211, 213–215, 219, 222, 224, 226, 236–240
Malhoit, François, 137, 141, 158, 159, 166
Maligne River, 102n.
Mallet, ———, 265
Mandan Indians, 38, 39n., 113n.
Mangeurs de lard. *See* Pork-eaters
Manitou, 51
Manitou Rapids, Rainy River, 104, 218, 238
Maple sugar, traded, 30, 237, 238, 276; making, 32n., 165, 233, 234, 236, 237, 238, 246, 267, 270, 271, 272, 273, 274, 276
Marabeau Portage, 101
Margoe, Indian, 272, 273, 274
Marin, Indian chief, 257, 258, 266, 269, 270, 271, 274, 277

Marte Portage, 117
Marten, 116; trapped, 222–224, 227–232; skins traded, 226, 228, 233, 235
Martin, ———, 198
Mattawa, settlement, 79n.
Mattawa River, route described, 67n., 68n., 79–81, 87, 106
Mauvais Mal, Indian, 130, 172, 173
Medicines, used by traders, 130, 131, 133, 135, 153, 167n., 168, 169, 177, 185, 206n., 207, 208, 217, 256; bleeding, 177, 206, 231, 274; traded, 262
Menominee Indians, 33, 246
Methye Portage, 16
Miami Indians, 14
Miccan Lake. *See* Namakan Lake
Michilimackinac, 33; fur post and traders, 5, 28, 29, 30, 31, 46, 47–50, 59, 86, 87n., 88, 89, 90n.; mission, 31; commandants, 34, 35n., 47, 49, 50; Indians, 34, 50
Michipicoten, 90
Midewiwin, 260n., 261
Migneron, Louis, 205
Milford, Conn., 11, 18, 19, 26, 27
Milieu Portage, 199
Mille Lacs post, 191, 196n., 200, 201, 203, 209
Miln, John, 112
Mink, 116, 184
Minnesota, fur trade, 3, 6
Minnesota Historical Society, 17
Minnesota River, Pond on, 6, 28, 44–46, 48, 51; described, 44, 45, 56; name, 111n.
Miquouanance, Indian chief, 269
Missions, 26n., 31, 247
Mississippi River, 33n., 39, 95n.; traders, 6, 11, 28, 30, 43, 45, 46; Indians, 8, 57; source, 13, 104, 105n.
Missouri River, Indians, 28, 34, 39n., 41, 51, 57; traders, 28, 112, 113n., 158n.
Mohawk River, 25n., 28
Moles, 116
Monin, David, 112, 113n.

INDEX   291

Monk, George H., 231, 232
Monongahela River, 18
Montagne à la Bosse, post, 137n.
Montagne de Foudre. *See* Thunder Mountain
Montagne des Oiseaux, traders, 126, 134, 136, 146, 153, 160, 174
Montcalm, Gen. Louis Joseph, 20, 21
Montour, Nicholas, 142, 154, 157, 160
Montreal, 30, 64, 69, 71n., 199n., 225, 263; fur trade center, 4, 5, 12, 14, 29, 68n., 101, 191; in French and Indian Wars, 26n., 27
Montreal Co., 96n.
Moose, 115, 125n.; skins and meat traded, 138, 234, 236, 238, 268, 269
Moose Lake, 100n.
Moose Portage, 99n., 117
Morgan, ———, 112, 113n.
Morice, Rev. A. G., 63, 64, 65n.
Morrison, William, 250n.
Morts Portage, 201
Mountain Portage, 75, 87, 196
Mouse River. *See* Souris River
Mufle, Indian, 208, 209
Munro, William, 137
Music, violin, 170
Musique Portage, 81, 87
Muskrat ("rats"), 116, 256; skins traded, 130, 214, 228, 255, 271

NABESS, ———, 179
Namai Kowagon, Indian village, 249n., 250
Namakagon River, 251n.
Namakan (Miccan) Lake, 102, 103n., 202, 239
Nelson, ———, 94
Nelson River, posts, 99n.
Nettley Creek, 109n.
Neuf portages, 99, 117
New Caledonia, B. C., 123, 126n.
New France, 26n.
New Jersey, 24, 25n.
New Northwest Company. *See* X. Y. Co.
New Orleans, La., 45, 46

New Portages. *See* Neuf portages
New York, troops, 19, 24, 25n.
New York City, 19, 28, 29, 47
Niagara Falls, portage, 28n., 82n.
Nipigon River, 91
Nipissing River, 80n., 82
Nolin, Augustin, 88, 89
Nolin, François, 170, 184, 195n., 197
Northwest Co., 82n., 84, 130n.; organized, 4, 11, 14; competition, 4, 91n., 95n., 96n., 99n., 123, 126, 127n., 134n., 138, 139, 141, 142n., 145, 157, 169, 191, 194n., 208, 210, 211, 212, 213, 214, 218, 219, 221, 225, 226, 246, 249, 252, 259, 276; merger with Hudson's Bay Co., 4, 103n., 124, 158n.; merger with X. Y. Co., 4, 127n., 191, 199n., 225, 246, 263, 264; posts, 5, 78n., 87n., 88n., 90, 91n., 92n., 93n., 95n., 96n., 98n., 100n., 101n., 103n., 107, 108, 109n., 112n., 113n., 115, 123, 125n., 126n., 134, 137n., 142n., 145, 157, 172, 190-194, 195n., 200n., 217, 218n., 225n., 245, 247, 263n.; traders, 16, 76, 91n., 95, 96n., 98n., 99n., 100n., 101n., 112, 113n., 115, 123, 126n., 127n., 137, 141, 142, 157, 158, 160, 170, 172, 189, 190, 195n., 200, 201n., 217n., 225n., 245, 247, 263n.; clerks, 63, 67, 95n., 137n., 142n., 157n., 160n., 170, 189, 190, 195n., 197n., 199n., 202n., 204, 226n., 230n., 231n., 249n.; partners, 64, 67n., 68n., 69n., 95n., 98n., 99n., 123, 124, 127n., 137n., 142n., 158n., 190, 194n., 225n.; ships, 89; border survey, 105n.; Selkirk troubles, 124, 189, 190; winter express, 149, 157, 158. *See also* Grand Portage, Trade goods, Voyageurs, specific posts and traders
Northwest Angle, 105n.
Northwest Passage, search for, 13, 14
North Wind, Indian, 172
Nut Hill, 125n., 130, 140
Nut Lake, 126

OCHRE RIVER, post, 112n.
Ojibway. *See* Chippewa
Okaquanatifs, Indian, 215
Oneida Lake, 28
Orignal. *See* Moose
Ormeaux, Adam Dollard des, 71n.
Osnaburgh Lake, 91n.
Oswegatchie, N. Y., 26, 27
Oswego, N. Y., 24, 26
Ottawa, Ont., site of, 73n.
Ottawa Indians, 32, 255, 256
Ottawa River, canoe route, 5, 29, 30, 67–79, 87. *See also* Long Sault
Otter, 59, 116; skins traded, 31, 45, 136, 228, 231, 233, 235, 237, 276
"Otter," 89, 94, 95, 96
Otter Head Point (Tête a la Loutre), 90n.
Oubitchigey, Indian, 169
Outarde, Indian hunter, 253, 255, 256, 259, 260, 261, 264
Outarde. *See* Fowl Portage
Owls, 116

PANGMAN, PETER, 95, 96n.
Pangman, Gregory & McLeod, 96n.
Pangman, Ross & Gregory, 12, 14n.
Paresseux Portage, 80, 81, 87, 195
Parisien, Hyacinthe, 205
Parisien Portage, 83, 87
Parrant, ———, 130, 160–165, 183
Partridge, 32, 35, 41
Partridge Portage, 98, 117
Pass au Travers, Indian, 135, 145, 146, 160, 165; son, 155, 160, 161, 165
Paul, Joseph, 198, 199n.
Payet, ———, 173
Peace River, 6, 16, 99n.
Peaux d'Ourson, Indian, 257, 259, 261–263, 274, 276
Peignecon, Indian, 198
Pelicans, 116
Pembina, fur post, 195n.
Pembina River, 142n.
Pemmican, defined, 132n.; making, 138, 161, 162, 164n., 174, 178, 179; traders' food, 164n., 166, 170, 171, 175, 184, 185

Pemmican War, 142n.
Pente Portage, 201
Perche, defined, 82n.
Perche Portage, 99, 117
Perdrix. *See* Partridge Portage
Perigné, Louis, 126, 130, 136, 146, 148, 153, 154, 157, 162, 163, 164, 167, 168, 171, 179, 180–184
Petit Bled, Indian, 149, 154, 160–163
Petit Boeuf, Indian, 158
Petit Corbeau, Indian, 132
Petit des Bois Bleus Portage, 102
Petit Jean, 157, 160, 165, 184, 185
Petit Mal, Indian, 179, 180
Petit Péché River, 207, 208
Petit Rocher, 101, 106, 117
Petit Rocher de Charette, 105, 117
Petit Sonant, Indian, 149, 154, 160, 161, 165, 241
Pic River, 90, 190, 197
Picotté, Indian, 211, 240
Pierre, Indian, 152, 157, 160
Pierro, Indian, 255, 256, 258, 259, 261–265, 268, 269, 273, 275–277
Pigeon River, portages, 97
Pigeons, 32
Pike and pickerel, 222, 223, 224, 227, 231, 254, 272, 273
Pike, Zebulon M., 225n.
Pine City, Minn., 253n.
Pine Fort, 112, 114
Pine Portage, Grand Portage route, 100n., 102, 117, 202
Pines, Indians, 194, 208, 209, 221, 223, 224, 231, 238
"Pinneshon," 38, 39
"Pipe," defined, 92n.
Pipestone National Monument, 51n.
Piquaquoite, ———, 135, 162, 163, 180
Pivard, Indian, 161
Plain Champs (Chant?) Portage, 80, 87, 197
Plante, ———, 149, 153, 156, 161, 167, 168, 169, 178, 206, 207
Plat (Plat Coté), Indian chief, 257n., 267, 268, 277

INDEX 293

Point Fortune, 64, 65, 71
Point Tessalon, 86, 87n., 88
Pointe à la Framboise, 92, 96
Pointe au Chapeaux. *See* Hat Point
"Pointe au Foutre," 107n., 138, 175
Pointe au Père, 92, 96
Pointe au Sable, 200
Pointe aux Pins, shipbuilding, 89, 94
Pointe du Mai, 102n.
Poitras, André, trader, 64
Pokegama Mission, 247
Pon and sons, Indians, 252, 256, 258, 266, 274, 277
Pond, Mrs. Nathan G., 17
Pond, Peter, 123; on Minnesota River, 6, 28, 44–46, 48, 51; narrative, 7, 11, 15, 17–59; sketch, 11–16, 18, 27; maps, 12–14, 104n.; in French and Indian Wars, 18–27; posts, 44, 96n., 104n., 112n., 123; among Yankton, 52–55
Poplar Villa, 64
Porcupine Mountain, 161n.
Pork-eaters, 68n., 92n., 93, 94, 191, 196n., 200; defined, 6
Portage du Fort, 75n.
Portage la Prairie, Assiniboine River, 38n., 111n., 112n., 137n., 141
Portages and portaging, methods, 75, 76, 78n., 88n., 97n., 98, 196n., 199n., listed, 87, 118. *See also* individual portages
Portelance, Joseph (Roy), 197n.
"Pose," 96; defined, 97n.
Potatoes, 32, 40; at Rainy Lake post, 213, 214, 220, 234, 239, 240
Pouchot, Capt. François, 26
Prairie de Travers, 181
Prairie du Chien, Wis., rendezvous, 34n., 44, 45, 46, 48, 49, 50, 51
Prairie Portage, 198; on Ottawa route, 87; on Grand Portage route, 101, 117
Premier, Indian chief, 103, 212, 213, 214, the younger, 161, 162, 173, 175, 176, 240
Prideaux, Gen. John, 24, 25
Priket, Richard, interpreter, 203, 204, 206–210, 212–221, 223, 225, 226, 228–241
Puan Indians, described, 34
Public Archives of Canada, 194, 245
Pumpkins, raised by Indians, 35, 40
Punk Hills. *See* Touchwood Hills

Qu'appelle River, 178; posts and traders, 64, 95n., 96n., 100n., 115, 125n., 137, 154, 168, 173, 175; name, 115n.; Indians, 139, 140n., 141, 151, 157, 160
Quebec, 13, 26n.
Queue de Porcèpic, Indian, 223, 230, 232, 235; nephew, 234, 235, 237

Rabbits, 35, 41, 130
Raboin, ———, 211, 212
Raccoons, 32, 45, 56, 116
Rainy Lake, 108n., 117, 195, 198; posts and traders, 6, 95n., 103, 104, 158n., 189–194, 199n., 200, 202n., 203–241; importance of post, 103n., 191; Indians, 103, 208, 209, 226, 228, 230–234; name, 103n.; post buildings, 191, 210–212, 214, 215, 218–221, 224, 226, 227, 229–231, 234–238; department employees listed, 204; post garden, 212–214, 220, 237–240. *See also* Faries
Rainy River, 6, 106, 194n., 238; described, 103, 104, 117, 191, 207n., 208–211; fishing, 207–210, 214–218, 222–228, 232. *See also* Faries
Rapid River, 220, 231, 235, 239
Rat Portage, 104, 105n., 117, 190
Rat River, 112n.
Réaume, Joseph, trader, 249, 250, 251, 253, 257, 263, 267–271, 276
Red Deer River, traders, 101n., 126, 127n., 141, 143, 145, 155, 156, 169, 170, 183, 184, 225n.; Indians, 150, 154, 173
Red Lake, 249n.
Red River of the North, 3, 108, 110, 125n., 171; traders and posts, 65, 68n., 95n., 96n., 109n., 123, 124, 127n., 137n., 139, 142n., 146, 148,

149, 152, 158n.; name, 97n.; Indians, 144, 150; fur route, 165, 179, 183
Red River Settlement, 109n., 124, 190
Rideau (Curtain) River, 73, 74, 102, 117
Rivière à la Biche. *See* Red Deer River
Rivière à la Coquille. *See* Shell River
Rivière aux Foin, 201
Rivière aux Rapides. *See* Rapid River
Rivière Blanche, 105, 106, 117
Rivière Creuse, 78, 79n.
Rivière des Chiens. *See* Dog River
Rivière du Milieu, 113, 114
Rivière du Moine, post, 79
Roche Captaine, 68, 79, 87
Roche Rouge, 104
Rocher Brûlé, 106, 117
Rocky Mountain dept., 137n., 142n.
Rognion (Kidney), Indian chief, 260
Rose Portage, 87
Ross, Donald, 97
Ross, John, death, 14, 15
Rossignol, François, 205
Rossignol, Joseph, 205
Roy, Baptiste, 129n., 130, 131, 133, 138, 144, 145, 152, 155, 156, 157, 161–164, 168, 176, 180
Roy, François, 129n., 131, 133–136, 165, 177, 179, 183
Rum. *See* Liquor

SABLE ISLAND, 104
Saganaga Lake, 101n., 117
St. Croix River, 246; Connor on, 6, 249–252; Indians, 8, 249, 251; source, 249n.; portages, 251
St. Germain, Hy., 198
St. Lawrence River, 5, 26n., 27, 67, 68, 72, 74
St. Louis River, 7, 69n., 95
St. Peter's River. *See* Minnesota River
St. Regis, battle, 64
St. Sulpice Seminary, 69n.
Ste. Anne's Church, 30, 68, 69, 79
Salt, 89, 142, 146, 149, 157, 161
Sandy Lake, 7, 95n., 246, 269
Sansfaçon, Joseph, 205

Sans Souci, Pierre, 204
Santa Fe, N. Mex., 41
Saskatchewan River, posts and traders, 12, 68n., 98n., 111n., 137n., 142n., 160n., 172
Sauk Indians, 35n., 40, 41, 43
Sault à la Biche, 109
Sault Ste. Marie, 67n., 79, 87n., 88, 106
Sauteau, Indian, 172, 175
Sauteaux Indians. *See* Chippewa
Savanna River, 102n., 199
Saws, pit, 228n., 230
Schenectady, N. Y., 25, 28
Second Connecticut Regiment, 20n.
Selkirk, Lord, 109n., 124, 189, 190
Semple, Robert, 190
Seraphin, ———, 249, 250, 259, 263–265, 268, 269–276
Serpent River. *See* Snake River
Seven Oaks, battle, 124
Seven Years' War, 4
Severight, Fred, 76
Shacobay. *See* Six
Shaw, Angus, 100, 158; sketch, 100n.
Shawcobai. *See* Six
Shell River, posts and traders, 95n., 141, 145, 158, 166, 170, 177, 178, 179
Silver, 42, 169
Sincire, ———, 198n., 199
Sioux, 8, 110, 114, 123; warfare, 7, 47, 48, 50, 85n., 109n., 112, 246, 257, 259, 266; Minnesota River, 28, 38n., 44, 45, 48, 49, 51; council, 49; calumets, 51; bands listed, 57. *See also* Yankton, other bands
Sisseton Indians, 57n.
Six, Indian, 259, 269, 271–277
Skunk, 116, 180
Slave Falls, 106n.
Slave Indians, 176n.
Slave River, posts, 96n.
Smallpox, 112, 155
Snake River, Connor's post, 245–247, 249–277
Snakes, 38, 39, 56, 111

INDEX   295

Sonnant Indians, 149n. *See also* Petit Sonant
Souris River, 113n., 115
South Wind, Indian, 172
Spain, traders, 113n.
Spunk Hills. *See* Touchwood Hills
Squirrels, 116
Stairway Portage, 100, 117
Steedman, William, 14
Stevens, Rev. Jedediah, 247
Stewart, Alexander, 160
Stone Indians. *See* Assiniboine
Stuart's Lake, 126n.
Sturgeon, 33, 116, 207, 209, 213–218, 234, 235, 237–240, 254, 255, 274
Sturgeon Lake, 12, 102n., 201
Sturgeon River, traders, 95n., 100n.
Superior, Wis., 248, 249n.
Sutherland, John, trader, 106, 126, 133, 138, 139, 147, 148, 151, 159, 163–166, 173–178
Sutherland, Mrs. John, 133
Swan River, 151; traders, 123, 126, 143, 146, 148, 152, 157, 162–168, 171, 180, 181; posts, 125n., 126, 134n., 144, 145, 157; brigade, 195n., 196, 197, 206, 207. *See also* Louis Perigné, other traders
Swans, 110, 131, 164, 171

Tabo, Indian, 130, 140, 172
Tadoussac, Que., 72
Talon Portage, 81, 87
Tapinawa, Indian, 218, 240
Tête à la Biche, 112
Tête Blanche, Indian, 158
Tête Jaune (Yellow Head), 258, 264, 266, 274
Thodey, Col. Michael, 25
Thompson, David, 12, 98n., 105n., 137n., 142n., 158n.
Thompson, J., 190
Thompson, Robert, 99
Thorburn, William, 95, 96n.
Three Rivers, Que., 4
Thunder, Indian, 129, 130, 134, 135, 136, 156, 169
Thunder Hill, 91

Thunder Mountain, 150, 180
Ticonderoga, in French and Indian Wars, 18n., 19, 20; battle, 21–24
Tiosaragointé, Thomas, 189, 204, 210, 214, 222, 223, 228, 232, 233
Toad (Crapaud), Indian, 139, 140, 142, 168, 180, 235; son, 177, 194, 210, 226, 239
Tobacco, 142; use in trade, 103, 129n., 134, 138, 140–142, 146–160, 165, 168, 170, 173, 174, 233, 250, 253, 257, 263, 265, 269, 276, 277
Todd, Isaac, 29
Todd & McGill, 29n.
Toisier, ———, 154
Tonnerre. *See* Thunder
Tortue Portage, 81, 87
Touchwood Hills, 125n., 140, 150n., 155, 156, 168
Trade goods, 31, 38, 42, 46, 54, 91, 107, 126, 127, 130, 131n., 137, 139, 141, 143–146, 150–152, 154, 156, 159, 167, 169, 170, 172, 173, 176, 183, 203, 235, 250, 252, 253, 276. *See also* Liquor, other specific items
Traineau, 219n., 220, 226, 228
Travois, 114n.
Treaties, *1783*, 3, 13, 104n.; *1794*, 13, 105n.
Tremblante River, 177n.
Tripe de Roche, 77
Troue Portage, 87
Trout, 32
Trout River, portages, 118
Turlington's balsam, 206, 217
Turnbull, Capt. George, 34, 35n.
Turtle River, post, 157, 158, 173

Umpherville, ———, 230, 236, 237, 239
Upper Red River. *See* Assiniboine River

Vaillant, ———, 212, 213, 215, 216, 217
Valle, ———, 133, 137, 141, 149, 157, 169, 211, 222, 223
Valois, Pierre, 67

Van Veghte, Capt. Dirck, 25n.
Vases Portages, on Ottawa, 81, 82, 87; on Grand Portage route, 117
Venison. *See* Deer
Vent du Nord, Indian, 130, 140, 143, 144, 159, 161
Vermilion, 257, 266
Vermilion Lake, 102; posts and traders, 191, 211, 212, 218n., 226, 227, 241; located, 202n.
Verrat, Indians, 209
Voyageurs, 3, 7, 8, 64, 206, 245; types, 5, 6, 67n., 68n., 72n., 92n., 204; songs, 5, 76n., 92; customs and ceremonies, 30, 65, 68n., 69, 71, 72n., 78n., 79n., 81, 84n., 86n., 90, 92n., 93, 96, 97n., 99, 102n., 135, 146, 193, 224, 227, 256, 257n., 262, 263; wages, 67n.; food, 68n., 86, 95, 102, 103, 107n., 108, 110, 111, 132n., 135, 148, 206n., 208; graves, 71, 79, 82, 84, 90, 200n.; clothing, 133, 141n., 159. *See also* Canoes, Pork-eaters, Portages and portaging
Vultures, 116

WABASH INDIANS, 14
Wabikekek, Indian, 235, 236
Wabitai, Indian, 266
Waden, Jean E., death, 12, 15
Wahpekuta Indians, 57n.
Wahpeton Indians, 57n.
Wampum, 42, 47, 56, 169
Watab Portage, 99n.
Wattap, 39n., 71, 210, 217, 238, 240, 241
Weasel, 116
Welles, ———, 158
West Indies, 27, 28
Whitefish, 32, 33, 89, 214, 215, 216, 217, 218
Whitefish Lake, post, 191, 209, 213, 216, 217, 222, 223, 225, 228, 231, 232, 233. *See also* Lake of the Woods

White Mud River, 112n., 153
Whiting, Col. Nathan, 20
Wild rice ("oats"), 33, 36, 193, 206, 211; traded, 37, 38, 208, 209, 210, 212, 241, 246, 250, 252, 253, 271, 276; traders' food, 37, 222, 226, 228, 229, 230, 249, 256, 266, 272, 275
Winnebago. *See* Puan Indians
Winnipeg, Man., 109n.
Winnipeg River, 214; described, 104–108; posts and traders, 105, 107, 126n., 138n., 191, 217, 226n., 227
Winnipegosis Lake, 185
Winslow, Gen. John, 18n.
Winterers, 6, 7, 68n., 92n., 93, 99, 195n.
Wisconsin River, route, 6, 35–37, 39, 40n., 45, 49
Wishaima, Indian, 267, 276
Wolfe, Gen. James, 26n.
Wolves, 55, 56, 116; skins traded, 45, 138, 148, 150, 164, 167, 169, 174, 175, 176, 178; hunted, 125n., 273
Wooden Horse Portage, 100, 117
Wright, Philemon, 73n.

X. Y. Co., 150, 151, 215; competition with Northwest, 4, 123, 127n., 134n., 138, 141n., 142, 145, 169, 191, 208, 210, 211, 212, 213, 214, 218, 219, 221, 225, 226, 246, 252, 259, 276; merger with Northwest, 4, 127n., 191, 199n., 225, 246, 263, 264; organized, 96n., 127n.; traders and posts, 191, 202, 206n., 207, 214, 216, 217, 220, 222, 223, 224, 226, 229, 233, 235, 238, 239, 240, 241, 249n., 250n., 251, 258n., 276

YALE UNIVERSITY, 17
Yankton Indians, described, 52–55, 56–59
Yellow River, 251
York Factory, 99n., 117

www.ingramcontent.com/pod-product-compliance
Lightning Source LLC
Chambersburg PA
CBHW020745160426
43192CB00006B/244